CONTENTS

'And be hanged by the neck until you are dead'
Introduction

RAYMOND GILLESPIE

DURING THE NINETEENTH CENTURY, death by judicial hanging was not a pleasant end. Before the scientific intervention by Samuel Haughton – the Trinity College professor of anatomy who introduced both the knot which broke the neck and the more precise calculation of the ratio of body weight and distance dropped – the victim strangled to death, a process that was far from instantaneous. The face would swell, especially the ears and lips, the eyelids would turn blue and the eyes red, and sometimes they were forced from their sockets. A bloody froth or mucus might escape from the mouth or nose and, very often, urine or faeces might be involuntarily expelled at the point of death. All this could happen even when the hangman was knowledgeable and efficient, but bungled executions were not unheard of. An incompetent hangman could either decapitate the victim or, alternatively, leave him or her dangling in the air for up to half an hour before death came.[1]

The despatching of the criminal to his final judgment involved a complex ritual. Before 1868, hangings took place in public and often attracted a large crowd – who were meant to be overawed by the spectacle but who in reality behaved the same as any other group wanting a dramatic and shocking day's entertainment.[2]

1

By the nineteenth century, the period with which the stories in this book are concerned, the golden age of hanging was drawing to a close. In the mid-seventeenth century, about fifty distinct crimes attracted the death penalty – by the beginning of the nineteenth century, this number had risen to 190 before declining rapidly after the 1830s. Moreover, from the mid-nineteenth century, death sentences tended to be commuted to life imprisonment or transportation. In Ireland, eighty-one murderers were hanged in 1813–14, a figure which had fallen to fifteen for the period 1857–63.[3] Despite this decline in the use of the death penalty, a person could still be hanged for murder, rape, piracy, arson and treason, as well as some thefts.

The hanging of a convicted criminal came at the end of a long and complex legal process, a process that possesses a continual fascination for those interested in the study of local history. A sentence of hanging could only be pronounced after a trial at which the relationship of victim and perpetrator was laid bare and, more importantly, the relationship between all parties and the community within which they lived and worked was examined. Breaches of the law, particularly those that carried the death penalty, were social crimes in which not just individuals but entire communities were involved. The reports of trials that led to sentences of execution, whether in official court transcripts or in newspapers, offer accounts of behaviour in terms of guilt or innocence and reflect the dominant value systems of the participants in the trial. Yet when combined with other sorts of historical evidence they tell us more than this. They reveal the social attitudes within the communities which determined the protagonists' fates, and make it possible to understand events that transcend those articulated in court. These wider communal attitudes were often determined not by the principles of law but by custom and material lives. In many respects, the fate of individuals accused of serious crimes reveals an alternative system of justice existing often parallel to official morality or religion. A case in point is the events surrounding the murder of Connell Boyle at Annagry, County Donegal, in 1898. The murder had no political overtones and the perpetrator was quickly caught, tried and imprisoned. Yet the local community was unsatisfied with the machinery of the state and it identified another perpetrator who may not have struck the fatal blow but who was nonetheless judged to be as guilty as the man in jail. The local community duly meted out its own form of punishment.[4]

Those who lived through the events described in the essays in this collection might have been inclined to classify the capital crimes which they heard of in different ways. The most obvious differentiation was between what might be regarded as an 'ordinary' crime and those which were termed 'agrarian'. While the nineteenth-century administration recognised this difference, and indeed published annual returns of agrarian outrages, they did not define either term specifically. However, contemporaries were clear that agrarian crimes comprised disputes between landlords and tenants. Their most serious form was the murder of a landlord or his (or her) agent. In practice, as the essays by Sean Bagnall, Joe Clarke, Frank Sweeney, Margaret Urwin and Patrick Vesey demonstrate, there were personal as well as agrarian considerations lying behind many 'agrarian' murders. Personal motives are most clear in what might be described as the 'ordinary' capital crimes and the stories told by Austin Stewart, Edward Wylie-Warren, Catherine Mullan, Susan Durack and Seán O'Sullivan explore these motives fully.

A diverse range of forces drove individuals to commit capital offences and so end their lives on the gallows or, if they were fortunate, in prison for life or transported. Some were rational but others were not. The murder by Joseph Dorey of his wife and child in Naul, County Dublin, in 1881 was undoubtedly the manifestation of what we would now recognise as psychiatric illness or insanity. As such, it provides an insight into a world which is rarely discussed but yet was well known to contemporaries. The condition was ascribed to a range of factors including religious enthusiasm, drunkenness, old age or reversal of fortune and, for more inexplicable cases, mania or melancholia. It is significant that Joseph Dorey was said to have taken to drinking neat whiskey the week before the murder. Whatever the reason for the crime, Joseph's profile was all too like those who were committed to lunatic asylums in post-Famine Ireland – poor, drawn from the peasantry, male (and more commonly single males) and in early middle age.[5]

That more conventional motives, such as family disputes over land and theft, could result in murder, are clear from the essays of Edward Wylie-Warren, Austin Stewart and Seán O'Sullivan. When the seventy-four-year-old John Conran murdered his wife in 1893, the crime seems to have been prompted by disagreement about the passage of land to the next generation. There were probably more cases of this than are fully documented since such a murder was regarded as an internal family matter and there was a certain reluctance among the farming community to discuss it openly. Thus, in 1872, one judge observed that, in such circumstances, the wider community seemed not to consider murder a crime at all.[6] In fact, in the mid-nineteenth century, family disputes were the biggest single cause of homicides.[7] Such cases provide a unique insight into local family relationships in an age when attitudes to land were changing rapidly.

The murder of the young bank cashier William Glass in Newtownstewart in 1871 – at the hands of probably the least likely of suspects and in the most violent of ways – was motivated by theft. Yet, as Austin Stewart makes clear, this was an intricate case and so provides an opportunity to examine how the apparently impersonal forces of the law actually operated in the world of a small community. While the law should have moved through clearly defined processes of collecting hard evidence, preparing a prosecution case and bringing the accused to trial, that did not happen in this instance. The case against the man convicted was circumstantial at best. Even when the charge was preferred against him, the murder weapon had not been located and the proceedings of the robbery not recovered. Moreover, the investigators could not find a motive and witnesses were thin on the ground. All this was reflected in the fact that the first trial of the accused was inconclusive – in the end three trials were required to secure a conviction. Despite this, local rumours were plentiful and had already identified the man the community regarded as the perpetrator of the crime even before his arrest. It is difficult to believe that the theoretically impersonal forces of the law were not moulded to reflect the powerful social pressures of small-town Ulster as manifest by gossip and rumour. As such, the case demonstrates the importance of local circumstances in influencing ostensibly centralised and standardised procedures.

Similar in terms of motivation to the Glass murder is the case discussed by Edward Wylie-Warren. In this case, the motive of greed was central to the murders committed but there must be some sympathy for Matthew Phibbs because of the disintegration of his family's business fortunes which changed Phibbs' life from a position of security and prosperity to that of a young man without work, home or income. That he should finally commit murder could be viewed as an inevitable conclusion to his fall in life.

Murder features so prominently in this book that it is possible to think that it was the only capital crime in nineteenth-century Ireland. This was far from the case. Susan Durack's essay on the rape of Sarah Sutton in 1799 is an important reminder that hanging was also the punishment for other crimes. In the early nineteenth century, the crime of rape was problematic. The legal principles involved in the prosecution of rape cases were poorly defined and the victim's case was tainted by the assumption that the suit was malicious and feigned.[8] This meant that the veracity of all the testimony was strongly challenged and the woman's reputation was contested. Thus, a charge of rape would be brought only after much consideration, although criminal conversation – the common law action which lay at the suit of a husband to recover damages against an adulterer – was a much more commonly prosecuted crime. If there were legal problems, there were even more deep-seated social problems in dealing with such a crime. An accusation of rape struck deeply at what was most dear to the world of the Anglo-Irish – their sense of honour, which manifested itself in a range of ways, most spectacularly in duelling. A trial for rape was, in effect, a challenge to the family honour. Moreover, it also reveals much about the attitudes to women in late eighteenth-century Ireland. In the story investigated here, Sarah Sutton was expected to maintain the family honour by remaining virtuous, though if, as the law held, this was true, the origin of her 'venereal complaint' remains unexplained and the possibility that she acquired this from her husband remains. The importance of the double standard in this society deserves to be explored.

Rape, family disputes, madness and murder motivated by greed no doubt provided suitably salacious reading for the consumers of the rapidly growing nineteenth-century press. However, the crime of agrarian murder generated a different set of reactions. These crimes were perceived as a much more fundamental threat to the social and political fabric of Ireland and whole communities became part of the action and were considered to be perpetrators. Statistically, the murder of landlords in mid-nineteenth-century Ireland may not have been as common as more impressionistic evidence suggests.[9] However, that is not to minimise their impact. The reconstruction of events surrounding the murder of a landlord reveals much more about the psychological impact of a local murder on a community than the bare statistical data compiled for political purposes.

Patrick Vesey's examination of the murder of Revd John Lloyd in Roscommon in 1847 provides an example of how the murder of one landlord in a specific social, political and religious setting generated fears out of proportion to those warranted by the actions. The murder of the Roscommon landlord Major Denis Mahon a month earlier, coupled with religious tensions generated by Protestant proselytism, had served to sharpen fears in a community where social relations were already stretched to breaking point by the economic pressures of overpopulation and food shortages. The murder of Revd John Lloyd on Sunday, 28 November 1847, seemed to focus the fears of the Protestant community on one event. A minister of the Established Church and a landlord (though not the owner of a large estate) who had evicted some of his tenants, he was assassinated shortly after he had left the pulpit of his own church at Aughrim, County Roscommon. Few had any doubt that this formed part of a conspiracy orchestrated locally by a secret society called the Molly Maguires. The subsequent trial of a number of men seemed to confirm these suppositions. That the twenty-five crown witnesses in the case had to be given police protection suggests popular support for those who committed the murder. Moreover, the fact that no landlords in the area were murdered after that of Lloyd suggests that the actions taken against the Molly Maguires following the murder of Lloyd had broken the conspiracy.

Conspiracy theories are, of course, comforting and have the merit of ensuring that the sort of random patterns of victimhood sometimes associated with murder can be imbued with a kind of logic. Hence landlords and the police greeted stories of the Molly Maguires and Ribbonism with enthusiasm and saw conspiracy and coherent motives in all sorts of agrarian violence in the mid-nineteenth century. While Ribbonism may have existed it was difficult to classify and hence quantify.[10] In many cases, the murder of landlords may have had complex and mixed motives. Seán Bagnall's analysis of the Kinlan murder on the outskirts of Dublin city in the early nineteenth century shows how the seeds sown in the 1798 Rebellion and in Emmet's rising of 1803 percolated down to the lower orders in subsequent years.

Conspiracy as a capital crime made it possible for the administration to take firm control in maintaining law and order, especially in areas prone to agitation against landlords. Frank Sweeney's examination of the motives behind the murder of Charlotte Hinds at Ballyconnell, County Cavan, in 1855 is an example of this. Charlotte was one of those landlords who adapted to the economic dictates of the years after the Famine and, in doing so, created tensions on her estate. The coverage of the crime in the newspapers portrayed it as another example of Ribbonism and a manifestation of the conspiracy which was clearly afoot to destroy the authority of the Westminster administration in Ireland. The gentry of Cavan agreed, seeing the whole episode as part of a large-scale Ribbon plot. Yet at the trial what was revealed was not a challenge to the might of the British Empire but a small group

7

of local tenants whose motives for murder were not immediately obvious. The gap between political perception and local realities was clearly very great.

Awareness of this difference between social relations in the parish or estate and how officialdom perceived those relations is an important tool for understanding how local society in nineteenth-century Ireland worked. The politicisation associated with the Land League and the Plan of Campaign inevitably had an impact on local communities, but the temptation to explain all rural violence in terms of this process alone needs to be resisted. Joe Clarke's reconstruction of the murder of the gamekeeper William Mahon at Ballyforan Bridge in 1879 not only provides an insight into the political background of such events but also engages with the sort of interpersonal grievances which could arise in a local community and in some cases could spill over into violence. Taken as an agrarian crime, the murder of William Mahon was a curious event. His injuries were consistent with being beaten to death rather than shot, which was the norm for dealing with landlords. The close proximity necessary for a beating, for example, contrasts strongly with the anonymous dynamiting of Weston House, the home of William Mahon's employer, which was carried out by one of those involved in the killing. The murder of Mahon has all the hallmarks of a local community, suspicious of the workings of the law, dealing in a violent way with a local problem – the activities of an overzealous gamekeeper. The murder rapidly became a political event and was interpreted within a wider framework of conspiracy, as those involved appeared in the context of an attack on a landlord's agent, an attack seen as typical of Fenian activity with its use of dynamite.

From a rather different perspective, Margaret Urwin's story of the 1880 murder of Charles Boyd, the nephew of a south Kilkenny landlord, who was the intended victim, demonstrates the political use of murder trials at a time of considerable tension. Relations between Boyd and his tenants were poor, perhaps because he was a recent arrival in the area and determined to make his property pay rather than allow it to be merely a symbol of status. As the local branch of the Land League was formed after Boyd's murder, it could not have been involved in the assassination, nonetheless it quickly capitalised on the publicity generated by it. The presence of bands and bonfires at the end of various stages of the investigation, and the public procession on the acquittal of the accused in 1881, have the hallmarks of the political ritual associated with Land League and other nationalist organisations of the late nineteenth century. However, the annual regatta, held a year to the day after the murder, brought forth the different attitudes within the community to the crime and shows how easily the split between nationalists and establishment could be awakened in everyday life.

Taken as a whole, these essays provide an important way of looking at the local, public and private worlds of nineteenth-century Ireland. Crime, and especially capital crime, touched almost every aspect of society. By directing the focus of historical analysis to these individual events of murder, theft and rape it is possible to examine something of the social dynamics of those worlds. Statistical analysis may help us to understand the incidence and geography of crime, especially agrarian crime, but the case studies of individual events in this book enable the dissection of motive to reveal a great deal about the inner workings of local societies.

Studies such as these make it possible to reconstruct the realities of local life. The insights gained are often at odds with what protagonists on either side of the political divide at the time wanted contemporaries, and later historians, to believe. Through an understanding of why some were prepared to risk ending their lives in such a shocking and violent way on the scaffold, we are better placed to understand how they chose to live their lives and this is one of the most important tenets and benefits of local history.

'I don't care where I am brought to, so long as you don't take me to hell'

Naul, County Dublin, 1881

CATHERINE MULLAN

THE VILLAGE OF NAUL, County Dublin, which derives its name from the Irish *an aill*, meaning 'the cliff', is approximately a fourteen-mile drive north from Dublin city. It is situated on the south bank of the Delvin river, which acts as a natural county boundary between Dublin and Meath. A wonderful hidden glen, known as the Vale of the Roches, completes the county boundary. The structural remains of two castles – Snowton Castle on the Meath side and Black Castle on the Dublin side – can be found at this point.

In the eighteenth century, the village grew under the patronage of the Hussey family of Westown House. By the late nineteenth century, the village had established itself as an industrial centre and today the remains of a mill complex at the bridge and a pair of lime kilns to the rear of the nearby mediaeval churchyard, give evidence to a once thriving industrial village.

In 1881, Mr Anthony Strong Hussey, justice of the peace, resided in Westown Demesne where his estate covered some 525 acres and contained a mansion, ornamental gardens and woods with pasture and tillage fields made up the remainder of the estate. The main entrance to the demesne stood on the northern outskirts of Naul. The ruins of the demesne house still stand but are a gaunt reminder of times past. Today, two large ornamental gates set between two tall ornamental granite piers stand proud announcing the once grand entrance, as does the elegant foot entrance gate adjoined to one of the granite piers. On the left-hand side of the main gates, there is a gate lodge, now part of a garden centre. Another lodge, which has been demolished but which was originally situated on the estate to the south of the town, provided a further entrance.

A young married couple, Joseph and Mary Dorey and their two children, a boy aged three and a baby girl aged six months, lived in this second lodge. Joseph Dorey was about thirty years of age, good looking, of middle stature with sandy-coloured hair and fair skin and was employed as a groom by Mr Hussey. He was known to possess a sober, cool and collected demeanour. Mary, his wife, was a local girl and her family, the Bennetts, resided in the townland of Loughmain, just outside the village. She was about twenty-five years old with dark hair and fair skin. It is believed that Joseph was not the father of the three-year-old boy who was born before their marriage, but this doesn't seem to have been a problem and the Doreys' neighbours considered them to be a happy, contented family.

Joseph and Mary Dorey had spent the evening of Monday 11 July 1881 chatting to Mary's sister, Margaret Bennett. They were in good form and their six-month old baby, Bridget, was the centre of attention, sitting on her mother's knee in their kitchen. Margaret, who was employed as a maid in the household of Mr Hussey, left her sister's home at a quarter to eight to return home.

The month of July was very warm – temperatures for the month as reported in *The Irish Times*, ranged from 57 to 71 degrees Fahrenheit – and Monday 11 July was another warm day. Local people had been sitting out or standing at their doors on that evening.

Mary Ronane, a housekeeper working for Mr Hussey, was awakened at about four or five o'clock on Tuesday morning, 12 July, by a knock on her bedroom window.[1] When she looked out, she saw Joseph Dorey but refused to entertain his requests for help. Within an hour and a half, Peter Sweeney, a labourer making his way to work, also encountered Joseph Dorey. Following a conversation with him, Sweeney immediately went to the RIC barracks in Naul where he informed the police of his suspicions that a murder had been committed.

Sergeant Delaney and Peter Sweeney made their way down to the gate lodge on the Westown estate but nothing could have prepared them for what they saw. As they entered the gate lodge, they were met with a still silence. Before their eyes, amidst the wrecked and strewn bedroom, lay the bodies of Mary Dorey and her six-month-old daughter, Bridget. They were both dead and horribly mutilated.

National newspapers reporting the crime detailed the results of the investigation held at two o'clock on the Tuesday afternoon, where evidence was given before Henry Alexander Hamilton Esq., JP, Captain Filgate, JP, and W. St Leger Woods, JP. Sergeant Delaney of the RIC stated that, following information received, he went to the gate lodge of Mr A. Strong Hussey of Westown and, on entering the gate lodge, found the bodies of Mary Dorey and her infant daughter, Bridget, lying in the bed. He described how he found a hatchet smeared with blood and at once proceeded to the pleasure gardens of Westown House where he found Joseph Dorey stripped to the waist. The sergeant arrested Dorey and charged him with the murder of his wife and child, cautioning him to say nothing that would incriminate him. When he did so, Dorey raised his voice and said, 'Criminate myself? Why I told everybody, and I will tell everybody.'

Following this initial formal investigation on 12 July, Sub-Inspector Shaw applied to the magistrates for the prisoner to be remanded. A date for trial was set for Saturday, 16 August, in order to obtain further information with a formal inquest set for Wednesday, 13 July before Dr Davies, the county coroner. The prisoner was removed in the evening to Kilmainham Gaol.

On 13 July, *The Irish Times*[2] and *Freeman's Journal*[3] ran headlines describing the double murder in Naul as a 'Dreadful Murder' and 'Fearful Murder'. *The Irish Times* reported that Joseph Dorey had cut his wife's throat and had attempted to cut the throat of his six-month-old daughter. Village rumour suggested that jealousy was the inciting motive to the crime. Although he was a sober, steady and respectable man, in the previous week while in attendance at the Bellewstown races, Joseph Dorey had, local people said, taken to drinking half-pints of raw whiskey.

On the day of the inquest, Dr Davies, opening the proceedings, addressed the jury, remarking on how great a sadness this particular occasion was to all in attendance.[4] He said that he was sure that the jurors in their lifetime had never been called on to participate in such a terrible case and explained that it was their duty to view the bodies and determine from the evidence available what had caused their deaths. Dr Davies advised the jurors that, if the attacker wilfully, knowingly and of malice aforethought deprived these two persons of their lives, it would be their duty to find a verdict of wilful murder. However, he directed that if any altercation had arisen between the attacker and his victims and the deed was done in the angry feelings that resulted, then they should find a verdict of guilty of manslaughter.

The jury then proceeded to the gate lodge to view the bodies. The weather was still warm and the bodies had lain undisturbed for nearly two days. It was midday when the jurors arrived at the scene of the crime, Dr Adrian was making an examination of the bodies. The jury entered silently and gathered around the corpses of Mary and baby Bridget Dorey whose mangled bodies lay side by side.

Margaret Bennett was the first to give evidence. She said her sister was about twenty-six years of age, was married with two children and that she last saw her alive in Mr Hussey's gate lodge where she lived on Monday, 11 July, at about eight o'clock in the evening. Margaret said her sister was sitting at the fireplace. Margaret continued saying that her sister appeared to be on good terms with Joseph, her husband, adding that she never saw them quarrelling. She said her brother-in-law seemed to be cool and collected and in his usual way that evening and then described how the eldest child, a three-year-old boy was in her father's house, because she had taken him there the previous Friday.

Dr Adrian was then called on to give his clinical evidence from his examination of the bodies. He began by stating that, on the right-hand side of Mary Dorey's skull, he found a compound fracture of the frontal and parietal bone which was four inches in length and from which all the cerebrum protruded. There was a compound fracture of the right arm, two inches above the elbow joint. Underneath that, there was a long incised wound exposing the abdominal muscles. There was an incised wound three inches long on the right knee joint and there was another large incised wound three inches long fracturing both bones of that leg. The skull of the child was completely severed from left to right above the ear, and the child's brains were scattered about the bed. He noted that hair matching that of Mary Dorey was visible on the hatchet.

After a short deliberation the jury handed in a verdict of wilful murder against Joseph Dorey for the deaths of his wife and child and on Saturday, 16 July 1881, he was charged on remand at the Balbriggan Petty Sessions.

As word spread locally that Joseph Dorey was to appear at Balbriggan Petty Sessions, a large crowd gathered around the train station in the town. As the train pulled in, an excited crowd of men occupied the platform. The train moved forward slowly until it stopped so that a door in the third-class carriage faced the station exit door. An order to clear the platform was given by a member of the RIC and the crowd was moved to outside the station. Joseph Dorey walked to the train carriage door and stood there for a short time, looking out. His appearance was listless and his expression apathetic. He had a smile on his lips and spoke to one of the policemen guarding him. Then he was marched, handcuffed and in the centre of a number of policemen, to the side entrance of the courthouse in the town.

Joseph Dorey had not had an easy time since his arrest the previous Tuesday. There was nothing glorious in his demean-our. His face and head were physically cut and bruised and his throat discoloured. The back of his coat was torn and his clothing in general was soiled and bedraggled. Both of his eyes were encircled by livid bruises, his forehead was also bruised and a wound on the upper back portion of his skull was covered with sticking plaster.

The magistrates presiding over the case were some of the leading landlords in counties Dublin and Meath – Mr Hans A. Hamilton (chairman), Captain M'Cartney Filgate, Mr St Ledger Woods, Henry St George Osborne Esq., Jr, and Captain the Honourable E. Preston, JP. Sub-Inspector Shaw of Balbriggan conducted the case for the crown and Dublin solicitor Mr Cane appeared for the prisoner.

Sub-Inspector Shaw informed the bench of the proceedings to date, stating that the prisoner had been brought before the magistrates the previous Tuesday and charged with a very serious criminal offence. He explained how, at that stage, he had merely asked the court to take evidence and grant a remand of the prisoner, but that subsequently an inquest had been held (on the previous Wednesday) at which the accused was not present. Shaw stated that a jury had found against the accused and, as a result of their decision, he had got a warrant from the coroner committing the prisoner to jail where he had been held on the warrant of the magistrates.

Mr Cane, as solicitor for the prisoner, thanked the sub-inspector for the firmness and impartiality he exhibited in the conduct of the case. Then the first witnesses were called.

Mrs Mary Collier stated that she was the wife of John Collier and they lived at Westown in the lodge on the opposite side of the main gate to the Doreys – about three or four yards away. She said she last saw Joseph and Mary Dorey at about six o'clock on Monday 11 July, when she called in to see the young mother before she went milking and found her sitting at the fireside with the baby on her knee. Later, when she returned from milking, Joseph had called in to her for a little sup of buttermilk to make whey. Mary Collier said she later dropped the milk into Mary and that was the last time she saw her alive. She said she had locked her door at eleven o'clock and had gone to bed. The evening and night she described as peaceable and no noise attracted her attention. In cross-examination by Mr Cane, she said that the Doreys were a very peaceable couple. She had known them for a year or so and had never seen the prisoner drunk, or even with a drink in his hand. On that night, he was sober, she said.

Margaret Bennett then gave her evidence. She said she lived at Loughmain, near Naul and that she remembered Monday, 11 July because she visited her sister's house around seven o'clock and stayed until a quarter to eight. Her sister's husband and youngest child were present and they all sat in the kitchen. She said that Joseph was sober and that the couple appeared to be on good terms.

Margaret Bennett then told the court that she had noticed Joseph was wearing a plaid shirt. At this point, the shirt found in the bed where the murdered bodies were discovered was produced for her to identifiy. Cross-examined by Mr Cane, Margaret confirmed that she had seen the couple daily over the previous year. She said she had not been able to go into the lodge when she heard of the death of her sister and niece – she had had to stop at Mrs Collier's house.

John Shiel was the third witness and said he lived on the opposite side of the road to Mr Hussey's gate lodges. Joseph and Mary Dorey lived to the left of the gate and he saw them there on Monday, 11 July after he came home from work. At about ten in the evening, he and his wife heard a strange wild screech or roar which came from outside. It was, he said, 'un-natural-like' but he could not say if it was the cry of a man or woman. He got up and went outside but didn't hear or see anything more. Cross-examined by Mr Cane, James Shiel said he knew Joseph Dorey for the last eleven years and always thought he lived on good terms with his wife.

Mary Ruane, Mr Hussey's housekeeper, said she heard a knock at her bedroom window about four or five o'clock on Tuesday morning. She opened the window shutters and saw Joseph Dorey standing outside. He muttered something about murdering his wife, but she could not really understand what he was saying. She thought perhaps it was another person he was talking about. She said she told him 'to go away and see your priest' and then closed her window but he knocked again and asked for a shirt. She then got up and dressed herself but, half an hour later, she noticed him standing on the gravel walk behind a rose tree. She described how he had a white handkerchief around his neck and thought by his appearance that he might be out of his mind or have drink taken.

Peter Sweeney described himself as a labourer on Mr Hussey's estate. He told the court that, when he was going to work at six o'clock on the morning of Tuesday, 12 July, he met Joseph Dorey. He greeted his neighbour, saying, 'Fine morning, Joe.' Dorey answered by saying that he could hardly speak. Sweeney said that Dorey's speech was so indistinctive that he could only make out a few words and thought that Dorey said someone had beaten him. It would not have been unusual to hear that an employee on a landlord's estate might have been attacked.[5] Agrarian unrest was at its height, with newspapers at the time carrying daily reports of attempted murders, shootings, beatings and boycotting of landowners, as well as many of the workers employed on estates. Peter Sweeney said that he continued to question Joseph Dorey about the incident and it slowly became clear to him that a dreadful double murder had been committed and that Joseph Dorey had taken part in the deed. He then asked the prisoner who had beaten him and Dorey replied, 'I murdered my wife and child last night.'

Having been asked further questions, Sweeney said that Dorey told him, 'Why man, the two are lying beyond. I beat them into jelly with a hatchet. I am a devil.' The witness said he asked Joseph Dorey if he was drunk and the prisoner replied, 'No, I took two tumblers of mulled porter.' When he asked Joseph what the cause of the murder was, the prisoner replied that, when he had jumped up and pointed at a statue and said, 'What's that?' his wife had replied that it was 'Joseph', and added, 'Don't you know his crooked head?' Dorey then whipped up the hatchet. 'I split her head. I knocked out her brains,' he told Sweeney. Sweeney told the court that, on hearing this, he went to the police barracks in Naul and reported the crime. The police accompanied him to Dorey's gate lodge where he found the hatchet standing up against the wall close to the door. He described how he saw the form of a woman lying dead, with a little cloth over her face and the blood flowing through it.

Sub-Constable William Jacob went through the inquest evidence.[6] He was re-examined about the facts connected with the finding of the bodies and the subsequent arrest of the prisoner in Mr Hussey's pleasure grounds. Jacob said that, on being arrested, the prisoner asked him where he was being taken to and he said he replied 'to the barracks'. Jacob then stated that Joseph Dorey had said to him, 'I don't care where I am brought to, so long as you don't take me to hell.' He said Sergeant Delaney searched the prisoner in the barracks and found a knife and two small statues made of chalk. One was an image of St Joseph, whose head was broken off, and the other was that of the Blessed Virgin. He confirmed finding the plaid shirt in the bed where the bodies lay. The shirt was again produced and identified. Sub-Constable Jacob confirmed he was present when the hatchet was found.

The next witness was Mr Anthony Strong Hussey who said he was a magistrate and the owner of Westown Demesne. He was not residing there at present but occasionally visited the estate. He confirmed that he knew the prisoner personally and that he had been in his employment as a groom for the past thirteen months and was previously in his father's employment. According to Mr Hussey, Joseph Dorey was always correct, sober and of very good character. He had never heard anything derogatory about him but had always heard that the prisoner and his wife lived on very good terms and he had never heard of any cause of quarrel between them.

Dr Edward Adrian, MB, of Balbriggan said he examined the bodies of the deceased to ascertain the nature of the injuries. In his view, the immediate cause of Mary Dorey's death was a compound fracture of the skull. He felt certain that her death must have been instantaneous. It was an incised wound but the head must have been struck with the back of the hatchet, as the skull was beaten into pulp. There was no haemorrhage from the lower part of the body except from the arms. In his view, the wounds on the lower part of the body were inflicted some time after death. There was profuse haemorrhaging from the wounds to the skull. As a result of the force of the impact, the brains and blood of both victims were scattered over the bed, wall and floor. The hatchet was then produced as evidence and it was identified as the instrument used in the attack.

In its report, the *Freeman's Journal* described the reaction of Joseph Dorey on seeing the exhibit of the bloodstained blade of the hatchet saying he 'looked at it eagerly and scanned the faces of the magistrates and those around while it was exposed, as if to witness the effect the sight of the weapon would produce'.

Sub-Inspector B. G. Shaw of Balbriggan RIC Barracks was the next to give evidence. He described entering the bedroom and finding about a square yard of the boarded floor at the foot of the bed smashed in, as if done with a hatchet.

The evidence for the prosecution then closed.

Solicitor Mr Cane obtained permission to have a conversation with his client at the end of the room. When they returned, Joseph Dorey sat down at the table reserved for solicitors while Mr Cane addressed the bench, saying that he would not discuss his defence in court. He described to the magistrates how his client Joseph Dorey had been put in a cell in Kilmainham Gaol with two other men. Such was his state of insanity that he attacked the two other prisoners and, as a result, suffered injuries to his face, throat and head. Mr Cane proposed to the magistrates that a prisoner in such a state of mind as Dorey should have been guarded and not butchered. At this point, he showed the prisoner's injuries to the court.

The magistrate, Mr Hamilton, then read a written statement that contained the charge against the prisoner and noted Dorey's refusal to enter his defence in that court. The document was handed to the prisoner who signed it. Joseph Dorey was formally committed to stand trial at the Commission of Oyer and Terminer on 4 August 1881 and was then returned by train from Balbriggan railway station to Kilmainham Gaol.

The opening of the Commission of Oyer and Terminer (a court that was constituted to hear felonies and misdemeanours and was based at the courthouse in Green Street, Dublin city) took place on 4 August 1881 as planned. It was officially opened by the Right Honourable Lord Mayor and Right Honourable Mr Justice Barry, Sir George Owens, high sheriff for the city and Mr Cusack, JP, high sheriff for the county in attendance. There was a large number of cases to be heard, with the result that the trial of Joseph Dorey did not commence until the following day.

When the trial opened on 5 August an application was entered by Mr J. A. Curran (instructed by Mr Gerald Byrne), for the defence, to postpone the trial until the next commission.[7] The reason for this application was that an affidavit had been made by Mr Byrne to the effect that he had only been assigned to the defence on 3 August and therefore he had not had sufficient time to prepare a defence. Curran also said he wished to communicate with the prisoner's friends in the country as a letter written by a doctor had been delivered to him stating that lunacy existed in the prisoner's family.

Mr Murphy, QC, and Mr W. O'Brien, who (instructed by Mr Anderson, crown solicitor) appeared for the prosecution, did not oppose the application. They were of the opinion that the case required further inquiry. Mr Justice Barry then postponed the trial until the next commission.

The next commission sat on 26 October 1881 when the following gentlemen were sworn in for jury service: Richard Ward (foreman), Hamilton D. Athol, John E. Berrie, James Conlon, John Fay, Francis Gibney, Lawrence Keeper Jr, and William F. Lalor. The trial judge was Mr Justice Barry.

Joseph Dorey pleaded his innocence saying he was not guilty. Having heard the evidence, the jury took only a short time to agree with him and return a verdict of not guilty, adding that the murder was the work of a man incited and inflamed by manic homicidal actions. The judge directed that the prisoner should be kept in confinement during the lord lieutenant's pleasure and sent Dorey to Dundrum Asylum.[8]

In 1893, some twelve years after his conviction, Joseph Dorey escaped from Dundrum Asylum and was never recaptured. There were no further traces of his whereabouts.

'I flatter myself we have strangled the evil in the bud'

Lisaville, Elphin, County Roscommon, 1847

PATRICK VESEY

AS REVD JOHN LLOYD, the parson of Aughrim parish in County Roscommon, entered his parish church for services on the morning of Sunday, 27 November 1847, he must have welcomed the hour or more of peaceful prayer and reflection that he would spend among his friends and co-religionists who could be trusted and depended upon in this quiet haven, away from the turbulent, worrisome world surrounding him. He was a member of the Lloyd family of Rockville and was also related to the Lloyds of Croghan, both prominent Roscommon families with large landholdings in the county who were all strongly unionist, anti-Repealites and staunch Protestants.

On that particular Sunday morning, the Church of Ireland congregation was still reeling from the shock of the brutal murder of Major Denis Mahon less that four weeks earlier. Mahon, of Strokestown House, was the Protestant proprietor of a large, overpopulated, poverty-stricken, subdivided, indebted estate and had been killed on 2 November 1847. His murder struck terror into every landlord in the county and Revd Lloyd must have harboured severe fears that his own situation could mark him out for a 'visit' by the Molly Maguires.[1] After all, he held over 500 acres of land near Carrick-on-Shannon where his tenants had lately 'combined' to avoid paying rent. A year earlier, he had evicted some of his tenants from land he held at Caltra, near Elphin, and in recent months he had caused 'notices to quit' to be served on other tenants of his in the same townland. It was dangerous to be a landlord in the Roscommon of the 1840s.

Though the River Shannon separated Roscommon from the midland counties of Leinster, the farming practices of the county in the 1840s had much more in common with the agrarian counties of that province than it did with its neighbours to the west. With the exception of the western regions of the county, Roscommon was traditionally a grazier county. Its tracts of rich limestone land favoured the production of milk, beef and mutton. In the 1840s, some estates in the area around the town of Strokestown, such as that of Major Mahon, were overpopulated, mismanaged, subdivided and inhabited by a mass of insolvent pauper tenants. However, in Elphin efforts were underway to rectify the situation and establish a prosperous tenantry on larger, commercially viable farms.

The population of Roscommon according to the 1841 census was 253,591. A decade later, the 1851 census put the population at 174,492, a decrease of over thirty per cent. The percentage decrease of the population in the area covered by this story was greater – the figures for 1841 and 1851 respectively were 50,798 and 30,288, a decline of more than forty per cent in ten years.

By the 1840s, possession of land was vital for survival in a rural county such as Roscommon. This decade witnessed a cycle of agrarian violence that began with the attempted assassination in 1843 of Richard Irwin, a Catholic landlord and magistrate, and continued with a campaign of violence to such an extent that, by 1847, the county was almost ungovernable. The violence was underpinned by the peasants and smallholders' quest for 'conacre' (where land was made available for letting on eleven-month leases to the landless without granting the tenant any legal right to the land). This conacre land would then be used to produce crops, mainly potatoes, for human consumption.[2] Failure to obtain a plot of conacre land would most often lead to destitution and starvation for the families of the landless labourers and cottiers (a class that, by 1847, was being eliminated from the Roscommon landscape due to the effects of the Famine). As the demand for land rose higher, the rent required to obtain it also began to spiral. Those tenant families in north Roscommon, who rented smaller farms comprising between one and ten acres, were also in a perilous economic position by 1847 because many were unable to meet their rental obligations. The landowners themselves were most often in financial difficulties due to a sharp drop in rental returns because of tenants' inability to pay, the obligation to pay rates to fund the fledgling poor law system and the accumulation of private debts. As the 1840s progressed, eviction became more common in north Roscommon.

Violence thrives most often in conditions of economic and social chaos. Desperate conditions often produce desperate responses. The Molly Maguires, supposedly named after an evicted widow woman, was a secret society that lacked any political agenda but was almost solely devoted to what they saw as redressing agrarian wrongs.[3] They attempted to force landowners to set conacre, lower rents or give 'abatements' (write-off some or all of the rent), prevent evictions and restrict anybody from occupying a farm from which the previous tenant had been ejected. Their methods were the threatening notice, most often posted but sometimes nailed to a tree or erected in a prominent location. Cattle were often driven off lands, stolen or shot, land supposedly required for conacre was 'turned', houses were attacked and damaged and landowners, land agents, drovers and herds were intimidated and attacked. Apart from Tipperary, Roscommon was the most disturbed county in Ireland during the Famine years.

Revd Lloyd was unfortunate that the areas of the county in which he ministered and possessed property were especially disturbed. He was doubly unfortunate in that he resided in an area where Molly Maguireism was strong, well organised and able to draw on the wider based Ribbon movement.[4] He had been visited at his home at Smith Hill in May 1846 by three masked Mollys who ordered him to increase his workmen's wages to one shilling a day. When Revd Lloyd refused they said they would pay him another visit if he did not comply with their orders and they 'hoped he would not put them to the necessity of using the detonators'.[5]

While landholding, rents and leases were the reasons for most landlords' unease with their tenants, Revd Lloyd had drawn attention to himself from another source which put him on the wrong side of the Catholic population from which most of the tenants came. During the late 1840s, north Roscommon witnessed not only scenes of destitution, famine, fever, evictions and violent assassinations, but it also experienced some of the sectarian bitterness generated by what became known as the 'second reformation'. This was the title given to the efforts of the Protestant missionary societies seeking new converts in Connacht and Munster. The Protestant missionary effort enjoyed its greatest success in the western areas of Galway and Mayo. The success enjoyed by Revd Nangle in and around Achill, County Mayo, caused a spirited and forceful reaction from the local Catholic clergy.[6] They claimed that most of those who embraced Protestantism in this period did so as a result of being tempted by offers of food and clothing. They put forward their views that, to obtain the soup offered as relief by the Protestants, it was necessary to attend the Protestant church on Sundays. Hence the derogatory term 'souper' was coined to describe those who switched religious allegiance in this period. Revd Lloyd's brother, Guy Lloyd of Croghan, was known as a militant Protestant and he offered free nourishment to the destitute. The descendents of those who availed of it were known as 'Croghan Soupers' afterwards and, indeed, this term can sometimes be heard today.

The Protestant bishop for the Diocese of Elphin had his palace in the town of that name, only three miles from where Revd Lloyd resided at Smith Hill. The bible distribution efforts organised by this bishop in Strokestown had encountered the heated opposition of the local parish priest, the fiery Father McDermott. Revd Lloyd's cousin, who was parson of the parish of Kilglass, was named in a heated exchange of letters between Father Brennan, the parish priest of Kilglass, and Captain Wynne, who distributed aid on behalf of the British Association for the Relief of Destitution in Ireland. It appears that Revd Lloyd's area of ministry overlapped with that of Father Brennan. Using the columns of the *Roscommon and Leitrim Gazette*, Father Brennan wrote to the relief society, stating that he was impressed by the great humanitarian efforts made by the society over the previous two years. However, he continued:

> I have been vigilant lest your benevolent intentions should be frustrated and the pure stream of charity be diverted from its legitimate course by having the fruits of your bounty rendered ancillary to the fell purposes of proselytism in the parish entrusted to my spiritual care, the parish of Kilglass. Activated by these motives I have reason to believe that your agent, Captain Wynne, gave 76 suits of clothes to a school kept here under the auspices of the Rev. Mr Lloyd, the Protestant rector of this parish, which school is notorious as being the hotbed of that system of which I complain.

He concluded by condemning the conduct of Captain Wynne who he described as a public official who had shown bias in the discharge of his duty. Captain Wynne was the poor law local inspector and, as such, would be deemed an eminently suitable person to be entrusted with distribution of food and clothing in an area which he knew intimately.

Captain Wynne replied, denying Father Brennan's charges and stated that he gave food and clothing to the schools which, in his opinion, needed it most. In a second letter, Father Brennan denounced the captain for supplying bread and clothes reserved for the Carrick-on-Shannon Poor Law Union to Revd Lloyd's schools in his parish. He wrote:

> ... it is lamentable to see how our famine stricken poor are treated by those well-paid officials, to whom are entrusted the means of relieving their wants. Here allow me to assure you that the bread you are distributing to the four schools in my parish is not fit for dogs and to those who will eat it for long will communicate certain death.

He then described the bread as 'black as my hat' and 'half-baked rye'. He declared the reason the captain had not distributed this bread to poor Protestant schools in the area was because they did not ask for it and he refuted the claim that he distributed it to all the Catholic schools, stating that non-Catholic schools had received some of the bread 'despite my frequent appeals to your tender mercies'. Father Brennan went on to claim that what he described as the Protestant Diocesan Proselytising school of the parson of this parish (Revd Lloyd) 'has been supplied and has been receiving extra supplies of clothes'. He further noted that:

> ... everyone within twenty miles of Kilglass has heard with disgust of the inroads made here upon our faith and church, by this very Protestant school, alias the factory where numbers of famine Protestants are manufactured. By your late disbursement of clothing to it, you [Captain Wynne] have become its very best supporter, and chiefly contributed to its accursed success. You indiscreetly sent him (Parson Lloyd) the clothing and it was only by accident I heard it. Such a bonus in Famine times, when the people are stark naked, would allure the most constant and faithful of the Catholic children. It would be difficult to resist so powerful a temptation in such depressed circumstances of the country. This adventitious aid coming from you immediately after the parson had my respected curate and myself summoned to the petty sessions of Rooskey, for entering this unhallowed school, much enhanced the value of your previous gift. I venture to say you did not send him half or quarter suits as you did to our schools.

Captain Wynne wrote the priest a short, curt answer in which he stated, 'Pardon me, in reply to state that your information on the various subjects upon which you touch in that letter appear to be strongly erroneous.'[7] On top of famine and tenant discontent about land issues, the prevalence of emotional religious issues only added further fury to the situation and the Lloyds were not far from the centres of controversy.

The years 1846 and 1847 were fateful ones for the Lloyds. The *Roscommon and Leitrim Gazette* of 30 May 1846 reported the death due to fever of the parson's brother, John, who had been the surgeon attached to the county infirmary at Roscommon. It was also reported that the deceased was a man of gentle and amenable disposition whose benevolence of feeling and kindly deportment towards even the poorest meant that he was deeply and universally regretted.

At the conclusion of service in the church of Aughrim on Sunday, 28 November 1847, Revd John Lloyd stepped down from the pulpit to spend some time among his parishioners. A short while later, he mounted his gig in the company of his servant, Patrick Rooney, drove away from the church grounds and headed for his home at Smith Hill. When they got to the townland of Lisaville, two miles from Elphin, two men armed with pistols appeared in front of the horse. Rooney was told to get down from the gig. Then one of the men held the reins of the horse and the other discharged his pistol at Revd Lloyd and 'immediately deprived the unfortunate gentleman of life'.

In a report dated 29 November 1847 to constabulary headquarters at Dublin Castle, Mr Blake, resident magistrate of Elphin, stated that the reason for this outrage was that the late Revd Lloyd had 'evicted some tenants who owed him arrears of rent last November from the lands of Caltra', some three miles from Elphin. Lloyd himself was a middleman on these lands. Blake further stated that it appeared there was an 'organised system of assassination got up against the landlords of this county'. He concluded by stating that the late Revd Lloyd was 'considered to be a most charitable, kind and humane man'.[8]

Revd Lloyd's murder immediately after that of Mahon struck terror into the proprietary class in County Roscommon. Lloyd's cousin, Gay Lloyd of Croghan, himself the owner of a large estate and a magistrate, expressed their viewpoint when he wrote of:

> ... the frightful alarm felt by the well-disposed subjects. The state of intimidation and the feeling of insecurity exceeds anything you can have any idea of. In truth no one will remain in this county that can leave unless some protection is offered.

Lloyd stated that the murdered clergyman 'was of the most kindly disposition, however, that was no protection to him'.[9]

Indeed, this was the gentry's dilemma. They saw themselves as loyal subjects, assisting in the civil administration of the area, coping as best they could with reduced or non-existent rental returns whilst endeavouring to provide whatever assistance was possible to the poor on their estates. Their lives were at risk, their economic position was, in many cases, desperate and they felt betrayed by their former allies, the Dublin administration and the government in London. The Molly Maguires had exalted in the murder of Major Mahon. Several warning notices, which they issued in the weeks following the 'taking down of the tyrant Mahon', testify to this. A warning was posted to Major Mahon's counsel, Maurice McCausland who resided in Fermanagh and owned 19,000 acres in north County Roscommon. McCausland was informed that a resolution had been passed 'to take down all tyrannizing landlords' and 'you are numbered among them'. He was further warned that, unless he wanted to 'share the same fate as his kinsman, the demon Major Mahon', he would need to forgive all rent arrears owed to him. The letter concluded by stating that a fund had been subscribed to by American emigrants for the purpose of shooting Roscommon landlords and two men had been appointed to travel to the 'northern county' to shoot him. The letters bore a Strokestown postmark.

The landowners and gentry appealed to politicians and the administration for support. A memorial from the magistrates of County Roscommon to the lord lieutenant informed him that the failure to arrest the murderers of Major Mahon and Revd Lloyd had given a 'sense of confidence to the assassins' and, unless the government acted with a strong hand, similar outrages would be committed in the immediate future. They stated that they had been reliably informed that 'Mr Lloyd's assassination is only one of several that are to follow and that the extermination of the landlords is resolved upon as a means of getting possession of their properties, that being a proprietor is alone a sufficient cause for assassination'. Amongst other measures, the magistrates suggested that all arms held by the lower classes be called in, that a townland in which a murder was committed be fined, that the revenue generated as a result should pay for information leading to the arrest and conviction of those responsible for the crime. They also proposed that, in such a townland, all outstanding rents should be collected by the police and military so that nobody in the townland would profit from murder. Though the magistrates were fully aware that destitution and poverty existed in most of the townlands of north Roscommon, they accepted that the vast majority of the poor were law abiding but they believed that their wretched destitution was being used as a cloak by a minority to justify violent and murderous acts.[10] This memorial was signed by twenty-four magistrates, including Guy Lloyd of Croghan.

In an editorial, the unionist inclined *Roscommon and Leitrim Gazette* deplored Revd Lloyd's murder and denounced the perpetrators in the strongest language. It stated that, in the thirty years it had been published, it never had to report an act as shocking as 'the assassination of this divine servant of the almighty' who was shot within an hour of descending from his pulpit. The writer noted that Revd Lloyd's residence at Smith Hill was the birthplace of Oliver Goldsmith, his ancestor. He also observed that the assassins had vanished into the local densely populated villages where 'shelter and opportunities for concealment' were afforded them.

The Revd Lloyd's funeral and internment at Elphin cathedral was reported as 'the largest and most respectable assembly of sorrowing friends and neighbours that we remember to have ever seen on a like occasion'. The *Roscommon and Leitrim Gazette* stated that almost all of those of respectability attending the funeral were carrying pistols and many were accompanied by members of the constabulary. Revd Lloyd was described as a 'truly charitable man, his generosity was profuse during the late trying season' and the opinion was expressed that 'his liberality of political and religious opinion could not be quarrelled with by the most sectarian'. The editorial concluded by stating that 'the most direful apprehensions prevail amongst the few of our nobility and gentry who are courageous to remain in this bloodstained land'[11] and hoped that the executive government would use the new powers about to become available to it under new legislation to protect the lives and properties of the inhabitants of the county, to prevent a recurrence of the 'disastrous scenes as the above, the horrors of which we feel are but very imperfectly detailed'.[12]

On 29 December, a month after Revd Lloyd was murdered, Father Brennan wrote a lengthy letter to the lord lieutenant in which he stated that the Molly Maguire society which at one time enjoyed widespread support in the parish of Kilglass had now through the:

> … *unrelenting efforts of my assistant Revd O'Beirne and myself in bringing these deluded miscreants to the altar and getting them to make public atonement for their conduct and promise the congregation that they would in future abandon not only that but every secret society. I flatter myself we have strangled the evil at its bud and put down Molly Maguireism in, at least, this locality.*

Brennan used his supposed success in stamping out the secret societies in his parish as the basis for an appeal to the lord lieu-tenant not to send extra constables into the area because, in its destitute state after the suffering of the Famine, Kilglass would be unable to meet the financial burden involved in supporting extra police.[13] Father Brennan enclosed with his letters an anonymous threatening letter which he had received, bearing a Dublin post-mark. He stated that the writers of the letters were a coterie of rabid persons for the purpose of organising religious bigotry and sectarian animosities which every good man should abhor. The threatening letter informed the priest that, due to the failure of the government to protect the lives and property of its subjects, the writers had sworn an oath:

> … *that for the life of every Protestant landlord or clergyman of this county [Roscommon] that is sacrificed by this monstrous conspiracy, that we will in retaliation take the life of a parish priest until we exter-minate the county of its vermin. Let me now give you fair warning when a murder is committed in future, one of your members may pre-pare for death.*

The letter ended with a drawing of a musket and a coffin. It was signed in blood by a group calling themselves 'Ireland's Defenders'.[14] There was something ironic in Brennan's condemnation of religious bigotry in his letters given his views and actions on Revd Lloyd's schools.

The parish of Kilglass was a disturbed area at the time the priest was writing. It is almost certain that the Molly Maguires were still active, despite the views expressed by the priest. One can see the level of fear, intimidation and anger felt by the Protestants after the murders of Major Mahon and Revd Lloyd in the threatening letters sent to priests by groups such as those styling themselves 'Ireland's Defenders'. By November 1847, it appeared to many that the rule of law had collapsed in the area between the towns of Carrick-on-Shannon, Elphin and Strokestown. Eviction, poverty, starvation, famine, fever and death were thinning the numbers of the poorer classes while insolvency, intimidation, emigration and murder were reducing the ranks of the landlords and gentry.

In the climate of fear that existed, many magistrates stopped attending meetings and courts. Of the ninety-six magistrates in the county, only thirty-two attended at Elphin to discuss their response to the assassination of Major Mahon.[15] Only twenty-three attended the similar meeting in relation to Lloyd's murder. The county administrators advised that, without extra powers, they would be unable to restore the county to peace and tranquillity.

The government in London responded by passing the Prevention of Crime and Outrage in Ireland Act, which came into force in December 1847 and enabled the lord lieutenant to use his judgement to proclaim a disturbed district. Such a declaration enabled the deployment of extra police and military in the proclaimed area, with extra powers of search or arrest, and the calling in of arms held by unauthorised persons. The act also contained sections dealing with murder, conspiracy to murder and accessory to murder after it had been committed. Armed with these powers, the administration made an all-out effort to crush agrarian unrest in the proclaimed areas of Roscommon, which included the baronies of Boyle and Ballintubber North.

The feelings of shock and horror felt by loyal subjects at the murder of Major Mahon on 2 November 1847 was nothing compared to the anger and helplessness which they felt at the murder of Revd Lloyd. The landed proprietors felt abandoned by the Irish executive and the British government. At the time it was not only Protestant property owners who feared the consequences of a possible repeal of the Act of Union. Many of the Catholic gentry also felt that repeal of this act would endanger their estates. In the landed society of mid-nineteenth-century Roscommon, upward movement was possible. Most of these 'new' gentry were ambitious Catholics who had often succeeded in acquiring quite large landed estates, despite the religious and civil disabilities under which their class had laboured in the previous century. On political, social, economic, and law and order issues, these Catholic gentry by and large shared the same opinion as their Protestant fellow proprietors. All were at one in demanding that the full vigour of the law be applied in the 'most disturbed' county. The chief supporters of the emancipation movement were the men of little or no property who were the people that required land at a 'fair rent' and their resistance to government, landlords and Protestantism was total.

The descent into near anarchy which occurred in north Roscommon between 1843 and 1847 and which caused such fears, began in September 1843 when Richard Irwin – landlord, middleman, land agent, magistrate and Roman Catholic – barely survived an assassination attempt on the Roscommon to Strokestown road. When Mahon was killed a reward was offered which was similar to the £250 reward offered by the administration for information leading to the arrest, prosecution and conviction of Lloyd's killer.[16] However, there was progress in the Lloyd inquiry within a short time. The police concentrated on Patrick Rooney who was a servant of the late Revd Lloyd and who was sitting alongside him on the day he was shot. He had seen the two men carrying pistols on the road and one of the men caught the reins of the horse and stopped them and ordered him from the gig. Whether willingly or under pressure from the police, Rooney told the court that Tom Donoghue was the man who went to the side of the gig where Lloyd was sitting and, after some remarks to the clergyman, shot him. He was positive that Donoghue was the man who fired the shot. With this information, the police were in a position to identify the ring of conspirators.

The resident magistrate at Elphin, Mr Blake, stated in a report how magistrates and a head constable from Elphin went to Ballinderry station and sought Constable O'Brien's help in arresting Donoghue, who he was informed 'lived three or four miles from Roscommon'. They had a name and a description but they did not know where Donoghue lived or who might be concealing him. In a strange area and with the displacement of people due to the prevailing famine and fever, it would be no simple matter to locate a specific person. With Constable O'Brien's assistance they succeeded because he was able to use his knowledge of the locality and his ability to speak Irish to track down the elusive man. In this quest, O'Brien called on a local woman, Mary Mac-Namara, for help.

MacNamara later sought to obtain financial reward for the information she supplied, writing to the lord lieutenant that Sergeant William O'Brien of Fourmilehouse police station came to her and begged her to tell him where Tom Donoghue was living and that she did so and the sergeant, accompanied by a head constable, went to Donoghue's house 'and the sergeant spoke in Irish for Donoghue to open his door and he then was taken'. She hoped that 'your lordship will show your kindness to me by giving me a trifle of money which my little family is in much need of, that your lordship values my public service, such as I have rendered in this case'.[17]

That O'Brien was an energetic and able policeman is without doubt. He distinguished himself in the Mahon murder inquiry. He arrested suspects locally and he even discovered where some suspects were residing in England, where they had fled after the murder. Constable O'Brien even succeeded in 'persuading' these suspects to return to Ireland and turn approvers (i.e. to give evidence for the prosecution against their former allies in crime). The Strokestown and Elphin areas were saturated with police and military after the murders of Mahon and Lloyd but O'Brien was the only policeman in either investigation who seemed to have a rapport with the local communities and it appears he had a good personal knowledge of the people of the Fourmilehouse area because he seemed to benefit from information supplied by a number of local informants.

In his reply to the sub-inspector of police at Roscommon, Constable O'Brien confirmed that Mary MacNamara had provided information. 'She did inform me of the particular place Donoghue resided, about four miles distant from this station.' O'Brien ended his letter by stating that, having acted on information supplied by Mary MacNamara, he had arrested suspects for the murder of Major Mahon and that he soon hoped to bring these murderers to justice.[18]

However, in what appears to be a display of professional jealousy of a colleague from another police district, the inspector stated: 'I am of the opinion Constable O'Brien did no more than his duty in accompanying the head constable when asked to do so.'[19] Crown solicitor Peter Keogh commended Constable O'Brien for the manner in which he performed his duty in relation to the Mahon murder inquiry.

The authorities received information of evidence coming from other sources. Horatio Nelson Lawder, a local landlord and magistrate, wrote to T. S. Redington at Dublin Castle:

I have to state that on the 6 December following the murder I received private information as did immediately lead to the arrest of the two actual murderers, namely John Flanagan and Thomas Donoghue and ten of their conspirators who planned and instigated the murder. The same informant also gave, through me, important private information respecting the murder of Major Mahon and other outrages.

Lawder also stated that a pledge was given to the informant that he would be rewarded financially for his information and he requested Redington to bring his letter to the attention of the lord lieutenant. He concluded by stating that 'only for the private information so given, the perpetrators of that diabolical murder would have escaped unpunished'. The informant discussed the information James Coughlan and Michael Walshe, two of the conspirators, could give and Lawder had them arrested. After much 'difficulty' these two gave a lot of information against the other conspirators. Another of the arrested conspirators was Michael Beirne who also turned approver.

With O'Brien and the RIC working in tandem, a number of the conspirators soon become informers and, by the time the conspirators and murderers were brought to court, the authorities were in a strong position to prove their case. However, John Flanagan would not stand trial – he died of ill-health in Roscommon Gaol shortly after his incarceration.

In his address to the grand jury at Roscommon Crown Court on the day prior to the commencement of the Spring Assizes, Baron Lefroy spoke of the list of cases to be heard. The judge said he was scarcely able to adequately address the jury members due to the appalling nature of some of the crimes committed. He continued 'one's heart sickens and spirit flags at the contemplation of the scenes about to be depicted'. He said such a hopeless mass of crime recorded on the court calendar presented a picture of a county totally demoralised and in the grip of despair.[20]

At the 1848 Spring Assizes in Roscommon town, Thomas Donoghue was charged 'with having discharged a pistol loaded with ball, at the Rev. Mr J. Lloyd of Lisavalley in this county on the 28 November 1847'. The prisoner appeared to be in a weak state of health as he had to be carried into the court by two prison guards and three doctors were called to establish that he was in a fit condition to stand trial. They stated that, in their opinion, he suffered from a physical ailment and that his weak state was due to fear. The attorney-general led for the prosecution and Mr Walter Bourke appeared for the prisoner.

The first witness for the prosecution was the co-conspirator Michael Walshe who had turned approver. He firmly placed Owen Beirne, a highly respected local man who was well-known to have strong opinions about the erring landlords of the locality, in the centre of the conspiracy. He stated that he lived at Garnorid-dawn and knew the late John Lloyd as he lived on part of the land of Smith Hill held by the late clergyman. He also knew Owen Beirne and saw Donoghue at Beirne's house and heard Beirne say they had no choice but to shoot Revd Lloyd. He then stated that Owen Beirne named Thomas Donoghue and John Flanagan as the men who would carry out the murder. Walshe then continued that he saw pistols in Beirne's house on the morning of the murder and saw Flanagan throw away a pistol near the scene of the murder later that day. Under questioning, he admitted that he was a Molly Maguire and that he had turned up landlords' lands but he swore that he never took a pistol or a gun from a man's house nor had he ever posted threatening notices.

Owen Beirne's brother, Martin, told the court that he went to Tom Donoghue's place of employment at Duram on Owen's instructions and asked Tom to come back with him to his brother's house the night before Lloyd was shot. He had never met Donoghue before or since. Under cross-examination by the defence, Martin said that he did not give any of this evidence when he was in jail on the charge of conspiring to murder Revd Lloyd, and didn't say anything 'until yesterday'. He did not know there was a reward offered in the case.

Patrick Rooney, who sat on the sidecar with Lloyd, had identified Donoghue as the man who actually fired the fatal shot and Walshe gave evidence of seeing Donoghue armed in Owen Beirne's house on the morning of the murder. A police constable named Reynolds testified that, whilst on patrol on the Roscommon to Elphin road on the night prior to the murder, he met Martin Beirne and a man whom he identified as Tom Donoghue near Cargins. A woman named Betty Reynolds stated in evidence that she worked for a Mr Luke Corr at Duram and that Thomas Donoghue was also employed there. She recalled that she saw a stranger come and speak with Donoghue. Luke Corr stated in court that he employed Donoghue, that he knew he was in poor circumstances and that Donoghue used to regularly call for his money on a Sunday but had not appeared for payment on Sunday, 28 November, the day Lloyd was shot. Whilst the main witnesses may have been influenced by monetary gain, these minor witnesses mentioned above could not expect to share in any reward.

Pat Holmes stated that, on the day of the murder, he was going towards Revd Lloyd's residence because he wished to speak to him. Then he saw the rector's gig approaching on the road and heard a shot, after which Revd Lloyd fell back in the gig. He saw the prisoner, Tom Donoghue, along with John Flanagan come from the area of the shot and saw them leave the road and enter the surrounding fields. Donoghue was carrying a pistol and Flanagan had a short gun. He later saw James Coughlin shake hands with the others and say 'well done, you have levelled the old chap'.

Thomas Breheney stated that he had attended the church in Aughrim on the day the rector was shot and had met two men on the road as he returned home. Then he identified Donoghue (though he did not know the prisoner before) as one of the men saying that he was carrying a pistol which he tried to hide. The other man carried a small gun. Breheney then denied that he was motivated by the reward offered in the case.

After the defence and the prosecution had addressed the jury, Baron Lefroy charged the jury at some length before they left their box. After about five minutes deliberation, the jury returned a verdict of guilty and the judge pronounced the death sentence on Thomas Donoghue.[21]

Donoghue's trial did not elicit any particular reason or motivation why the clergyman was murdered. However, in July 1848 at the assizes in Roscommon, Judge Baron Lefroy again presided when Owen Beirne was charged with conspiring to murder Revd Lloyd. More detail emerged during the course of this trial as to the reasons why Lloyd was shot, how the murder was planned and effected. The objectives the conspirators hoped to gain by their actions also became clearer. The attorney-general again led for the crown and Mr Bourke and Mr Harkon, QC, appeared for the defence.

Michael Walshe was again the first witness called and stated that, on the evening of the fair at Croghan held on 28 October 1847, a group of men, including himself, met Owen Beirne on the road and, during the course of their discussion, they talked about ways of improving their living conditions. They had been refused employment on the public relief works in Caltra whereas men from Raheen, a townland a few miles away, had been given employment. They felt aggrieved about this as they saw the Raheen men as outsiders who had been given preferential treatment. Owen Beirne appears to have been a leader to the men of his area, so they sought his advice. He rejected a suggestion that they should steal or kill some of the Revd Lloyd's cattle and then seek employment on the public works. Owen Beirne told them that, as they all had received notices to quit their farms and houses from Revd Lloyd, their only option was to shoot him so that they would have the land to themselves. Walshe continued that Owen Beirne said that they should each contribute £1 to a fund to hire an assassin. However, on that particular day, the men dispersed without reaching a decision. Walshe continued that he was at Owen Beirne's house early on the day of the murder and saw John Flanagan and Thomas Donoghue there. It was a rainy morning, that later turned to snow – he heard Tom Donoghue say he was afraid the guns might not fire because of the damp weather. Owen Beirne appeared agitated that morning and was continuously 'out and into the house'. Under cross-examination by the defence, Walshe stated that all his family were ill on that day with the fever which was rampant in the area at the time. He then conceded that he failed to warn Revd Lloyd of the conspiracy against his life.

Witness Martin Beirne, Owen Beirne's brother, stated that he had received 2s.6d. for contacting Thomas Donoghue and bringing him to Owen Beirne's house. He confirmed that he swore information about two weeks after the murder, when he was himself in jail charged with being one of the conspirators because he knew a reward for information was on offer. Patrick Rooney and Patrick Holmes repeated the evidence they had given at the Donoghue trial. After ten minutes deliberation in their room, the jury returned a verdict of guilty and the judge sentenced Owen Beirne to death.

It was usual in nineteenth-century Ireland for people under sentence of death to petition the lord lieutenant for clemency. Both Thomas Donoghue and Owen Beirne forwarded petitions to Dublin Castle for the consideration of Lord Clarendon. The papers relating to the Beirne petition are lost, but the Donoghue petition is in the National Archives in Dublin. It is dated 6 March 1848 and signed by the prisoner himself. He stated that he was persuaded to murder the Revd Mr Lloyd (this was underlined in the original) and when the crime was about to be perpetrated he desisted (this last word underlined) but held the reins of the horse (last three words underlined) till another committed the foul deed. Donoghue asked that the sentence of death be commuted to transportation for life and he requested that, if his excellency could not extend this mercy to him, then his body should be given to his friends and 'not to have been buried within the precincts of the gaol' (the words 'friends' and 'precincts' are underlined).

Fathers Hanly and Quinn – parish priest and curate respectively of Kilbride parish, in which the condemned man had resided – had signed the petition as did, surprisingly, Sub-Inspector Blakeney, who was leading the Mahon murder inquiry at this same time. The last paper in the petition contains the lord lieutenant's response 'let the law take its course'. Thomas Donoghue was hanged at Roscommon on 22 March 1848 with only a small number of people present to witness the event.

On 8 August, the principal conspirator, Owen Beirne, was to be hanged at Roscommon (along with Patrick Hasty who was one of the organisers of Major Mahon's murder). The authorities were expecting trouble and drafted in extra police and military – the day before the executions, a platoon of infantry from Athlone marched to Roscommon. On the morning a number of the Cavalry Regiment and the Scots Greys rode into the town. In what was to be the last public hanging in Roscommon, over 4,000 people came to watch as the men were hanged in the square in front of the gaol. It is probable that this large turnout was due to the unfortunate men's involvement in the Molly Maguires and the wider based Ribbon movement. The men confessed their guilt, urged anybody still involved with the secret societies to heed their priests and cease illegal activities.

Ironically, the person who was in charge of the executions was John Hackett, the under-sheriff of Roscommon whose cattle were driven to Croghan Fair in October 1847 by some of the conspirators. It was on their way home from this fair that the advice of Owen Beirne, as to what course of action might be taken to improve their economic conditions, was sought.

The last rites were administered to those about to be hanged by Father John Madden, the parish priest at Roscommon, who was known for his close connection with the magistrates in the county. Owen Beirne and Patrick Hasty were then executed and their bodies were left hanging for a short time. The town remained quiet and the military returned to their barracks. The multitudes looking on were cowed. The agrarian resistance movement and those from whom it had drawn its support were either in America, dead, or, if living, demoralised.

At the Spring Assizes in Roscommon in 1849, another of Owen Beirne's brothers, Michael, was tried as another of the co-conspirators in the murder of Revd Lloyd during which the same witnesses gave more or less the same evidence. It emerged at this trial that Revd Lloyd had quite an amount of land let to tenants in the Caltra area and that the conspirators were in arrears with their rent. Some had made no payment for the past three years and Lloyd had started eviction proceedings. Michael Walshe, the approver, said at this trial that he had heard Owen Beirne say that 'nothing would do but to civilize that dog, parson Lloyd'.[22]

The jury found Michael Beirne not guilty and the other prisoners still in jail awaiting trial for their part in the conspiracy were released on bail and were never put on trial. Having convicted and executed two men for their involvement in Lloyd's murder and, mindful of the acquittal of Michael Beirne, the authorities sought the advice of the attorney-general 'as to the advisability of further proceedings'. The attorney-general was of the opinion that it was 'not advisable to proceed further with the case and, therefore, the witnesses should not be further detained at the public expense'.[23]

It had taken a considerable period of time before progress had been made in the investigation into the murder of Major Mahon. Indeed, the magistrates had initially despaired of bringing the perpetrators of that crime to justice. The conspiracy to murder Mahon had been months in the planning and lax in its execution. Public houses in Strokestown were the meeting places where the plan was put together and roles assigned to those involved. It was only on the third attempt that the conspirators succeeded in killing Mahon. Owen Beirne appears to have been a more efficient organiser than Patrick Hasty and Andrew Connor, the chief organisers of the Mahon killing. Beirne had made his plans, collected the funds and had the parson killed one month to the day he first put the proposal to his neighbours. What emerged at the trials was a picture of a determined, resourceful and efficient character, one who was head and shoulders above his fellow conspirators in confidence, intellect and ability. Ironically, it appears that it was information given in relation to the Lloyd murder that led to the convictions obtained in the less well-organised Mahon killing.[24]

In a report written after the last of the Lloyd trials had been heard, the crown solicitor agreed that the information provided by Lawder's informant was vital in securing convictions. This informant, who was not named in the surviving writings of either Lawder or Keogh, was granted £100 reward by Keogh, who felt that the witnesses Patrick Holmes and Patrick Rooney should have first claim to the remaining reward money. He noted that they were not involved in the conspiracy and swore their evidence shortly after the murder was committed. Keogh stated that the servant Holmes identified Donoghue as the man who fired the fatal shot and he also reported that Rooney proved that Flanagan and Donoghue were the men he saw jumping off the road into the field with guns in their hands after Lloyd had been murdered.

Keogh further stated that the other witnesses – namely Michael Walshe, Martin Beirne and James Coughlan – were of a different order. They were all more or less involved in the conspiracy. Keogh believed Walshe had been present at all meetings held to arrange and effect the murder. He had seen Flanagan and Donoghue leave Beirne's house with pistols on the morning of the murder and, after the fatal deed had been committed, Flanagan had given him the pistols to hide. (He later brought the police to the spot where the weapons were concealed.) James Coughlan swore in court that he was at a few of the early meetings by accident when the murder was being planned and that he took no active part in the conspiracy. Keogh knew this information was false and was aware that Coughlan was present near the murder scene and that he shook hands with Flanagan and Donoghue and congratulated them saying 'you have downed the old boy'. Keogh wrote that Martin Beirne gave evidence of receiving money for travelling ten miles on the night before the murder to inform Donoghue that Owen Beirne wished to see him, though Keogh believed that Martin Beirne was not aware of the purpose for which Donoghue was required. Although Keogh believed that Walshe and Martin Beirne should be financially rewarded for becoming crown witnesses he recommended 'that a marked distinction be made in the amount of remuneration to be awarded to James Coughlan'.[25]

After three trials and two executions, the question of the guilt of the hanged men remains. The convictions obtained were based primarily on the evidence of Rooney, Holmes, Michael Walshe and Martin Beirne. All four were in poor circumstances so that the prospect of sharing the reward offered may have encouraged them to give evidence. Rooney was Lloyd's servant and appears to have been closely attached to his dead employer. It is significant that Walshe and Beirne did not offer information until after they were arrested and even then Walshe's information was only extracted with 'difficulty'. Both men were also sure that, if they failed to turn approver, they would most likely be tried themselves for their part in the conspiracy.

It may or may not be relevant that Donoghue resided in the parish of Kilbride. It was at Kilbride that Andrew Connor of Strokestown arranged for Major Mahon to be shot. It may also be relevant that Richard Irwin of Rathmoyle House, a Catholic landlord, middleman and magistrate, was attacked by armed men while he travelled through the parish of Kilbride in 1843 and barely escaped with his life.

As those executed and those on whose evidence they were convicted lived in close proximity the fallout from the Lloyd affair must have been felt in the Elphin area for generations. There were initially twenty-five crown witnesses, all of whom had to be given police protection. The fear felt by the witnesses for the safety of their families can be seen in their memorials to the lord lieutenant. James Coughlan wrote that, because he was being detained in Roscommon Gaol, his mother was left 'in distress and poverty, compelled to stay in everyman's corner who is pleased to give her the shelter of the night and very few willing to give her that [because of] anger towards me'.[26]

Patrick Rooney requested the lord lieutenant to take 'my family which is only four in number under your protection as they stand in danger in the middle of the friends of those persons that are yet to be tried'.[27]

Peter Keogh, the crown solicitor for Roscommon, stated in a report that:

[he had] made particular enquiry as to the truth of the statement in Rooney's memorial and ascertained that hard feeling exists against the family of Rooney amongst the friends of the prisoners in the midst of whom they are living. This hard feeling has increased in consequence of Owen Beirne having been convicted at the last assizes and subsequently executed, and his brother, Michael, being one of the prisoners to be tried at the next assizes.[28]

The plight of Martin Beirne's family was evident from the memorial of Thomas Padden, a 'turnkey' at Roscommon Gaol. It appears that, on the authority of the magistrate Mr Lawder, Padden had extended the protection of his own home to Beirne's family. Padden wrote that, on 1 August, the wife and children of Martin Beirne,

> ... came into this town without any means or money to support them and would have ultimately perished with hunger were it not for your memorialist taking compassion on them, and took them into his house and supported them from that time up to the present. The said family having been deprived of all means in consequence of the husband's incarceration and the general destitution of the county against herself and family in consequence of the prosecution.[29]

Mr Blake, magistrate of Elphin, wrote to his superiors at Dublin Castle informing them that he had been 'repeatedly applied to' by the wife of Michael Walshe to arrange for her to be sent to Ballybough Depot in Dublin. The magistrate noted that Mrs Walshe and her three children were already under protection in Roscommon but she still did not feel secure. Blake observed that:

> I think it very advisable that this request should be complied with as Michael Walshe who will be a most important witness at next assizes in the trial of the conspiracy to murder the Rev. Mr Lloyd and he will be dissatisfied if his wife is not allowed to Ballybough and being an odd tempered man may fail in giving his evidence properly if he has any reason for being dissatisfied.'[30]

Padden had not received any remuneration for maintaining Beirne's family and he wrote to request the lord lieutenant to arrange that Peter Keogh pay him for his efforts. It appeared that though he had proclaimed himself 'but a poor man' in his memorial, Padden had to wait some considerable time for his money. In a report written over a year later Keogh stated that 'the amount due to Thomas Padden for the maintenance of the family of Martin Beirne from the 1 August to the 21 September 1848 inclusive, at the rate of £1 per week is £7-3-6'.[31] The county inspector at Roscommon subsequently had that sum paid to Padden.

In view of what he saw as a 'real threat', Keogh arranged for all the families of the principal witnesses to receive police protection at the police depot in Ballybough in Dublin.

Because of concerns for their personal safety, it was decided that the witnesses could not return to their localities in Roscommon. The principal witnesses – Rooney, Holmes, Walshe, Coughlan, Martin Beirne and their families – were given a free passage to New Orleans. Before they boarded ship, they were each given sums of money to purchase 'outfits' and, on disembarking in America, were provided with further small sums of money. Even in the allotment of allowances for clothes and pocket money, the authorities were more generous to three of the witnesses who had been most useful. Walshe and Martin Beirne received £5 each to purchase an 'outfit' and £10 on arrival in New Orleans. Holmes and Rooney were each given £10 to buy 'outfits' and a further £25 on their arrival in New Orleans. In a letter to the chief secretary's office, Peter Keogh stated that the expenses of the crown witnesses' families including provisions, beds, bedding and clothing material would be £93.0s.0d. and that there would be a vessel waiting to receive them on 12 January 1849.[32]

Whilst the killing of Major Mahon, which occurred on 2 November 1847, was the highest profile murder ever committed in County Roscommon, the assassination of Revd Lloyd a few weeks later was the pinnacle of the campaign of agrarian violence in the county which had begun some years earlier. The eviction of tenants was always a contentious issue in rural Ireland. The issuing of notices to quit, such as those received by Lloyd's tenants, was enough to evoke feelings of fear, desperation and dread which were compounded by the failure of the potato crop and the almost total disintegration of rural society of north Roscommon by 1847. Of further relevance was the fact that Lloyd resided in a part of the county where the Molly Maguires were armed, well organised and appeared to enjoy the support of many of the smaller tenant farmers. The arrests and executions following the

Mahon and Lloyd murders, coupled with intense police activity in the Elphin and Strokestown areas, broke the grip of the secret societies. The Molly Maguires were never to murder again in Roscommon. During the 1840s, Roscommon had experienced a level of agrarian related crime second only to Tipperary. By 1850, arrests, executions, evictions, emigration, starvation, fever and death had massively reduced the population of the county.

The decade of poverty and violence was followed by one of peace and prosperity. Landlordism survived the Famine and the next two decades were to be its Indian summer.

Revd John Lloyd was of the wrong religion, was a member of the wrong social class and resided in the most violent part of a very violent county. He had evicted before and was about to evict again, so the assassins struck. This was the most chilling atrocity perpetrated by the Molly Maguires in Roscommon but, despite the close proximity in time and location of the two murders, it was the Mahon affair that received national and international attention, due mainly to the involvement of the local parish priest and the Roman Catholic Bishop of Elphin in the controversy. Major Mahon's deeds – good or bad, depending on your viewpoint – are today commemorated at Strokestown in the National Famine Museum. In contrast, the murder of the clergyman less than ten miles away is uncommemorated and largely unremembered.

And what of the tenant farmers? A series of land acts introduced a system of peasant property rights by which each farmer owned his own farm. The twentieth century brought independence, the Irish Republic and the EC, but the emigration trail taken by so many from Roscommon from the depressed 1840s onwards never ceased and the drift from the land has continued unabated and is evident in the deserted farmsteads and silent homesteads of today. Only the fading memories of the bitter struggles of the past are sometimes recalled by older generations.

'The eagerness of the lower orders to press the case against the prisoner'

Ballymote, County Sligo, 1861

EDWARD WYLIE-WARREN

BALLYMOTE IS A SMALL country town in the barony of Corran, in a part of south County Sligo, in the north-west of Ireland. It is situated within an area that, according to Archdeacon O'Rorke, 'is of exceeding rich lands' and has always been a place of some importance because of its strategic position at the junction of the five roads that radiated out to Sligo via Collooney, to Coolaney, the pass through the Ox Mountains called the Ladies Brae, to Ballina and the north coast of County Mayo and to Castlebaldwin in east Sligo.

In any description of Ballymote, the castle has to be mentioned since its presence was the reason for the growth of the town. It occupies a low-lying site to the south-west that, even today, is outside the urban area of the town. The building of the castle was started during the fourteenth century by Richard De Burgh, the Red Earl, and, for all its active life, was the strongest castle in Connacht guarding the pass through the marsh to its flank.

The town boasts only one other building of antiquity, the Franciscan Abbey that alas is also a ruin. Very little is known about the abbey but its style of architecture suggests that it was built in the fifteenth century. Surprisingly, Solomon O'Droma and Manus O'Duigenan did not write the famous *Book of Bally-mote* (c.1391) in the abbey but in the castle. The book, which now resides as a precious relic in the Royal Irish Academy in Dublin, sheds little light on local happenings as it is concerned almost entirely with more national events.

It was a Fitzmaurice, Lord Shelbourne, who, following the example of the landed aristocracy in England by attempting to participate in the Industrial Revolution during the eighteenth century, first attempted to introduce industry to the Ballymote locality by building a linen mill. At its peak, the mill employed some 300 people, most of whom were imported Protestant weavers from the north of Ireland. The venture was a very expensive failure. Arthur Young, a commentator of the time said, 'Lord Shel-burne paid well for his Protestant weavers; for falling into the hands of rascals he lost £5,000 by the business, with only seventeen Protestant families, and twenty-six or twenty-seven looms established for it.'[1]

Shelbourne's successor tried even harder to found a local industry but also failed. He built slated cottages for the more important weavers, a handsome inn and a large house for the master weaver. This business was almost defunct when Lord Shelbourne's descendant, Lord Orkney, sold the Ballymote estate to Sir Robert Gore-Booth in 1833.

In spite of these failures, the town of Ballymote had started its modern development. The first bank, The Provincial Bank of Ireland, arrived in 1826. On the darker side of human enterprise, a bridewell was found necessary and was built in 1815 for the sum of £600.[2] Communication with the rest of Ireland was by water, foot or horse. Public transport was provided by private enterprise. For Ballymote, this consisted of a two-horse car that ran from Ballymote to Sligo on Tuesdays and Saturdays and a one-horse car that connected with the Dublin to Sligo mail coach by running twice daily between Ballymote and Drumfin.[3]

This small amount of development was totally insufficient to provide employment to the great number of subsistence farmers who faced starvation because of the failure of the potato crops, a failure that was serious in 1845 and almost total in 1846. The suffering in the Ballymote area was considerable but was not as severe as in other parts of the west of Ireland.

Sir Robert Gore-Booth was made of sterner stuff than his predecessors. He was obviously endowed with an acute level of business acumen making considerable improvements in his estates and was considered a progressive landlord granting leases for small commercial purposes. By this action, he was largely responsible for the growth of the town and the provision of more shops and specialist tradesmen. In fact, according to O'Rorke, during the late nineteenth century, the only noticeable non-religious pre-Gore-Booth building was the Bridewell. A stone-built Anglican church was built in 1818 followed by a much grander Roman Catholic edifice in 1848, built at a cost of £2,500, a great sum at that time. These two churches were at opposite ends of the town. The neo-gothic Roman Catholic church was rebuilt in 1857 and the enterprise was undertaken by Canon Tighe – to suit his own architectural tastes – and is the present building.

By 1861, the weaving trade had almost disappeared from the area and the principal activity was farming and the supply of goods and services to the farming community. Sir Robert Gore-Booth was the main landlord of the town and much of the surrounding countryside, but the estates of the Coopers, Major O'Hara, C. L'Estrange and Gethin also influenced the town.

The area around the junction of Main Street and Market Street was the primary retail centre of Ballymote. The properties were mixed between residential houses that had been purpose built or modified to become shops with residential accommodation. The individual plots certainly marched side by side and it seems likely that the houses were built as a terrace. It was not possible to gain access from the side of the structure, suggesting that there was an unbroken façade. The buildings were built against a steep slope with almost certainly some excavation being required to facilitate the rear portion and rear yard. From the rear of the backyards, the land rose exceedingly steeply to the back and the rear gardens were reached by a series of steps. A field at the rear completely overlooked the roof of the shops. At the rear of each backyard, a portion of land was left unfenced so that it was possible to gain acess to the backyards of each house.

The term 'shop' seemed to have been reserved for the actual sales area of a retail unit while the whole building, including the living accommodation, was termed 'a house'. In addition to the trades mentioned above, there was a drapery business that had ceased trading some years before the events of this story and had been replaced in another premises under different management. Main Street ran along the bottom of a valley that rose to the east and climbed from its junction with Market Street to reach a prominence overlooking the town below. Market Street climbed steeply at right angles to Main Street to reach a plateau on which was situated the Church of Ireland building and provided an area of level ground on which, to this day, a market is held. From this plateau, it is possible to see the shop premises of Main Street below. There seemed to have been a sense of fraternity between the shopkeepers even if they were in competition. It was, in fact, a very tight knit community.

William Callaghan's shop had a good location on Main Street immediately opposite the junction with Market Street where it had traded successfully for many years. However, William Callaghan was a very elderly man, in 1861 he was about ninety-four years old and frail in his physique. In recent years, he had stopped opening his shop early in the day and quite often failed to open at all, especially on a Monday. His wife Florence normally called Fanny, was some twenty years his junior. The shop sold the usual array of a general grocery store and Fanny Callaghan was the main stay of that section of the business. As well as being a grocery shop, Callaghan was a dealer in skins and there was an outhouse at the rear of the main building in which they were stored. Within the community, it was generally held that William Callaghan was fairly well off financially – there was a common belief that he always had several thousand pounds in cash on the premises. At this time, the third member of the household was Anne Mooney, who was about fourteen and was the daughter of a small cottage farmer from outside the town. She worked as a general domestic help to the Callaghans. For the previous few years, a man and a woman had also helped the Callaghans in a personal capacity. The man habitually shaved William Callaghan and brushed his coat daily. The woman also claimed to have brushed his coat on a regular basis.

One neighbour of the Callaghans was another shopkeeper, Mr O'Brian, but, on the other side, the adjoining property was vacant and very neglected and stood on the Main Street as a monument to the ill-luck and personal failings which some families had to endure. It had been a well-stocked drapery shop owned by a Mr Phibbs who, unfortunately, died leaving a widow, two daughters and three sons. One son died soon afterwards and one went to America. One daughter married but died within a short time leaving the youngest son, Matthew Phibbs, then aged fourteen, and the remaining daughter to run the shop. This arrangement continued with sufficient success to provide a living for the two siblings and their mother until the daughter married. Tragically, this daughter also died leaving Matthew to run the business on his own. Within a short time, it was common knowledge that Matthew was drinking heavily and he began to develop a reputation for dissolute living. It was no surprise to anyone in the town that the business collapsed after a few years. Eventually, the shop's stock was sold at auction by his creditors and Matthew and his mother lost their home. The mother took two rooms in a house nearby, on the opposite side of the road, and Matthew went off to find his fortune. He returned periodically and stayed with his mother before departing for fresh pastures once more. But the dilapidated premises adjoining the Callaghans remained closed and fell into disrepair.

The month of January 1861 started cold and dry. There was not much interest on 7 January, the first Monday of the month, when the Callaghans' shop did not open at all. The couple's age was understood by the community and, unlike many of their neighbouring shopkeepers, they were wealthy enough and relatively independent to choose their times of opening as it suited them.

Not only did the Callaghans' shop not open on the Monday, it did not open on the Tuesday either. Even more mysterious was the fact that no one had seen either Fanny or William Callaghan, or Anne Mooney, throughout the whole of Tuesday – although Anne had been prominent in the town the previous evening. Robert Morrison, who had a shop in the same street near to the Callaghans, did not note the fact until another neighbour, Charles Gillmore, came into the shop and remarked about the Callaghans shop being closed before concluding 'they are all dead' as a humorous remark. As the evening wore on, Luke M'Hugh, Henry Rogers, Edward Hunt and I. O'Brien, the immediate neighbours of the Callaghans, called into Morrison's shop and a general discussion ensued concerning the absence of the Callaghans. It would seem that the main issue was the non-appearance of Anne Mooney, since she was considered to have been a considerate, diligent and caring girl who would not have left the Callaghans all day without a reason and no reason was known to the assembled neighbours. The non-appearance of the elderly couple was not considered so remarkable as their lifestyle was somewhat sedentary because of the age and frailty of Mr Callaghan. No decision was taken regarding any action and there was a general consensus that matters should be left until the following morning.

But Edward Hunt felt very uneasy after the meeting and, when he closed up his shop at around eight or nine o'clock that evening, he and Luke M'Hugh decided to call next door to the Callaghans where they knocked loudly on the door. Hunt even peered through the letterbox but was not able to see anything unusual in the darkness. Frustrated, they returned to their respective homes having decided that there was nothing more they could do that evening.

Unknown to the men, Anne Mooney's friend, Catherine Mulligan, who was employed by another neighbour the Fords, had spoken to Anne Mooney on the Monday evening sometime between seven or eight o'clock when the Ford shop closed. However, when the Callaghans' shop didn't open on the Tuesday morning, she was concerned enough to call at the Callaghans' house, knock loudly and to look through the letterbox. She could see that the passage door was open but was unable to attract anyone's attention. She then took a stepladder and placed it on the garden wall and from that point called again for her friend without getting any response. She was unable to see anything obviously amiss and so did nothing further. She could hear the Callaghans' back door slapping during the day.

The Callaghans' shop did not open on the Wednesday morning. This caused serious alarm within the immediate neighbourhood and a number of the neighbouring male shopkeepers – Robert Morrison, James Gormley, Pat Flanagan and Luke M'Hugh formed an action group. They decided to go to Mr O'Brian's shop since it was immediately adjacent to the Callaghans' property and gain access through the back gardens. The gardens of these properties were separated by stone walls, too high to climb over without ladders. However, the gardens backed onto a lane next to a ploughed field that was accessible by gates from each garden. The Callaghans' gate was open and so the men went through to the rear of the building where they found that the back door was open as well. They called out loudly but received no response. They then entered the hallway calling out all the time. Most of the premises in that part of Main Street were of a similar plan and so, knowing that the residential portion of the establishment was on the first floor, they went upstairs.

The Callaghans' premises consisted of a two-storey building. The front of the ground floor had been converted or was purpose built as a shop having the benefit of two good windows facing the street separated by the central shop door. A second door opened onto the street at the side and gave access to a hallway, that was also connected to the shop by a doorway. The staircase came off the hall which continued rearwards to the kitchen. A second door in the kitchen gave another access to the shop behind the rear counter. There were four rooms on the first floor, two to the front of the property of which the larger of the two was used as a parlour. This room was described as being well-furnished with modern furniture. The second front room was William Callaghan's bedroom which normally, in addition to the bed, contained a desk or chest of drawers. Fanny Callaghan's bedroom was the larger of two at the rear of the house while the fourth and smallest of the rooms was that of the maid and was furnished as a bedsitting-room. An unusual item within this room was a table set out as an altar on which religious statues and paraphernalia had been placed.

Outside, a courtyard was formed at the rear of the house and around it were situated a brew-house, a small room used for the storage of skins and a coal or turf house opposite the draw well. This courtyard separated the main building from the well-laid-out garden accessed through an arbour and a few steps to a gate. This opened out to another garden, accessible through rising stone steps, which contained a second arbour and gate. At the rear of this upper garden was the gate giving access to a rudimentary lane running across the openings from the main road properties and which separated them from the ploughed field. The gardens had been tended lovingly over a long period.

Inside the house at the top of the stairs, there was a landing onto which all the first floor doors opened. The group of neighbouring shopkeepers noticed that all the doors were open, except one. They also noticed that the dining table had been fully laid out for supper with a place set for a guest. Robert Morrison, Luke M'Hugh and James Gormley opened the closed door and went into William Callaghan's bedroom. The first thing they noticed was the dreadful sight of Callaghan lying in the bed with his head and face covered with a bloodstained pillow. Robert Morrison lifted a corner of the pillow and looked under and saw that the victim was quite dead – his throat had been cut and his body was cold. Morrison quickly replaced the pillow and they all went back down the stairs to the shop in something of a hysterical condition, shouting that the occupants were all murdered, although the other victims had not yet been discovered. They found Fanny Callaghan's body lying behind the counter at the rear of the shop and saw that her throat had also been cut. Initially, there was no sign of Anne Mooney but the extent of the outrage soon became apparent with the discovery of her body in the coal house. Her throat had been cut and she seemed to have been thrown to one side. Morrison was chosen to go for the police while the rest of the team remained on guard at the shop.

An inquest was opened on 10 January 1861.[4] Constable James Garland, who was the policeman that returned with Robert Morrison and searched the premises, gave evidence. He gained entrance to the house in the same way as the neighbours, by climbing over the 'mearing wall'. He made straight for Mr Callaghan's bedroom where he found the body on the bed. The deceased was lying on his back with his hands drawn towards his breast and the right hand grasping the blanket. His nightcap was partly drawn over his eyes. The policeman removed the bloodstained pillow and determined that Mr Callaghan's throat had been cut and that there was a little froth coming out from the cut. He also noticed that the upper part of the body was cold. He then examined the contents and state of the room. He noted that there was a small box on the chest of drawers that gave signs of having been 'knocked about'. In it, the constable found a pocket book holding three £1 notes, an envelope addressed to Mr Callaghan and various items of correspondence concerning shop business as well as some oil paper and tea paper.[5] All had bloodstains on them. There were also signs of blood on the bottom of the box.

Constable Garland then went downstairs to examine the shop but was unable to open the door from the hallway until he had help from two other policemen because Mrs Callaghan's feet were against the door. She was lying on her back behind the counter and her head was turned to the left so that her throat was exposed showing that it had been cut on the side. The constable then turned his attention to the shop. He found an open drawer with a few copper coins including a four-penny piece in it and noted that there were bloodstains to the side of the drawer. Lying around were pieces of paper on which there were traces of blood, as if someone had attempted to wipe bloodstained fingers. One piece showed this very clearly. Constable Garland's next duty was to examine the coal house containing the body of Anne Mooney. She was lying on her right side as if thrown there and in addition to her hair being clotted with blood it was very clear that her throat had been cut.

Constable Garland's next action was to make a more detailed examination of the murder scene to see if there was any indication of the identity of the murderer or murderers. In Mrs Callaghan's room, he found a waistcoat and a woman's gown hanging behind the door with blood on each. In the opposite room, there was a very dirty, well-worn pair of trousers, which were also blood-stained. The looking glass in Mrs Callaghan's bedroom appeared to have smears of blood on it. In the parlour, he noted that the table had been prepared for dinner, there was even punch in some of the glasses. The kitchen yielded a can that contained water stained with blood as if someone had tried to wash his or her hands. He saw a clothes horse on which a cloth hung with blood-stains on both sides, again as if someone had wiped their hands on it. In a small room on the left, there was a jug with a blood-stained handle and a spot of blood on the kitchen curtain.

In addition to establishing the cause of death, one of the responsibilities of an inquest is to attribute blame or guilt. In a closely knit, rural community, the traits and character of the inhabitants are always well-known and when crimes are committed local intelligence is fairly adept in narrowing the field of suspects to the minimum. The Callaghan and Phibbs families had traded side by side for many years and it was common knowledge within the community that, although Mr Callaghan had the reputation of being somewhat eccentric, he was of a jovial disposition and had befriended young Matthew Phibbs during his efforts to continue his father's business. Certainly there was local knowledge of Matthew's circumstances, and particularly that he had attempted to borrow money from all and sundry in the locality. It seemed very probable that it was Matthew who was to have been the guest for dinner on that evening Monday, 7 January 1861. Speculation would suggest that there was an immediate suspicion among the group of neighbours who were in the vicinity of the murder victim's house that Matthew Phibbs was the culprit and this suspicion was obviously passed on to the constable. There was also knowledge of his likely whereabouts because the policeman was able to go directly to the home of his mother where he always stayed when he visited Ballymote. Once there, the rooms were searched.

Mrs Phibbs seemed to have been living in fairly straitened circumstances occupying as she did only two rooms in the upper part of a house that she shared with another lady, Bridget Fall. The house was situated on the opposite side of Main Street to the Callaghans'. Mrs Phibbs had only one bed but on it she had two ticks, one of which she would place in another room for herself when giving up her own bed when Matthew stayed with her.[6] Garland found what appeared to him to be bloodstains on one of the ticks while the other one was very clean. On a pillow on Mrs Phibbs' bed, he found an even clearer drop of blood, which appeared dried and rubbed, but no further signs of blood were found on any other bedclothes or on any of the rest of the clothes in the room. The two ticks had been placed one on top of the other in Mrs Phibbs' bed and it was on the top one that the stains were found. Mrs Phibbs stated to the constable that it was her feather bed and that her son had occupied the smaller room.

Mrs Phibbs was not entirely destitute. Her source of income was not disclosed and was not relevant to the inquest. She still had one son who resided in America who may have remitted some money or she may have been the recipient of charity or poor law relief. Mrs Bridget Hunt asserted that, on Monday, 7 January, she had been commissioned by Mrs Phibbs to go and get a loaf of bread and was given half a crown to do so. That was some three hours after dark and the shops were still open. (Mr Morrison closed his shop sometime around eight or nine o'clock.) The centre of the town would have been well lit and lively during the winter evenings. Mrs Hunt had been instructed by Mrs Phibbs to make sure that the loaf was fresh as her son was going away to Sligo in the morning.

Two brothers, surgeons Joseph and William Longhead, conducted the autopsies. Their evidence was that William Callaghan's throat had been cut from ear to ear with a sharp knife or razor and the cut was so deep as to have cut into the trachea and the oesophagus. In addition, there was a fracture to the skull in the region of the temporal bone, which was depressed. The wound was consistent with that inflicted by the corner of a heavy object. In fact, the constable found a half brick in the victim's bed clothes. Fanny Callaghan and Anne Mooney had similar wounds to their throats but Anne had also been struck on the head with the corner of a heavy object such as a brick. Her skull was fractured. Taking into consideration the state of the bodies and the cold temperature that was being experienced that early January, the surgeons were of the opinion that the deaths could have occurred during the night of Monday, 7 January 1861.

Evidence was called as to when any of the victims had last been seen alive. James Hunt had delivered coal on the Monday and saw Fanny Callaghan in the shop at dusk. He noted that the kitchen and back doors were closed. He was under the impression that they were preparing dinner. Catherine Mulligan spoke to Fanny Callaghan and Anne Mooney at dusk between six and seven o'clock on the Monday evening. No one saw any of the victims alive after that time.

The inquest was then directed towards identifying the murderer and was concerned with the movements and pecuniary situation of Matthew Phibbs and what amounted to rudimentary forensic evidence.

The following day, 11 January, Mounted Constable Pat Forgery was sent to Riverstown to arrest Matthew Phibbs on suspicion of murder. He made the arrest in the doorway of Pat Conway's inn and took Phibbs to the barracks where he was searched. Three razors were found, one of which had blood on the heel. Phibbs also had on him the very considerable sum of £17.17s.¹/₂d. that included £3.10s.0d. in gold and bank notes, some of which were stuck together with blood. When arrested Matthew Phibbs was wearing a dark-grey top coat that was identified as having been purchased by him on Wednesday, 9 January in Sligo, where he threw away a similar coat that was in good condition. Two other men were also arrested but soon released.

Thomas Scanlon gave Phibbs 'no help', by which he meant that he did not lend or give him any money when Phibbs came into his shop after breakfast on Monday, 7 January. Bartholomew Cawley said that, on the morning of Saturday 5 January, Phibbs came to his house and bought some cakes for which he paid. He saw him later at the back of William Callaghan's property where he stood on the wall bounding the Callaghans' garden at about twelve or one o'clock while people were at mass. Cawley said that Phibbs looked as if he was surveying the back of the Callaghans' house. Other witnesses corroborated this statement.

Luke Feeney and Owen Cawley were working in the field behind the shops and saw Phibbs come out of the opening by the rear of the separating wall of the Callaghans' premises on Tuesday morning sometime between ten and eleven o'clock. They saw him walk to the rear of Dr Longhead's garden, quite slowly at first, but then he hurried on towards the east through the ploughed field breaking into a run towards the Sligo road. Bridget Fall, who occupied the lower part of the house that she shared with Mrs Phibbs, saw Matthew between eight and nine o'clock in the evening of Monday, 7 January when she didn't see any marks on his face or fingers and he seemed sober. She said that, although he could let himself in or out without her knowing, there was no fire lit on the Tuesday morning, as he usually did when he stayed with his mother, so she didn't think he'd been home. She didn't see him again until he was a prisoner. She said that Mrs Phibbs wondered where her son had gone. Mrs Fall was very distressed in the witness box and gave her evidence somewhat reluctantly. Eventually, she said that she knew nothing more about the murders and she was permitted to stand down.

Mary Flaherty lived four miles out from the town on the Sligo road towards Major O'Hara's property where she kept a public house. In giving her evidence, she said that Phibbs had entered the pub between midnight and one o'clock Tuesday morning when he seemed sober and had no marks on him. He paid a shilling for some tobacco and a whiskey and a few pence that he owed. Oliver Hanley knew Matthew Phibbs and also saw him on Tuesday morning near Flaherty's house. Evidence was given that, on the day before Matthew Phibbs had been detained by the police in Riverstown, after a small boy had reported that 'a man of quality' was drunk and a danger to himself. Phibbs had been placed in a cell to sleep off the effect of the drink. It was discovered that he had a considerable sum of money on him amounting to over £22, and some of the bank notes were stuck together with what appeared to be blood. There was much speculation in the court as to what had happened to the balance of the money from one day to the next.

The remainder of the evidence concerned the finding of bloodstains, the identification of a coat and the allegation that the prisoner had marks on his face and that one of his fingers had something white on it. The verdict of the Coroner's Court was that Matthew Phibbs had caused the deaths through wilful murder. He was then handcuffed and taken on a car between two armed policemen to the gaol in Sligo where he arrived at 7.40 p.m.

The *Sligo Independent* of 19 January 1861 carried an article that purported to give a detailed analysis of Phibbs' character through phrenology.[7] No close examination of his head had been carried out and the article was written based on observation of the subject in the dock from the well of the court. It was severely critical, in fact condemnatory and prejudicial, regarding the psychological make-up of the accused.[8]

Matthew Phibbs appeared at the assizes in March 1861 with the Right Hon. Justice Fitzgerald entering the crown court and taking his seat on the bench at 9.30 a.m. the prisoner was placed at the bar where he was formally charged with the wilful murder of William Callaghan. A panel of jurors was finally assembled after Phibbs objected to several people. Some measure of the public, and in consequence political, interest in the case was reflected by the fact that there were four senior counsel acting for the prosecution. Leading the prosecution was Mr Burke, QC, aided by Mr Colcannon, QC, Mr Carlton, QC, and Mr Baker, QC. For the defence, there was only Mr Sidney who was instructed by Mr Edward Pollock.

It was part of the prosecution's case that Phibbs was without financial means and this was not contested by the defence. Documentary evidence was produced to show that he had made a formal petition to procure aid and relief for his defence in court. Consequently, a defence lawyer had been provided to act for him. There had been a system of what amounted to a form of legal aid by statute from the time of Henry VII whereby an accused person could issue writs for no charge and would have an attorney assigned to him suing *in forma pauperis*. By the middle of the nineteenth century, this system had decayed to the point that only in the case of crimes carrying capital punishment, mainly murder, was counsel appointed by the court. The Henry VII statute was repealed in 1883.

Mr Burke opened the case for the crown with a good précis of the case against Phibbs, who was described as having no fixed abode. Apart from outlining the evidence to be presented by the prosecution during the trial, Burke laboured the acceptability of circumstantial evidence because reliance on it alone was somewhat unusual at that date. He told the court, 'It is not a case of positive testimony as no person saw the prisoner committing the act. It is allowing to circumstance ... It depends on a train of a series of circumstances.'

In the intervening time, the prosecution lawyers were well aided by the police who had been very busy and, in addition to the reinforcing of the inquest information, produced some small items of new but highly relevant information.

Perhaps unusual in an Irish context at that time was the fact that there was no reluctance by witnesses to come forward to give evidence. The overwhelming feeling of revulsion also prompted people to volunteer information. An example of this phenomenon is the story of a paper chase initiated by the voluntary evidence of John Kertins who described himself as a railway worker who did not work the same hours as the majority of employed people. He had been in Mrs Flaherty's pub on the Sligo road on the morning of Tuesday, 8 January 1861, when Phibbs had come in for a glass of whiskey and tobacco. Although he did not know Phibbs, he followed him on the road towards Sligo when he saw him take out some papers from his pocket, tear some of them into pieces and throw them down. Kertins kicked them as he walked through them. A little further on Phibbs took out more papers and stuffed them into a ditch. It was not until a couple of days later when Kertins heard of the Ballymote murder that he thought of the paper tearing and stuffing incident and how peculiar it had been. When the significance of the incident in relation to the murder dawned on him he went back to the ditch and found some of the papers. Most were torn into strips but he did find an entire envelope addressed to William Callaghan. He took this to James Mulligan who was described in court as being 'a man of Mr Cogan's'. Mr Mulligan in turn passed them on to Mr James M'Hugh, another man of Mr Cogan's. M'Hugh next passed them on to Catherine Gethin who gave them to Mr B. D. Cogan. (Mr Cogan was the deputy sheriff of the county and the phrase 'a man of' meant that they were employed by the deputy sheriff and were responsible to him.) Catherine Gethin was the wife of a local magistrate and part of the county establishment.

Within our modern context, the path along which the evidence travelled to reach the sheriff was convoluted but it demonstrates the stratification of Sligo society in the nineteenth century. The envelope was presented as evidence in the court and it had been clearly addressed to William Callaghan. The post master, William Longhead, and the postman, John Flanagan, both swore that the letter had passed through the post office and had been delivered to Mr Callaghan.

Bartholomew Cawley recollected that Phibbs had come to his house sometime between twelve and one o'clock on Sunday, 6 January 1861, and purchased a half biscuit for which he paid.

Later the same morning, he saw Phibbs standing at the rear of the Callaghans' premises by the gate looking at the rear of the building. He then observed Phibbs stand on the party wall between the gardens where he appeared to be surveying the rear of the Callaghans' property quite intently.

The crown made much of the evidence that Phibbs had been in dire financial straits before the time of the murder. In addition there were verbal depositions that he had sought loans or gifts from many people. This the prosecution contrasted with the purchase in shops in the town of Sligo of a new coat, new cap and boots by the accused the day after the murders paying thirty-six shillings for them mainly in half-crowns. Another example of his extravagance was Phibbs' hiring of a car at two shillings to take him to Sligo from Riverstown, a distance of thirteen and a half miles when most people would have walked such a distance.[9]

Phibbs' defence depended almost entirely upon the rhetoric of his counsel, Mr Sidney, who made a long emotional plea to the jury to consider the agony of an elderly mother, the youth of the defendant – he was in his early twenties – and pointing out that no one had witnessed the murders. He used the well-worn phrase 'it's better for ninety-nine guilty men go free than one innocent man be hanged'. He also stated that Phibbs could not answer in court for himself. The judge later rebutted this statement and said that in law the accused was perfectly entitled to give evidence on his own behalf if he chose to do so.

In his summing up, the Right Honourable Justice Fitzgerald paid a lot of attention to the position of circumstantial evidence in this case and précised the case for the prosecution and complimented the defence barrister, Mr Sidney, on the eloquence of his speech for the defence. There seemed to be little doubt in the judge's mind that the case for the prosecution was proved beyond any doubt by the time that he sent the jury out to consider its verdict. Indeed the general public had no doubts about Matthew Phibbs' guilt either.

However, the matter was not to be settled so quickly. The jury was not able to reach a verdict and was sent out again and again.

By eleven o'clock that evening, the street outside the courthouse was thronged with people and, when a bugle sounded at ten minutes past midnight, there was a virtual stampede to get into the court for the verdict. There was considerable confusion and noise in the court where it was estimated by the *Sligo Champion* that there were over five thousand people crammed into the space. The deputy sheriff, B. D. Cogan had to threaten to clear the court unless order was restored. To the judge's obvious annoyance, the foreman of the jury stated that they were unable to give a unanimous verdict since they were hung, eleven to one, and there was no likelihood of resolving the matter. The judge was quite willing to sit at an immediate retrial but, as the lawyers had already left Sligo, the judge held over a retrial until the next assizes.

The new trial commenced on Tuesday, 9 July 1861 under the Honourable Judge Hayes. For the prosecution, Mr Burke, QC, was again leading with Mr Colcannon and Mr Carlton assisting. Mr Sidney continued as the sole advocate for the defence. Virtually no new evidence was produced. Significantly though, many witnesses seemed to have improved their memory since the previous trial with the elaboration of detail that most probably came from lengthy conferences with the police and with the prosecuting counsel. There were minor discrepancies from the depositions given at the inquest and the earlier trial of which much was made by Mr Sidney, who at one stage made the striking comment about 'the eagerness of the lower orders to press the case against the prisoner and to suppress, as much as they could, anything that would be favourable to him'. This was minimised by the judge in his summing up. The speeches of the leading counsels were as eloquent as before. The jury retired but this time the guilty verdict came after only two hours of deliberation and was unanimous.

The judge's black cap, which was in fact a triangle of black material, was placed over his wig by the court usher, and Judge Hayes pronounced the death sentence, but not naming a date for the execution. Phibbs seemed to visibly shrink. Two warders helped him and escorted him back to the prison.

In prison, the condemned man was never left alone and a turnkey named Bell slept in the same cell with him. According to the *Sligo Champion*, the prisoner at last began to exhibit remorse and poured out a confession to Bell. The confession was made to the turnkey because the prisoner's request that a Primitive Wesleyan preacher, Mr Lindsey, be allowed to visit him had been refused by the Gaol Superintendence Board.

In his confession to Bell, Phibbs told of the hiding place in which he had hidden items that he had stolen from the Callaghans. On his day off, the turnkey went to Ballymote and found the turnip field in which the items were buried. The field was on Mr Gethin's property and was situated about 300 yards behind the victim's house. Bell dug up two large silver spoons, six silver teaspoons, a case of pistols, a watch, a watch chain and seal. Phibbs had said that he had hidden £14 in money wrapped in a piece of material but Bell swore that he was unable to find it. He reported back to the prisoner who told him that the money had been wrapped in a cloth and hidden under a rock. Bell enlisted the help of the neighbours of the murdered couple and a big search was mounted to no avail. Phibbs described the cloth and it was almost certainly the one described by a witness at the trial as having been found snagged on a bush. No trace of the money was ever found.

Instead of being pleased and congratulating Bell on his initiative, the Gaol Superintendence Board suspended him from duty. They charged that he had acted improperly by searching for the stolen goods instead of informing the relevant authorities. This was the same board who were denying the condemned man his spiritual advisor. Bell was later reinstated but was kept far away from the prisoner.

By 1861, the *Sligo Champion*, *Sligo Chronicle* and *Sligo Independent* were the three papers competing strongly against one another in County Sligo. In fact, throughout the whole of the progress of the trials, the reporting of the murders and the prison life of the perpetrator, they indulged in bitter recriminations against one another with accusations of salaciousness, bias, slander and downright misinformation. This competition did result in a universal attempt to seem public spirited. The *Champion* took every opportunity to castigate the establishment exposing religious and social bias and making the authorities accountable to the public. The county gaol in Sligo was the responsibility of the grand jury who had formed a subcommittee – the Gaol Superintendence Board (often called the Gaol Board of Superintendence) – to take over the general administration and establish the ethos of the prison. By statute, there had to be three chaplains in attendance for the spiritual welfare of the prisoners, a Roman Catholic priest, a Church of Ireland minister and a Presbyterian minister. The condemned man requested that a Primitive Wesleyan minister Mr Lindsay should visit him and administer to his religious needs and give him comfort. When the Gaol Superintendence Board refused this request, the *Sligo Champion* instigated a vigorous campaign showing how appalled they were at the bigotry demonstrated. They also made much of the fact that there was not one Roman Catholic on the board. However, the board stood firm. Eventually, the deputy sheriff intervened and gave permission for Mr Lindsay to visit Phibbs and to administer relief to him.

In the weeks after his guilt had been proven, Matthew Phibbs started to exhibit extreme remorse and religious fervour clinging on to the hope of forgiveness from an all-loving God. While in this state of mind, he made a detailed confession to prison officials substantiating all that had been alleged during the inquest and the two trials. He also, however, added to the substance of the hard facts by revealing his thoughts and intentions prior to the murders.

He stated that he and his mother were destitute and that he had neither job nor any immediate prospect of one. In this pecuniary state, he had made his way back to his roots in Ballymote hoping that acquaintances would rally round and come to his aid. In this he was bitterly disappointed. He approached several people but they simply turned him away or gave him derisory sums to be rid of him. The image of old Mr Callaghan kept coming to him and thoughts of all the money the old man was reputed to keep on the premises and his age and feebleness caused him to start thinking that, in reality, it would be a mercy to end this feeble life and to help himself to some of the money in the house. He said that his first impulse was to break into the house and steal the money without hurting anyone. His second thought was to steal the money and kill Mr Callaghan. At no time did he intend to hurt either Fanny or Anne Mooney.

In the event, as he entered the rear yard of the premises, he was accosted by the maid who asked him what he was doing there. He panicked and hit the girl on the head with a half brick that was lying on the ground. He then cut her throat and threw the body into the coal house. As he entered the shop through the kitchen door, he met Fanny Callaghan and, this time, he did not hesitate. He grabbed her and cut her throat while they were behind the shop's rear counter. The murder of the old man was calculated and deliberate – Phibbs hit him with another piece of brick and then cut his throat with one of the razors that he had carried for the purpose. Phibbs claimed that he was in a disassociated mental state throughout the whole time he was in the Callaghans' house and he continued to be in that state during the days afterwards until the time of his arrest.

A memorial, in effect a petition, made in the name of Phibbs' mother was sent to Queen Victoria who in turn referred it to the lord lieutenant of Ireland. The memorial pleaded for a commutation of the death sentence on the grounds that the evidence was circumstantial, that there had been evidence accepted by the court to which the defending counsel objected and finally on the grounds of the youth of the defendant. The lord lieutenant's reply was short and to the point:

> Mrs Mary Phibbs – your memorial, addressed to the Queen on behalf of your son, Matthew Phibbs, having been referred to the Lord Lieutenant for his decision. I have to inform you that on full consideration of all the circumstances of the case, his Excellency feels it to be his painful duty to leave the law to take its course. I am your obedient servant.[10]

The *Sligo Champion*, in spite of its condemnation of its rivals for salaciousness, gave the fullest account of the last public execution to be held in Sligo. Public execution was banned altogether within Britain and Ireland in 1868. It had been twenty-six years since the previous public execution in Sligo, when two men convicted for murder in Tireragh were hanged at the same site. However, for all the intervening years, 'the unsightly, disgusting gallows has been allowed to remain outside the gaol for all to see'.

No description of the gallows is extant but it would seem to have been built on the common British plan which was a stout timber platform some twelve feet off the ground supported by heavy timber stanchions. In the centre of the platform would have been a trapdoor secured by a metal lever. Two heavy uprights supported a substantial beam running across and above the platform and its trapdoor at about ten feet above it. A set of steps provided access from a doorway of the press-room to the gallows platform.[11] There was no resident hangman in Ireland and each capital punishment required the executioner to be brought over from England. In this case, the principal English hangman was occupied with another execution in England and so his assistant was sent over in his place. He arrived in the gaol a few days prior to the date for the execution.[12]

Unfortunately, there is no copy of the gaol minute book extant before July 1864 to give us any detail of the construction and maintenance of either the gallows or of the arrangements necessary for the execution, but the minute book does give us some idea of the financial implication involved in the execution of a J. McDade in 1875, which was carried out in Sligo Gaol as public executions had been banned in 1868. There had been a small amount of inflation since 1861 but the figures given do bear a relationship to the Phibbs' execution. On Saturday, 3 April 1875, the gaol minute book recorded that the Gaol Superintendence Board issued a cheque to Messrs Hunt and Sons for £22 for the erection of the gallows and the sum of £23.16s.0d. for rebuilding the execution shed's roof. Of course, for the 1861 execution, there was no shed and its associated expenses since the hanging was to be public and in the open air of the market yard. They issued a cheque for £13.10s.0d. to William Alexander to cover his fee as hangman and his expenses. For extra turnkey expenses, they allocated £5 and £4.4s.0d. to Thomas Armstrong and Thomas Graham respectively. These payments were a considerable burden on the prison budget.

During the Saturday before the execution of Matthew Phibbs, some 150 extra police were drafted to Sligo to preserve law and order but, in fact, the town seems to have been rather subdued. The prisoner appeared to have been composed within himself attending the prison chapel on the Sunday, praying and singing hymns with the prison chaplain and with Mr Lindsay. He wrote a farewell letter to his mother but declined food.

At about 7.30 a.m. on the morning of Monday, 19 August 1861, a vast crowd gathered around the scaffold and at that time the deputy sheriff, the prison doctor, Dr Lynn, and the governor of the gaol entered the prisoner's cell to tell him that it was time for his execution. At this point, all of Phibbs' composure left him as the full horror of what was to befall registered in his consciousness and he had to be physically helped to the press-room. Here, he met a fairly nervous hangman who seemed rather reluctant to approach him until he sensed that Phibbs was even more nervous and was not going to attack him. The hangman was a short, thick-set man who had his face covered with a black gauze type material that concealed his features. He stated that this was his seventh execution but, judging from his performance, he had learned little from his previous six efforts.

Phibbs' arms were bound at the elbows behind his back and a black hood was placed over his head. The condemned man was never to see the light of day again. There was a short delay as they awaited the Dublin coach in case there was a stay of execution but none came and the party made its way from the press-room to mount the four steps to the scaffold. The blindfolded Phibbs stumbled on the steps and had to be assisted to mount the platform. The executioner threw a rope over the beam but he did so from the wrong side and the rope became snagged, twisted and stuck. Phibbs, still with his head covered, was taken down the steps to the press-room until the rope could be untangled. This was not easily accomplished and, in the end, the deputy sheriff sent for a ladder and personally climbed up and released the rope which was then placed in the correct position.

The condemned man was again brought up from the press-room and placed on the centre of the trapdoor with the noose of the rope laced around his neck. By 1861, the object of hanging was not to kill by strangulation but to dislocate or fracture the top three vertebrae in the neck damaging the vital components of the spinal chord to produce death, virtually instantaneously. The hangman pulled a lever at the side of the scaffold and Phibbs fell about eight feet with the rope biting into his neck. The body convulsed for about two minutes and then remained still swinging gently from side to side. As the bolt was drawn there was a deep collective moan, more a sigh, from the great crowd followed by total silence. The body was left hanging for about forty-five minutes before it was cut down enabling the doctor to pronounce that life was extinct.

But a rumour quickly spread in the area and gained general acceptance that Phibbs was not dead at all. It was said that, when Phibbs was taken down to the press-room during the problem with the rope, a dummy was clothed in exactly the same manner as him and that it was this dummy, complete with black hood, that was carried up the steps and hanged in place of the condemned man. This switch was engineered by friends of Phibbs, who was subsequently secreted out of the county.

Even this was not enough for the populace and the next rumour to gain popular circulation was that Phibbs had become completely mentally deranged and had taken to wandering around Ballymote at night seeking fresh victims. This final tale was so firmly believed that many properties in Ballymote had stout iron bars fixed to their ground floor windows – and, according to J. C. McDonagh, even in 1934 many of windows of the area still had these original iron bars.[13]

'They have been sent back to their desolate home, broken spirited and hopeless'

Shanbogh, South Kilkenny, 1880

MARGARET URWIN

THE TOWNLAND OF SHANBOGH, meaning 'old settlement', is pleasantly situated in the parish of Rosbercon and slopes gently down to the River Barrow, which it touches at one point.[1] It comprises 978 statute acres and, in the nineteenth century, was an area of mixed farming, with livestock out to pasture as well as the cultivation of oats and barley.[2] This part of south Kilkenny was Irish speaking before the Famine of the 1840s and, in the 1901 census, some of the older inhabitants are recorded as still being Irish speakers. Adjoining Shanbogh was the beautiful demesne of Annaghs, owned by Mr Walter Sweetman, JP.

The 1848–49 Encumbered Estates acts allowed for the sale of Irish estates that had been mortgaged and whose owners, because of the Famine, were unable to meet their obligations. It was hoped that English investors would be attracted to buy Irish estates and thereby transform Irish agriculture. The plight of the existing tenants was not considered and they were unprotected by the legislation. In actual fact, these estates were generally bought by speculators. Shanbogh had been in the ownership of the Warburton family who possessed thousands of acres throughout the country. They were obviously unable to meet their obligations because, on 2 February 1872, the townland was put up for sale in six lots, excluding the graveyard and glebe, by the Landed Estates Court. In a sale that was completed on 4 June 1872 three of the six lots, comprising 863 acres, were purchased for £10,280[3] by Thomas Boyd, who already held the tenancy of a lot[4] containing eighty acres that he went on to purchase on 24 January 1873 for a further £1,500.[5] He was, rather curiously, enabled to purchase the major portion of land through a mortgage provided by Father Edmond Walsh, one of the Roman Catholic curates of Rosbercon parish.[6]

Thomas Boyd, a member of the Church of Ireland and a native of Macmurrough on the other side of New Ross in County Wexford, appeared to be a man of substance – apart from a lucrative solicitor's practice in New Ross (many of his clients were of the landlord class and Boyd acted for them in pursuing their tenants for outstanding rents), he also had substantial business interests in County Wexford and was the crown prosecutor for County Tipperary and sessional crown solicitor for County Kilkenny. His purchase of Shanbogh, and some 470 acres in County Wexford (in the parishes of Bannow and Rathangan) during the same decade, made Boyd a landlord in his own right.

His grandfather, James Boyd, a native of Kent in England and of Huguenot ancestry, had founded the family in New Ross in the eighteenth century. One of his sons, John, who became a merchant, married Hannah Hogan and they had a large family. Thomas, born in 1818, was the third son and fourth child of the marriage and he himself married Frances Thorp of Chilcomb Lodge, situated in the townland of Raheen (beside Shanbogh), in May 1852.[7] Frances' family held property in Dublin where her two brothers practised as solicitors out of Kildare Street.[8] Thomas and Frances were married in St Anne's Church, Dawson Street, and set up home at Chilcomb. Their house was an imposing mansion containing eighteen rooms with seven windows to the front. They had six children – four daughters and two sons. Their eldest child, Caroline Harriet Crosby, was born in 1853. She was followed by the first son, John Thomas Evans, around 1855.

Hannah Matilda was born around 1857 and Charles Daniel on 10 September 1859. Two other daughters, Dorothea Elizabeth and Frances Katherine, were born in the 1860s.[9]

When Boyd purchased Shanbogh, he acquired some thirty tenants with the property and decided to have the land revalued soon after its acquisition, probably with the intention of raising rents. In any event, the revaluation did lead to increases in rent for the tenants. Twenty-five of them agreed to pay the increase demanded, the five exceptions were: two brothers, Richard and Michael Phelan; their sister, Anastasia Holden, whose late husband, Michael, was a brother of Margaret, Michael Phelan's wife; Margaret Forristal; and John Shea. Interestingly, apart from Shea, these tenants were the largest farmers on the estate.[10] Of the remaining tenants, another five held substantial farms while the remaining twenty were smallholders.

These five tenants were paying considerably higher rents than the others at the time Boyd acquired the land. Richard Phelan and John Shea were paying £1.1s.0d. per acre; Anastasia Holden was paying £1 per acre; Michael Phelan was paying 19s.0d; and Margaret Forristal, at 16s.0d. per acre, paid the lowest of the five. However, the remaining tenants holding over ten acres were paying varying rents of anything between 9s.0d. and 15s.0d. per acre. When Boyd himself had been a tenant, he had been paying 14s.0d. per acre for his holding. Therefore, it is not surprising that these tenants objected to a proposed increase in their rents.[11]

In April 1879, Michael Davitt founded the Land League at Irishtown, County Mayo. In October of that year, he and a number of colleagues organised a meeting in Dublin of tenant representatives from all over Ireland and the Irish National Land League was established with Charles Stewart Parnell as its president. Although the Land League had not yet been formed in counties Kilkenny and Wexford, by the summer of 1880 tenant farmers throughout the country had become more focused on their circumstances. A great land meeting was held in New Ross on 26 September 1880, attended by Parnell, and branches of the league were set up throughout the surrounding area soon afterwards.

In the spring of 1880, Tom Boyd gave lime and seed potatoes to his compliant tenants, which he claimed was equivalent to a twenty-five per cent rent reduction.[12] He succeeded in removing his tenant with the largest holding, Margaret Forristal and her family and gained possession of her farm by paying her compensation under the Land Act. She moved with her family to another part of County Kilkenny and one of her descendants is the present Bishop of Ossory, the Most Revd Laurence Forristal.[13]

By 1880, tensions were rising between the Phelan and Holden families and Boyd, and he had already placed the collection of their rents in the hands of his Dublin agent because, as he later claimed, he had become frightened of them due to a warning he received from one of his employees. The widow Anastasia Holden lived close to Shanbogh Crossroads with her two sons, John and James, and a daughter, Anastasia. Boyd began proceedings against the widow, claiming she owed him £169 for outstanding rent. A writ was served on her on 7 May 1880 which resulted in one-third of the outstanding amount being paid with a second third due to be paid on 10 August.[14]

Michael Phelan had died in 1878 and his eldest son, James, succeeded to the tenancy of their eighty-eight-acre farm. James and his wife, Johanna, lived at Shanbogh Crossroads along with his mother, Margaret, his two younger brothers, John and Walter, and his sister, Anastasia. Richard Phelan, Michael's younger brother, lived on his 106-acre farm beside Shanbogh churchyard with his wife, also named Johanna, and their sons, Michael, James and Jeremiah.

Another factor increasing tensions in the neighbourhood, and bad feeling towards the Boyds, was the case of Bridget Doolin (Dowling), a widow from Jamestown, a townland situated in the parish of Glenmore, near Shanbogh. Mrs Doolin, a tenant of the Revd John Lymbery of Fethard Castle, County Wexford, had been struggling to make ends meet since her husband's death in 1867 and, after thirteen years of hardship, she was in arrears with her rent. Rather surprisingly, Evans, eldest son of Tom Boyd, came to her rescue by paying the outstanding amount. However,

Bridget claimed that he began demanding more and more payment in kind – grazing his cattle and sheep on her land, making her hand over hay, barley, oats and livestock, as well as a plough and harrow and even her two cars so that she was put in the position of being unable to till her land or attend church, fair or market. She alleged to Hugh Mahon, reporter with the *New Ross Standard*, and its sister paper, *Wexford People*, that, as a result of Evans Boyd's demands, she and her family would have starved without the help of her kind neighbours. She maintained that Boyd was attempting to force her and her family to abandon her farm and emigrate so that he might acquire it.[15]

The story, from Evans' point of view, was rather different. He claimed that Bridget Doolin had been on the verge of being evicted and had pleaded with him to pay the rent due and to take possession of the farm himself. He had since worked the farm, supporting the widow and her family. However, on seeing the prospect of a good harvest, Mrs Doolin had turned Evans' cattle off her land, saying he had no written agreement with her.[16]

Whatever the real truth of the matter, things were coming to a head by the beginning of August 1880. In the first week of that month, several attempts were made by Evans Boyd to graze his cattle on Doolin's farm but they were vigorously resisted. On one occasion, bailiffs were sent to force the cattle onto the land but they were out on the road again by nightfall. Eventually, on Friday, 6 August, all the neighbours from the surrounding countryside, who manifestly took Bridget Doolin's part in the dispute, arrived at Jamestown with scythes, pitchforks, sticks and other weapons but the bailiffs failed to appear.

It was at the instigation of Walter, youngest brother of James Phelan, that the dispute between Evans Boyd and Bridget Doolin became public knowledge. He had made the acquaintance of Hugh Mahon at a cricket match in Thomastown some weeks previously. (In those days cricket was the game of the people in the south-east of the country before the rise of the GAA and before Kilkenny became famous for its hurlers.) At the invitation of Mahon, Walter Phelan visited the offices of the *New Ross*

Standard on Saturday evening, 7 August when he told the reporter of the Doolin case and agreed to accompany him to Jamestown on the following morning to hear the widow's grievances at first hand.

The *New Ross Standard* and the *Wexford People* were sympathetic to land reform and the aims of the Land League. The editor, Edward Walsh of Wexford, was to become a prominent member of that organisation and was subsequently jailed for his activities. Hugh Mahon, then only twenty-three years old, was a native of County Offaly, who had emigrated with his family to the United States at the age of ten where he learned the printing trade. He returned to Ireland to take up the post of reporter with the *New Ross Standard* some months before these events.[17]

Every Sunday afternoon, except when the weather was wet, it was Tom Boyd's custom to drive with one or more members of his family to his out-farm at Shanbogh, approximately half a mile from his home and less than two miles from New Ross. On the fateful Sunday of 8 August 1880, he left Chilcomb Lodge at about 4.15 p.m. accompanied by his son, Evans. They were a little later than usual because Evans, who suffered from a spinal complaint, was unwell. On this occasion his younger son, Charles, who was home on holiday from Trinity College Dublin and Gladwell Boyd, a nephew from Kilkenny, were also with him. Gladwell was on a visit to Chilcomb and opted to drive the 'outside' car. Tom Boyd sat with him on the right-hand side while his two sons sat on the left. The road, which was at that time the new Waterford road, ran for some distance close to the River Barrow. It was a fine, open road and many townspeople favoured it for walks on fine Sunday afternoons.

The four men on the car were conversing casually about the ripening corn in the adjoining fields as they reached the point where the townlands of Shanbogh and Annaghs met. At a corner of a field on the left-hand side of the road, there was a thick, double hedge, a perfect place of concealment. As the car approached, a disguised and masked man jumped out from the hedge. He appeared to the men on the car to be dancing and

Tom Boyd's first impression was that he was a mummer. There was an ancient custom in the area of mummers entertaining at harvest gatherings. However, this notion was soon dispelled when the man was quickly followed out onto the road by two others. They were disguised from head to toe in white canvas smocks (ulsters) and leggings, their faces were covered by red masks and they wore women's white linen caps. More threateningly, they were each carrying rifles with fixed bayonets. It was later confirmed that the weapons were breech-loading Enfield rifles of the 1871 design formerly used by the military. This design of rifle had been replaced by a newer model and the older ones were now fairly widely available for purchase. It subsequently emerged that the weapons used in the attack had been cut 'under the iron ring, which secures the barrel to it' to make them more portable and for the purpose of easier concealment.[18]

The first assailant moved around to the right-hand side of the car while the two other men faced Evans and Charles on the left. One of the bayonets was raised so close to Evans' face that it almost entered his mouth. He struck at it and, as he did so, the trigger was pulled and a bullet grazed his leg, burning his trousers. The other two rifles were discharged almost simultaneously. The shot aimed at Tom Boyd was deflected by Gladwell, who hit the gun with his whip. This resulted in Boyd senior suffering only a minor wound to the shoulder. Charles, however, was not so lucky. A bullet entered his left side a little below the heart, passed through the lung and exited to the right of his spine. The same bullet then penetrated through his father's back but did not inflict a serious wound. All of these actions occurred within a few seconds. Tom Boyd grabbed the whip and drove on rapidly, shouting, 'Murderers'. The assailants pursued the car for only a short distance before giving up. Gladwell had jumped off the car and, quickly making his way through the fields, returned to Chilcomb Lodge and raised the alarm.

When the occupants of the car reached the farmyard it was discovered that Charles was seriously injured. He was taken home to Chilcomb on a door improvising for a stretcher, but despite the best efforts of his two uncles, doctors James Boyd of Bannow and John Boyd of New Ross, he breathed his last at 1.30 p.m. on Monday, 9 August 1880. Charles was dead, one month short of his twenty-first birthday, having successfully completed his law degree and awaiting a call to the bar. At his inquest, the medical cause of death was given as wounding of the peritoneum and lung – the verdict was death caused by gunshot wound.[19]

On the evening of the shootings, gentry from all the surrounding districts began arriving at Chilcomb Lodge to offer their sympathy and support. Later, Charles' friend, John Fegan, described how he had seen him crossing the bridge of New Ross just half an hour before he was shot, in perfect health and smoking a cigar. When Charles was laid to rest in St Mary's Cemetery, New Ross, on Thursday, 12 August, many prominent people were in attendance. Townspeople, farmers and gentry – including: Colonel Tottenham; several justices of the peace; Mr A. Cherry, proprietor of Cherry's Brewery; John Colfer, solicitor; two New Ross doctors; several Poor Law Guardians; and the sub-sheriff, Mr Wilkinson – gathered in large numbers.[20] Motions of sympathy were passed by New Ross Harbour Commissioners, New Ross Board of Guardians and New Ross Town Commissioners in the week following the murder; the murder was also mentioned in the House of Commons, which gives an indication of the family's status. On Sunday, 15 August, at eleven o'clock mass in Rosbercon, Father Edward Walsh (who had succeeded Father Edmond Walsh, who gave Tom Boyd his mortgage, in 1872) expressed his outrage and abhorrence of the crime. The landlord of Shanbogh appears to have made a habit of cultivating the friendship of the Catholic curates of Rosbercon as Father Walsh informed his congregation that he had been present at Chilcomb Lodge when Charles Boyd passed away and had also attended his funeral.[21]

However, Father Walsh's condemnation and outrage was far from universal, particularly after several arrests were made. Within an hour of the shootings, John and Walter Phelan were arrested, followed shortly afterwards by their sister, Anastasia, and first cousin, Michael, son of Richard Phelan. Thomas Murphy of Brownsford, a brother of Johanna Phelan (James' wife), was arrested at four o'clock on Monday morning and James Holden, son of Anastasia Holden, was taken into custody later that day. On Tuesday, 10 August, nineteen-year-old James, another son of Richard Phelan, was arrested. Two unfortunate tramps from Waterford, Patrick Thompson and Thomas Power, who were in the wrong place at the wrong time – walking along the Waterford road at the time of the shootings – were also arrested and held in custody until the following Saturday when they were released without charge. Thomas Doyle, a former employee of Tom Boyd's who was now working for Walter Sweetman of Annaghs, was arrested on 20 August and was formally charged with being the third assassin. Doyle was a tenant of Boyd holding less than two acres of land.

The arrests caused bitterness and indignation among the tenant farmers and labourers for miles around and there was speculation in the immediate aftermath that there was nothing to connect any of those arrested with the shootings other than the proximity of their homes to the scene of the crime. It emerged during the magisterial inquiry, held towards the end of August, that Evans Boyd claimed to have recognised John and Walter Phelan at the scene. It also transpired that Thomas Breen, a 'carman', claimed to have recognised John Phelan. Breen, who was in the habit of allowing his horse to graze along the roadside, was some distance from where the shootings occurred but maintained that, when the mask slipped off the face of the assailant who was pursuing Gladwell Boyd, he was able to identify John Phelan. Conversely, rumours began to circulate that three strangers had been seen at various places in the locality on the day of the attack. These rumours were to gain momentum and would form part of the evidence in the actual trial when neighbours would come forward to make this claim.

The rifles used in the attack and two of the disguises were recovered in a barley field belonging to James Phelan, while the third disguise was found in one of James Holden's fields. During this period, threats were made against the Boyds in the form of placards displayed in New Ross and Arthurstown, both in County Wexford. The message at New Ross read:

Death to the Boyds and all landlords
Rory of the Hills
Tom Boyd and Evans Boyd your day of doom is near
I'm watching you and the bloody Leigh of Rosegarland.[22]

In Arthurstown, a small deal coffin was left on a pier at the entrance gate to the demesne of Captain Chichester, who was land agent to his brother, Lord Templemore. On the lid of the coffin was written: 'Boyd first – Chichester next'. Boyd acted as land agent for Lord Templemore. It was deemed necessary to provide round-the-clock protection for Boyd's family at Chilcomb Lodge and a bullet-proof shed large enough to accommodate twelve policemen and with portholes for firing outward was brought from Waterford and erected at his residence. The reporter, Hugh Mahon, was later charged with printing an offensive placard but it is unclear whether it was the one displayed in New Ross.[23]

On 16 August, three hundred men and women from the surrounding districts arrived in Shanbogh to save the harvests of the Phelans and Holdens. They came from as far away as Whitechurch, County Wexford, and Slieverue, near Waterford. Many of them were strangers in Shanbogh but were there to show solidarity with and support to their fellow tenant farmers in their hour of need. When Bridget Doolin's corn was ripe, J. G. Dooley of Rosbercon used his threshing machine to cut it, assisted by Mrs Doolin's friends and neighbours, and then took the grain to his store in Rosbercon before Evans Boyd could get hold of it.[24]

The magisterial inquiry was held over three days, 21, 23 and 30 August in the grand jury room in Kilkenny. Walter Sweetman of Annaghs was one of the magistrates. On the first day, James Holden, Michael and James Phelan and Anastasia Phelan were informed that the charges against them were being withdrawn but they were not released until Monday, 23 August. Walter and

John Phelan, and Thomas Doyle were charged with being the three assassins while Thomas Murphy was charged with being an accessory to the crime. John Phelan was described as a 'young man of stout build' while both he and Walter were said to be of 'respectable appearance'. Thomas Doyle was described as a 'thick-set heavy looking man of about thirty-five or forty years of age'. Thomas Murphy was described as being middle-aged and having 'the appearance of a comfortable farmer'. Murphy was soon released, the charges against him having been withdrawn. There was rejoicing when these five prisoners returned home and tar barrels were lit on the hills overlooking New Ross while St Mary's Fife and Drum Band paraded through the town.

On the final day of the hearings Evans Boyd described the terrible event as follows:

> I saw the third man put the gun to his shoulder and point it at my stomach. I put my right leg up and as I did he raised it to my mouth making offers as if to stab me. I struck down the bayonet with my left hand, and just then the shot went off, burning the leg of my trousers, and making a hole in it. I know Walter Phelan and John Phelan. I see them in court now. Walter Phelan is the man who attempted to stab and fired the shot at me. John Phelan is the man who fired the shot at my brother, Charles. When Walter Phelan was endeavouring to stab me he was growling like a dog and said, 'Not one shot.' I replied, 'No one will fall off this car. I know two of you if not the third.' The car then passed on; it never stopped all through. They were not completely disguised. The backs of their heads were plain to be seen, and their eyes; and the man that fired at me, when he settled himself to put himself into attitude to fire, showed a darkish-coloured trousers at his thigh. I can positively swear to Walter Phelan's voice on that occasion.

At the end of the inquiry, Thomas Doyle was released, as there was no evidence against him. It was said that the only reason he was arrested was because of an indiscreet remark he made to a policeman. His twelve-year-old daughter, who was said to be a 'simpleton', was also taken into custody for a number of days about this time. Walter and John Phelan were committed to prison to be tried at the next assizes.[25]

The carman Thomas Breen, who had sworn evidence of identifying John Phelan, had become a very unpopular man in the locality. He was taken back to New Ross from Kilkenny by the Waterford steamer accompanied by a strong escort of police and was hissed at by a crowd gathered at the landing stage. He had previously been attacked in Kilkenny by a plasterer named Robert Davies, and George Allen, a blacksmith from Irishtown, had assaulted him in New Ross (the two men were sent to trial for these offences) and the inhabitants of Irishtown burned an effigy bearing the inscription: 'Thomas Breen, informer.' Breen was brought to the scene of the crime for the purpose of measuring the distance between the spot where he had stood and the place where the shots were fired. John Colfer, solicitor for the Phelans, claimed at the inquiry that Breen's evidence was unreliable and that he had contradicted himself several times. The prosecution obviously shared this opinion because he was not called to testify at the trial.[26]

Also adding to the tension in the area was the fact that Robin Brazil, a tailor who lived in a cabin beside James Phelan's farmhouse at Shanbogh Crossroads, had been held in custody without charge since shortly after the attack and was not freed until early September. As a tailor, he had undertaken jobs for the constabulary and his sewing, particularly his buttonholes, was compared to the workmanship of the disguises, which were said to be very well made. On his release, he claimed he had been offered financial inducements to 'tell the truth'. His twenty-five-year-old daughter, Mary, who had also been held in custody, was released around the same time.[27]

Four other young women, who were also being held in custody as witnesses for the prosecution, had been transferred to Richmond Avenue in Dublin from Kilkenny at the end of the magisterial inquiry. They had gone willingly enough believing it would be for only a very short time but the crown solicitor, George Bolton, claimed they, like Thomas Breen, would be intimidated if they were allowed to return home. The women were

Mary Anne Connolly, an employee of John Maloney, Walter Sweetman's gamekeeper; Ellen Green, James Phelan's domestic servant and sisters Mary and Margaret Cashin. Their continued detention also caused great resentment in the neighbourhood and locals insisted that the intimidation George Bolton claimed the women needed protection from was actually coming from agents of the crown. An order of *habeas corpus* was applied for by John Colfer, in respect of the Cashin sisters – Mary, aged nineteen, and Margaret, who was just fourteen – on behalf of their father, Michael, who held about three acres of land from Boyd. A conditional order of *habeas corpus* was granted and the girls were released immediately and restored to their father.[28]

However, Mary Anne Connolly and Ellen Green were left behind. They were over twenty-one years of age and so couldn't be claimed by their parents. They were also at a disadvantage because, unlike the Cashins, they could neither read nor write. Both were being held simply because they were close to the scene of the shooting. Mary Anne Connolly had been in the field where the assailants concealed themselves and was milking her employer's cow when the attack occurred. As she was opening the field gate the assassins ran past on the road in the act of following the Boyd car. She said she did not recognise any of the men. Ellen Green had been living in James Phelan's house for some three months prior to the shootings. At the moment the shots were fired, she was standing at Shanbogh Crossroads and saw three people in disguise running across the fields from the Waterford road towards Shanbogh churchyard but lost sight of them when they reached the churchyard.

The police exerted great pressure on Ellen Green because of her residency in the house of one of the accused. A reward of £200 had been offered for private information on the murder and this sum was offered to Ellen to entice her to give information on the making of the disguises. It would have taken Ellen Green, or any young woman in her situation, more than twenty-five years to earn such an amount but she held firm against the inducement. She was questioned at length by George Bolton, who asked if she had ever seen guns in James Phelan's house. Bolton also asked if any of the men she had seen running to the churchyard was lame. (James Holden had been suffering from an ankle sprain at the time of the attack.) Ellen Green answered 'No' to both these questions.

She was questioned as to who used to visit the house and who was in the house on the evening before the murder and replied that on the evening prior to the murder the Phelan family and Miss Grant, a cousin of the Phelans from Slieverue near Waterford, had been in the house and that only Thomas Murphy had visited. She confirmed that Mary Grant had been staying there for about a week before the attack and left on the following Tuesday. George Bolton continued his questioning of Ellen, repeatedly asking her whether or not Miss Grant, or anyone else in the house, had been sewing during the week prior to the murder or if she suspected that Mary Grant and Mary Brazil were the seamstresses involved. She again replied, 'No'. She was then asked if Mary Grant and James Holden were courting and replied that she didn't know but thought it unlikely because they were closely related.[29] Mary Anne and Ellen were eventually released on 5 October 1880, after Father Patrick Furlong of New Ross drew attention to their plight.

Unlike Thomas Breen, these young women, including Thomas Doyle's daughter, had not given any information that would be helpful to the prosecution case. Yet they were taken away from their families in the hope, it would seem, of eliciting some new information from them by keeping them in custody. It is interesting to note that, without exception, they were the children of poor and landless parents, people with no clout. The four older females were all in service, even Margaret Cashin at fourteen years old. The prosecution appears to have assumed that young women of their status would be easy to bribe.

A report was published in the *Daily Express* soon after the conclusion of the magisterial inquiry, claiming that Walter Phelan and James Holden had visited the house of Denis McGrath of Ballywilliam, County Wexford, on the Sunday prior to the attack.

It was suggested that the rifles were procured during this visit as it was reported that a parcel was seen being placed in their car. However, the version of events given by James Holden and Denis McGrath was rather different. Holden admitted they had visited McGrath on the day in question but he asserted that the purpose of the visit was twofold. First, the Phelans kept a stallion and, having a number of customers in the Ballywilliam area, Walter's purpose in being at McGrath's was to collect money due by several persons in the neighbourhood. James Holden claimed the second object of his visit was to arrange a coursing match between one of his greyhounds and one of McGrath's. Denis McGrath complained that the police had ransacked his house and had made enquiries at the local railway station about the possible arrival of any parcels for him. His cousin, who had recently arrived from Liverpool in poor health, was arrested but was released very quickly without charge. All the lines of investigation the police followed drew a blank.[30]

On 20 September, nearly a month after the conclusion of the magisterial inquiry, a meeting of farmers and townsmen was held in the office of the *New Ross Standard* for the purpose of establishing a fund – to be called the Shanbogh Defence Fund – to finance the defence of the Phelan brothers. The prime mover and main organiser was the New Ross curate, Father Patrick Furlong, who had brought the plight of the young women in custody to the attention of the public. Father Furlong was a native of Our Lady's Island parish in south County Wexford and had been serving in New Ross since 1871.[31] He was a staunch nationalist who was loved by his parishioners but was not highly regarded by his parish priest.[32] Father Furlong was elected treasurer of the Shangbogh Defence Fund and Hugh Mahon was appointed secretary. The priest announced that, following a request from him to the Irish National Land League, he had already received a £40 donation.[33] Over the following weeks and months, the cause of the Phelans grew in popularity and donations came flooding in from counties Wexford, Kilkenny, Carlow and Waterford as well as from America. There was overwhelming support from New Ross.

By the time the Waterford Winter Assizes were opened on 9 December, a powerful defence team had been engaged. These were Peter O'Brien, QC, C. H. Hemphill, QC, and David Lynch, BL, instructed by John Colfer, solicitor. Peter O'Brien eventually became Lord Chief Justice of Ireland in 1889. He was a formidable defence lawyer but gained a notorious reputation among Catholics in his role as a prosecution counsel with the ability to pack juries to gain convictions against them.[34]

When the case came before Waterford Winter Assizes it was postponed on the application of the crown solicitor for Kilkenny and Waterford, whose application was made on the ground that the crime was believed to be agrarian; that many of the jurors were intimidated by fear of injury to their families in the event of them reaching a verdict not concurring with popular sentiment; and that fifty-nine members of the jury panel were said to have been seen at a recent Land League meeting in Waterford. For these reasons, he suggested that a fair and impartial trial could not be had.[35] The case was set to be heard at the Kilkenny Spring Assizes to be held on 12 March 1881.

However, when the Spring Assizes opened, the case of Walter and John was once again postponed. The crown solicitor succeeded in obtaining a further adjournment for similar reasons as those given at Waterford.[36] In a letter from Kilkenny Prison to Hugh Mahon, Walter Phelan expressed his disappointment that the judge had not opposed this second adjournment of their trial in the interest of justice and humanity. He wrote of the 'hellish contrivance' of the prosecution in trying to 'get up a case' against them. He insisted there were no grounds for the accusation made against them but that it was simply malice on the part of the person who made it. He acknowledged the kindness shown towards him by the prison officials, the only difficulty for both of them was being separated from their friends. He declared that separation affected him most acutely but he was comforted by the belief that they could not be held 'longer than July'.[37]

On 23 March 1881, in a totally unexpected move, Bailiff Hammond arrived at Shanbogh and served formal notices on Richard

Phelan and James Phelan to quit their farms by 29 September. The notices were signed by Tom Boyd. The rents of both parties had been paid and no reason was given for these proceedings. There were rumours that Boyd had gone so far as to have a clause inserted in his will that, should he die before the deadline, his executors were to carry out his intentions in relation to the two families and have them cleared off the land.[38]

When the New Ross branch of the Land League was established in late 1880, James Holden and Richard Phelan had immediately become active members. Holden attended a huge meeting at Wellington Bridge on 24 October, which attracted crowds from all over south Wexford and further afield. The Phelan notices to quit came up for discussion at the next meeting of the New Ross branch. The secretary, Peter Pope, made remarks about Boyd being a professional man with no experience of farming, but, having capital of about £1,500 or £2,000, he had borrowed some £10,000 to purchase Shanbogh and become a 'lord of the soil'. This, Pope suggested, gave him powers to 'throw on the waves of the world families whose ancestors were respected and respectable when Boyd's were cutting faggots on the hillsides for a living'.[39]

The case dealing with Hugh Mahon's charge of printing an offensive placard was due to come up in court on 27 May 1881. A letter from the solicitor John Colfer to barrister David Lynch instructed him to act for the journalist and informed him that Mahon was required to produce the original manuscript of the placard. Mahon had admitted printing the document but there was no original as he had printed it 'out of his head'. Colfer was anxious that Mahon should not be compelled to admit to this action, as he might be liable to a criminal prosecution, specifically an incitement to a breach of the law. The letter concluded by asking Lynch to appear for James Holden and James Phelan as well as Mahon. No mention was made of the nature of the charges against Holden and Phelan, but Colfer appealed to Lynch to ensure that the three were treated fairly and 'not subjected to an examination for the purpose of entrapping them'. This letter suggests that Mahon was more deeply involved with the Phelans than might otherwise be assumed.[40]

The trial of the Phelan brothers was finally set for hearing at Queen's Bench in Dublin on 27 June 1881. Two days beforehand, Hugh Mahon interviewed the Phelan brothers at Richmond Prison and found them both in good health and spirits. They acknowledged the kind and considerate treatment they had received from the governor and warders of the jail and mentioned that the chaplain, Father Donegan of Harold's Cross, had brought his band to play outside the prison for them as a 'special compliment to the young men from New Ross'. Mahon reported that they had endeared themselves to everyone in and around the prison by their quiet courtesy and gentle demeanour.[41]

The jury was composed of businessmen and tradesmen of the city of Dublin, with four members being described as 'gentlemen'. The occupations of the remaining eight were listed as builder, merchant, grocer, merchant tailor, bookbinder, bookkeeper, carriage-builder and upholsterer. The prosecution decided, apparently at the last minute, that the two brothers should be tried separately and that Walter should be put on trial first. It seems this decision was based on the fact that Walter had a less watertight alibi than John. When asked in court, Walter pleaded not guilty to the charge of murder.

The most important witness for the prosecution was Evans Boyd, who swore positively that two of the assailants were John and Walter Phelan and he repeated the evidence he had given to the magisterial inquiry. Tom Boyd and his nephew, Gladwell, described the event from their perspectives but agreed they were unable to identify any of the men who had attacked them. Hugh Mahon was called by the prosecution to give an account of his visit to Bridget Doolin's house on that Sunday morning in the company of Walter Phelan. He was questioned closely about the time of day he parted from Phelan at Shanbogh before returning home to New Ross to which he replied that it was 'fully half-past three'. During cross-examination, the defence counsel highlighted Mahon's claim that Phelan had twice pressed him to go into the house with him and that Mahon had declined the invitation. The defence insisted this would suggest that Walter Phelan had been in no hurry to keep an assignment with co-conspirators in order to murder his landlord and his two sons.

The defence concentrated on a card party held in James Phelan's house on the afternoon of the attack. Richard Phelan's son James, Pat Carroll, Robin Brazil and Thomas Doyle were the card players and gave evidence that the fifth player at the table had been John Phelan who had remained with them throughout the critical period thus giving him a very strong alibi. However, Walter's alibi was not quite so watertight and the issue of time became a vital factor. The attack took place at about 4.30 p.m. Walter had returned home from his trip to Jamestown, at 'fully half-past three' according to the evidence of Mahon. When his mother was examined, she testified that he had come in requesting his dinner at 'a quarter to four'. She had told him there was no dinner left and he would have to make do with bread and butter. Ellen Green, who was spending the afternoon across the road in Brazils, said she saw Walter go into his own house 'between three and four o'clock'.

Pat Carroll's evidence was that he arrived at the Phelans 'after four o'clock' while Margaret Phelan put Carroll's time of arrival at 4.10 p.m. Carroll stated that when he sat down to play cards, he noticed Walter 'on the water sill' and that about three minutes later he called his cousin, James, to the door where he spoke with him in private for a couple of minutes before leaving the house. He claimed that only 'about four minutes' had elapsed before Mary Brazil came rushing in to impart the news that 'three queer fellows in white' were coming up through the fields. This would have occurred immediately after the attack. Strangely, this highly unusual event elicited no response from the card players. Carroll testified that he had been in Phelans for only seven or eight minutes in total when Mary Brazil arrived.

Evidence was given that James Phelan, the holder of the tenancy, along with his sister, Anastasia, his brother-in-law Thomas Murphy, and the visiting cousin, Mary Grant, had embarked on a trip to Inistioge on that Sunday afternoon and had taken a boat up river from Annaghs. However, they only got as far as Rosbercon because the boat was too small to hold them all. They disembarked at Chilcomb Pier and spent the afternoon in a public house in Rosbercon, remaining there until after five o'clock. Thomas Murphy then went home to Brownsford with the others accompanying him part of the way.

Much was made by the prosecution of what they called 'this ostentatious departure' of the one on whom suspicion would most likely have fallen had he remained at Shanbogh for the afternoon. In order to support Evans Boyd's claim of being able to identify John and Walter Phelan, the prosecution posed the question as to why he had not claimed that James Phelan, the actual tenant, was one of the attackers. It was suggested that, if he were lying, he would certainly have pointed the finger at James Phelan. There may also have been some confusion as to the identity of the two women as, rather oddly, Anastasia had been arrested and held for a considerable time although she was also on the trip, while Johanna, James' wife, who remained at Shanbogh all day, was never taken into custody.

The defence pressed the point as to whether or not Evans Boyd had actually identified the Phelan brothers at the scene or if it was rather something that occurred to him in the course of the following days. Thomas Byrne, a police constable on leave at the home of his parents-in-law, was called to give evidence. Byrne's wife was the daughter of John Maloney, Walter Sweetman's game-keeper and the employer of Mary Anne Connolly. The constable was, at that time, stationed in Taghmon, County Wexford, and had previously served at New Ross, where he had met his wife. He agreed that he knew the Boyd family but denied knowing the Phelans. He claimed he had been taking an afternoon nap when the shootings occurred. His mother-in-law had woken him immediately and told him what had happened and as he made his way out to the road, he met Evans Boyd coming out of his farmyard. The policeman asked Boyd if he had recognised any of the assailants but, according to Byrne, Boyd replied that it wasn't possible 'because they were masked to the ground'. The prosecution tried to discredit this witness by pointing out that a charge was pending against him accusing him of 'inactivity' in the wake of the attack and furthermore that a charge had been made against him two years previously of having lied to his superior officer.

Witnesses for the defence were called who claimed to have seen three strange men in the locality after the murder. The most important of these was John Dalton of Kilbrahan. He confirmed that his father's farm bordered Shanbogh. He stated that he had seen two men dressed in white close to his home at about five o'clock that evening. He lost sight of them but they reappeared within a few minutes, having changed into dark clothes, and began walking in the direction of Slievecarragh, another town-land bordering Shanbogh. A third man then walked past him, enquiring if he had seen the two other men. Dalton swore he had never seen these men before. Two other local farmers gave evidence of seeing three strangers at about six o'clock at Browns-town, which is over three miles from Shanbogh. Both farmers declared that the strangers had been travelling in the direction of Mullinavat, a village some distance away that had a railway station.[42]

Johanna Phelan, James' wife, claimed to have been out in the haggard all afternoon, protecting her turkeys against a fox that had been spotted during the previous week. One might be scep-tical of a young woman being willing to spend a Sunday after-noon in this manner while her husband and other family mem-bers went off on an excursion, but poultry-keeping was a very im-portant source of income for women in rural Ireland and Johanna Phelan might well be expected to guard her turkeys if a fox was known to be on the prowl.[43] On the other hand, she could have been acting as a 'lookout' and early reports of the shootings had mentioned a young woman waving a red handkerchief in the vicinity of Phelans' house immediately before the attack took place. However, no mention was made of a handkerchief at the trial. Johanna gave evidence that she had seen Walter a few minutes before she heard shots being fired. The prosecution challenged this evidence claiming that in her deposition she had said she had not seen Walter since he departed for Jamestown with Mahon. She suggested this was due to embarrassment because of the circumstances in which she had seen him – he had been in the act of pulling up his trousers in a nearby field.

The prosecution also mentioned discrepancies in the testimonies of other witnesses. They claimed that Robin Brazil had stated in his deposition that Walter had not come into the house at all that afternoon until he was arrested close to six o'clock. Margaret Phelan had originally stated that Walter left the house 'about a quarter of an hour' before Mary Brazil arrived and not four minutes earlier as she testified at the trial.

Peter O'Brien, QC, summing up for the defence, posed the question as to why John Phelan was not on trial based on Evans Boyd's evidence. He suggested the reason was that John had a watertight alibi. Therefore, if Boyd's evidence relating to John was wrong, could his testimony regarding Walter be relied upon? He again referred to Walter's visit to Jamestown with Hugh Mahon and the fact that Walter was in no hurry to 'shake Mahon off' on arrival back at his home in Shanbogh. He reminded the jury that Tom Boyd had stated he was actually later than usual in leaving home on that Sunday and concluded by suggesting it would be shocking if the jury were to believe that Mary Brazil, Robin Brazil, Mary Cashin, James Phelan and Margaret Phelan were all perjurers.

Mr Ryan, on behalf of the prosecution, was scathing in his contempt at the suggestion that three strangers had travelled from Tipperary, where Boyd was crown prosecutor, determined to exterminate him and his two sons. They would have had to cover a distance of some thirty or forty miles. He said it was a wild claim to suppose that these men would have the temerity to travel to a strange part of the country, in broad daylight, to commit a murder on a busy road. If some person in Tipperary had a grudge against Tom Boyd, they had many opportunities to attack and murder him while he was on business in that county. He also raised the question as to how such strangers could know about Boyd's habits or the perfect place of concealment from which an excellent view of anyone approaching from Chilcomb could be had for 500 yards. He suggested that such men would not have risked trespassing in a stranger's cornfield to abandon their weapons and disguises.

Ryan went on to point out that Walter Phelan had proved he was vindictive towards the Boyds by going to Hugh Mahon with the story of Bridget Doolin. He asked why, if Evans Boyd was lying, had he not claimed that James Phelan, the actual tenant, was one of the assailants? He couldn't have known that James had gone to Rosbercon for the whole afternoon.

Ryan demonstrated how slow the reaction of Constable Thomas Byrne had been, a policeman on the spot at the scene of the crime, pointing out that the Boyds had ample time to drive from the site of the attack to their farmyard and Evans, although suffering from a spinal complaint, then had time to get a gun, load it, lay it beside his father and have a conversation with him, go out in the fields to assist in catching a horse, come back out onto the road and, having done all that, only then did he meet the constable walking up towards the farmyard.

The lord chief justice, during his summing up, wondered why the police had arrested Walter and John Phelan immediately after the crime if Evans Boyd had not identified them at the scene. He posed the question as to why they should have been selected when there were thirty other tenants on the townland to choose from. It was, however, pointed out to him by the defence that others were also arrested very soon afterwards.[44]

Even if the Phelan brothers were innocent, it seems fairly certain that the culprits were locals. The attackers knew of Tom Boyd's habit of going for a drive on Sunday afternoons, knew the ideal place to hide (indeed, Boyd would later claim that he had seen Walter Phelan and James Holden on the Sunday before the attack within a few yards of that spot) and made their way confidently into James Phelan's and James Holden's fields in order to dispose of their disguises and weapons, no doubt satisfied that the local inhabitants would not try to capture or follow them.

As in all murder cases, it is necessary to examine possible motives. Who had a motive for wanting Boyd and his sons dead? At the time of the murder, the local family with the most obvious motive was the Holden family. They owed a considerable amount of rent and Boyd was due to move against them within two days of the murder. He had not hesitated to repossess Margaret Forristal's farm at the earliest opportunity, so the Holdens had good reason to fear that he would retake their farm as well. Also at that time, Boyd was expanding his farm business on his land at Shanbogh and building work was in progress, something that may have added to the tenants' feeling of insecurity.

The timing of Walter Phelan's visit to Hugh Mahon, on the evening prior to the murder, to inform him of Evans Boyd's dispute with Bridget Doolin, could have been deliberately chosen. Mahon admitted during the trial that he had not heard of the dispute from anybody else. Phelan readily agreed to accompany Mahon to the widow's house on the following morning being, in all probability, aware that the story would appear in the next issue of the newspaper. His intention may have been to focus attention away from the Phelans and Holdens by suggesting that somebody else might have a motive for wanting the Boyds out of the way. However, for this to be the case Walter would have had to be a man before his time, adept at manipulating the media. The journalist himself, the more experienced and better educated Mahon, may have had a role to play, as he was later prepared to print offensive placards, an incident in which he was linked with James Holden and James Phelan.

On that same evening, Walter Phelan and Thomas Murphy, brother-in-law of James Phelan, left a Rosbercon pub about nine o'clock and returned to Shanbogh Crossroads with a bottle of whiskey. According to the testimony of Ellen Green, all the Phelans were present as well as Murphy and the visiting cousin, Mary Grant. All, with the exception of the teetotaller, Walter, enjoyed a glass of punch and Murphy remained at the house overnight. Ellen did not mention that James Holden or any of Richard Phelan's family were there, but they could have been. Although it may have been a friendly gathering it could well have been a meeting of the conspirators to make the final preparations for the attack. It seems likely that, at some point on the Saturday evening, the weapons and disguises were deposited in the hideout under cover of darkness.

During the card game on the Sunday afternoon, no surprise was expressed or curiosity shown when Mary Brazil informed the card players of the 'three queer fellows in white'. On the contrary, play continued without comment.

The evidence of John Dalton and two other witnesses was that they had seen three strangers in the locality on the evening of the murder. However, it later emerged that Dalton's brother, Richard, had made a statement to the effect that he was on the boundary of Shanbogh and Slievecarragh at around the same time as John but saw no sign of the mysterious strangers. John Dalton and the other witnesses, although not holding land from Boyd, were tenant farmers and might have been willing to support one of their own in his difficulty.

Constable Thomas Byrne gave evidence that he did not know the Phelans prior to the murder but, obviously, his wife, the daughter of the Annaghs gamekeeper, knew them well, having grown up on the adjoining townland. In an article published in a penny dreadful entitled *Famous Crimes* some years after the murder, an illustration showed Byrne's wife preventing him from rushing after the assailants.[45] When all these factors are taken into consideration it would appear that the murder may have been the result of a conspiracy involving the whole townland and beyond.

The jury reached the only possible decision available to them, based on the evidence presented and they acquitted Walter Phelan after little more than half an hour's deliberation, the only real evidence against him being his identification by Evans Boyd. However, he and his brother were held in custody for a further night pending another charge against him (of shooting at the Boyds) and a decision on whether or not to put John on trial. It was decided to take no further action and they were both released the following morning.

The acquitted men were expected to arrive at Ballywilliam by the seven o'clock train on Friday, 1 July 1881. Three or four hundred supporters assembled at the railway station headed by the Ballywilliam Fife and Drum Band. However, John Phelan arrived alone. As soon as he stepped onto the platform, the band struck up 'God Save Ireland'. A procession was formed which led John all the way to New Ross. About a mile outside the town, the procession was met by the New Ross Brass Band along with a number of people carrying burning torches. Arches of greenery with roses had been erected at various points along the route and there was none better than that hung across the street of Rosbercon, from where the prisoner made his way home after almost eleven months' absence. Walter was reported to have left the train before it arrived in Ballywilliam station and to have made his way home quietly. Sadly, he was reported to be suffering from 'brain fever' and there were fears for his sanity.[46]

On Sunday, 10 July, a massive Land League meeting was held in Irishtown, New Ross, with 10,000 people in attendance. The town was decorated with green boughs, flags and banners and about twenty bands were present. The flamboyant Father David O'Hanlon Walsh of Knocktartan, County Wexford, rode into town on horseback followed by about 3,000 people cheering wildly. (His family had been evicted from their home on the previous Thursday, the day of Walter Phelan's acquittal, having refused, on principle, to pay what they considered to be an exorbitant rent. They were tenants of Colonel Tottenham and Tom Boyd was their land agent.)[47] Two platforms had been erected – one for speakers and the other for women. On the speakers' platform, Father Furlong of New Ross, Father Doyle of Ramsgrange and three MPs – Redmond, Sexton and Healy – were gathered. It was expected that the Phelan brothers would be present too, but they didn't appear. The condition of Walter, who had shown signs of 'mental derangement' since his return home, had worsened and Father Furlong had anointed him. His physician, Dr Meehan, said that with care there were hopes for his recovery.[48]

Soon after the excitement of the Phelans' acquittal and homecoming had abated, retaliation and counter-retaliation began in earnest. Intimidation of Boyd's workmen was stepped up. On 9 July 1881, one such incident occurred in the village of Rosbercon. The police named the instigator as John Phelan of Garanbehy, Rosbercon, a first cousin of John and Walter. He was described as being about forty years of age, married and a comfortable farmer of good character. Tom Boyd's traction engine was being driven through the village by an employee while a second man was walking in front carrying a red flag. John Phelan is alleged to have said to the man with the flag, 'Can you not get other work but carrying that flag? Down with Boyd.' He also 'hooted' and 'groaned' Mr Boyd's name and used similar expressions to the man driving the engine. A large number of people were present and they also hooted and groaned and called on the men not to work for Boyd.

On 4 August, Sub-Inspector Wilson of New Ross wrote that feeling against the Boyd family appeared to be increasing daily and that they were being subjected to all sorts of annoyances. Every effort was being made to induce his workmen to leave his employment. He claimed that the Phelans and Holdens were connected in Wexford and Kilkenny and that they exercised much influence for evil on the people. He recommended the arrest of John Phelan to prevent further occurrences of intimidation.

Sub-Inspector Webb of Thomastown wrote in October that Boyd and his family had been completely boycotted and that all his old workmen had left his employment, including the traction engine driver. John Phelan of Garanbehy was arrested on 26 October under the Protection of Persons and Property Act (1881) and was interned without trial for the maximum period of three months. (He was released on 28 January 1882.)[49]

Boyd's difficulty with his workmen cannot be doubted as, towards the end of July, large numbers of farm labourers from as far away as Cork were brought to his farm for the purpose of cutting his hay. They were escorted by a number of policemen and their arrival and departure proceeded very quietly.[50]

The New Ross Regatta was an important annual event for the

town and surrounding districts. In July 1881, a special meeting was convened by the regatta committee of New Ross Boat Club for the purpose of deciding a suitable date to hold the event. After some discussion, Monday, 8 August was decided upon by a motion of the chairman Mr A. Cherry, which was seconded by Mr D. Murphy. It was agreed unanimously and nobody present reminded the meeting that the date chosen was the first anniversary of Charles Boyd's murder. When the date was announced publicly the following day, the *Daily Express* accused the members of sectarianism. However, five Protestants had attended the meeting, including the chairman.

As a result of the outcry, when the next meeting was held to organise the regatta, the issue of the date was introduced and there was a proposal to change it. This led to a heated debate and a vote was taken. The result was that three members voted for the date to change – they were the only Protestants in attendance – while the other ten members voted in favour of retaining the original date. As a result, Mr McConkey of the Bank of Ireland; Mr John Fegan, watchmaker and friend of Charles Boyd; and Mr Williams, draper, walked out of the meeting. Mr Cherry does not appear to have been present but he later presided at the regatta.[51]

Another consequence of the committee's persistence in their determination to hold the regatta on the controversial date was that Evans Boyd tendered his resignation as captain of the Boat Club. However, the regatta proceeded on 8 August and was declared 'a magnificent and triumphant success' and the 'greatest yet witnessed on the river Barrow'.[52]

While one can accept that the date was originally fixed inadvertently, it might be expected that common decency would have dictated that, when the significance of the date was realised, an alternative would have been chosen to avoid further offence to a grieving family. However, other events were unfolding at that particular time which caused feeling against the Boyds to run high and reports on the success of the regatta were nothing short of triumphalist in tone.

On 26 July 1881, Anastasia Holden and her family were

evicted from their 110-acre farm, which they had held for centuries. On the day, a force of forty policemen, under the command of Sub-Inspector Wilson, left New Ross shortly after eleven o'clock and were joined in Rosbercon by a large number of policemen under the command of sub-inspectors Webb of Thomastown and Yates of Piltown. The detachment of the 20th Hussars, stationed at New Ross, headed the march to Shanbogh where Colonel Mollen, the resident magistrate of Waterford, met them.

When requests to gain admittance to Holdens' dwelling house were answered by torrents of boiling water, it was decided to proceed to Mr Boyd's out-farm to procure a crowbar and sledgehammer. This was done and, after about an hour's hammering, the door swung off its hinges. However when the door was removed, it was discovered that a well-built stone wall still barred the entrance to the house – all the time the water continued to pour out, drenching the bailiffs around the head and face. Eventually the wall was dismantled. The bailiffs were ordered to enter and only did so when several policemen were posted before the door with fixed bayonets. The police followed the bailiffs into the house where they found John Holden, older brother of James, standing on the stairs threatening them with a pitchfork. After a short stand-off, John was disarmed.

Throughout the proceedings James Holden remained standing in the yard, appearing to be unconcerned. He was requested by Colonel Mollen to intervene by asking those inside to give themselves up but refused to do so. His brother, John, was arrested and his sister, Anastasia, was charged with having thrown water over the sheriff's officers. She denied being present in the house while the door was broken in. The bailiff removed all the furniture and left it out in the laneway. At the end, Mrs Holden, assisted by her daughter, left the house. Possession was given to the sheriff as representative of Mr John Gray, who had purchased the interest of the farm in the Bankruptcy Court and six emergency men were installed. When John Holden was about to be conveyed to jail, James asked that a car be procured for him, as John was in delicate health. However, this was refused and he was forced to walk to Rosbercon. It was five o'clock by the time the police withdrew from Shanbogh. After the eviction, those workmen still with Boyd declared unanimously that they would never do a stroke of work on Mrs Holden's farm.[53]

Father Furlong wrote to the central branch of the Land League in August requesting further assistance in paying off outstanding debts in relation to the trial and the whole legal battle. He stated that the legal fees were £702 while other expenses, including the provision of wholesome food to the prisoners for the duration of their incarceration, had amounted to another couple of hundred pounds. He informed the committee of the sad circumstances in which the Phelans now found themselves. He wrote:

> They have been sent back to their desolate home, broken spirited and hopeless, one of them wrecked perhaps for life in mind and body, to find staring them in the face the sentence of eviction and extermination which their infatuated landlord has pronounced against them and their kith and kin.

This statement highlights the ongoing mental problems of Walter Phelan and it also supports the belief that Boyd was intent on removing the Phelans from their farm.[54]

Just a few days into the New Year of 1882, Robin Brazil, the tailor who had been accused of making the disguises for the attack on the Boyds, was evicted from his cabin at Shanbogh Crossroads. His rent was £2 per annum and he was one year in arrears. He had barricaded himself into his home but was forced out within half an hour. Another tenant of Boyd's who had also formerly been an employee, John Cullen, was evicted at the same time. Cullen held a cottage and half an acre from Boyd at a rent of £2.10s.0d. He offered to pay but it was refused and he was turned out on the road with his wife and eight children.[55]

In March, Mr J. G. Dooley of Rosbercon, who had taken away the corn from the Widow Doolin's farm at Jamestown in August 1880, agreed to pay Evans Boyd £150 for the farm and, in return, Boyd agreed to give up all claim on her land.[56]

In June, after a three-day investigation, Constable Thomas

Byrne was at last acquitted of the charge of inactivity on the day of Charles Boyd's murder. However, in a move that could only be regarded as vindictive, he was transferred to County Monaghan, 230 miles away. It was claimed that such a transfer was not on record since the formation of the force.[57]

On 24 January 1884, the final chapter in Boyd's attempts to have the two Phelan families evicted was played out in the Court of Appeal. He appealed to have them removed on the basis that they held only year-to-year tenancies. He lost the appeal, ending a three-year battle over the farms at Shanbogh.[58]

The outcome must have brought relief and a sense of security to James and Richard Phelan and their families. However, the victory was of little comfort to Walter. He had not recovered from the ordeal of his imprisonment and trial and had been committed to Kilkenny District Mental Asylum in February 1883.[59] Although he was acquitted by the Dublin jury of the murder of Charles Boyd, and was spared the hangman's noose, he nevertheless served a life sentence in that he never regained his health and spent the remainder of his long life behind the walls of the Kilkenny hospital. He died there on 3 March 1944, aged eighty-seven years.

Why were Boyd's tenants prepared to take the drastic step of shooting their landlord at that time, before the Land League was even established in the area? The answer would appear to be fear of losing their farms. Their ancestors had worked those farms, some of them for centuries, while Boyd was a blow-in, one of the new breed of speculators who were buying up land from the Landed Estates Court. These men had no background or history in farming but had made their money in business or the professions. Boyd was not a wealthy man in cash terms and had been forced to borrow the bulk of the purchase price of the townland from the most unexpected source, a Roman Catholic curate of the tenants' own parish. This transaction is likely to have been common knowledge among Boyd's tenants as is suggested by the remarks of Peter Pope at the New Ross Land League meeting. Men like the Phelans and Holdens probably resented such a man 'lording it' over them while to some extent they had been prepared to tolerate the patronage of a landed family such as the Warburtons, who sold the land to Boyd.

Few of those associated with the murder prospered. John Phelan and James Holden never married and never had homes of their own. John lived out his life with his brother, James, while James Holden, after the eviction of his family, went to live and work with Richard Phelan where he remained for the rest of his days.[60]

Evans Boyd married Mary Crawford, whose brother was married to Evans' sister, Dorothea. They had one son, Thomas Crawford Boyd born in 1886, who became a medical officer in the British army in India and chief inspector of hospitals there. However, Evans and his wife divorced soon after the birth of Thomas Crawford and both remarried.[61] Evans died very suddenly as a result of a stroke on St Stephen's Day 1900, very close to the spot where his brother was murdered twenty years earlier. He was just forty-five years of age.[62]

His father survived until March 1904, by which time he had reached the age of eighty-five.[63] Both Tom and Evans Boyd had become notorious during the decade of the 1880s as the agents of Colonel Tottenham. Evans had the dubious distinction of being the designer of a special battering ram that assisted in the eviction of David Foley of Ballykerogue, County Wexford, from his home in November 1887.[64] In Tom Boyd's will his effects were valued at £8,847. However, this figure included the value of a considerable amount of land. Despite having acquired the townland of Shanbogh over thirty years previously, two mortgages were still outstanding on it for more than £3,500 – £1,887 excluding interest being due to the Association for the Propagation of the Faith (a Catholic organisation) and £1,750 due to Lieutenant Colonel Frederick Tottenham. His life assurance policies did little more than clear his bank overdraft with the National Bank in New Ross (his policies realised £3,798 while his overdraft was £3,392).[65] He was obviously a man who did not keep a tight rein on his purse strings. Chilcomb Lodge was demolished in the late twentieth century and Thomas Boyd's descendants – those of

Evans, Dorothea and Frances – are scattered.

Richard Phelan's family has disappeared, as have the Holdens. However, on a positive note, James and Johanna Phelan had one surviving daughter, Johanna, whose descendants still hold the farm at Shanbogh Crossroads to this day.

'Put the saddle on the right horse'
Borklemore, West Wicklow, 1893

SEÁN O'SULLIVAN

THE TOWNLAND OF BORKLEMORE, which on the map looks like an intrusion into the neighbouring county of Carlow, is actually a part of Wicklow.[1] Today, it is still a quiet rural area halfway between the village of Kiltegan in Wicklow and the town of Hacketstown in Carlow. In the 1890s, under the shelter of a small hillock at the end of a laneway some forty yards from the main road, there stood a long farmhouse with a central kitchen and a room behind the fireplace, called the upper room, and a room at the bottom of the kitchen, called the lower, or servant's, room. The summit of Lugnacuilla Mountain could be clearly seen from the back of the house and, further to the left, Keadeen Mountain dominated. To the west and south the low green hills sloped down into the rich land of Carlow. It was in this beautiful and peaceful setting that the worlds of three people were shattered during a night in May 1893.

The owner of the house was seventy-four-year-old John Conran, a comfortable farmer of thirty-nine statute acres. He lived with his wife, Margaret, who was ten years his junior, and Mary Farrell, their elderly housekeeper who, although able-bodied, was in poor health and was generally looked after by Margaret. The Conrans had been married about thirty-four years but had no family – their two children had both died in infancy.

John Conran had been suffering from severe rheumatism for some years and could only walk with the aid of two sticks. This ailment severely limited his ability to work the farm so he employed a local neighbour's boy, ten-year-old Michael Byrne, who helped around the house, and William Dunne of Tinneclash who did most of the farm work. The Conrans' day-to-day activities were fairly mundane – perhaps a visit from the odd neighbour or travelling person bringing some news from the outside world or perhaps the shooting of an intruding crow or woodquest that was threatening the cabbage or potatoes.[2]

At about six-thirty on the morning of Tuesday, 16 May 1893, young Michael Byrne made his way up the lane to the Conrans' house to start his day's work. As he rounded the corner from the lane into the yard of the house, he was surprised to find his master, John Conran, gesticulating and shouting at the window of the upper room. As Michael ran towards him, Conran told him to run for their neighbour, Mr Jackson, and get him to come to the house immediately. At that minute, William Dunne came around the corner and into the yard. Conran told him that the two women had been murdered by an intruder during the night and that he himself was locked inside the house – he had heard the intruder lock the door from the outside and then throw away the key. Conran told Dunne to raise the door off the hinges but Dunne had already searched around and found the key about seven or eight yards from the front door. Mrs Keating, a relative of Margaret Conran, then arrived with young Michael Byrne whom she had met on the road. Michael was immediately sent to get his mother. When Dunne and Mrs Keating opened the door to the lower room, they saw that the two women were dead. William Dunne then went to Hacketstown police station and reported the tragedy.[3]

Sergeant D'Alton arrived at the house in Borklemore within a short time and found John Conran sitting in the kitchen. When the sergeant asked him what had happened Conran replied, 'Was it not a terrible thing that my wife and the girl were shot last night?' Then D'Alton found Margaret Conran lying on her back on the earthen floor of the lower room with her head towards the door and her feet partly under the bed. When he examined her, he found blood on her head and on the floor. Mary Farrell was lying on the bed and there was a lot of blood on the pillow and bedclothes. D'Alton then examined the kitchen and noticed a shotgun placed over the fireplace. He realised it had recently been fired when he saw powder on the nozzle. He also noticed a cracked cap on the nipple of the gun. When he searched the kitchen further, he found a flask of gunpowder, a canister containing a lot of shot and a paper case containing wads for guns in the chimney place.

On Wednesday, 17 May, an inquest was held at one o'clock in Mrs Lowe's public house in Kiltegan with John Conran as the principal witness.[4] He said that his wife was baking a cake when he went to bed on Monday night, 15 May. He woke at about eleven 'with his water' and heard a sort of moan. Then two shots rang out in quick succession – at this juncture Conran clapped his hands to illustrate the timing of the shots. He crawled out of bed and got his two sticks before making his way to the door leading to the central kitchen, where he saw a man he did not know who was wearing a hat, had his face blackened and the collar of his coat pulled up around his neck. The intruder was holding the key to the kitchen door leading to the outside. Conran thought that he heard the footsteps of another person outside, but couldn't be certain. The intruder then went out and locked the door behind him and Conran said he thought he heard the key being thrown away. When Conran made his way to the door and tried to open it by lifting the latch, it didn't open because it was securely locked. He then went to the lower room but there was no light there so he made his way back to his own upper room, struck a match, lit the lamp and then went back to the lower room:

> When I saw the state they were in I laid down my sticks and stretched down to my wife who was lying on the broad of her back. She was quite cold. I was so feeble I could not lift her up. I saw the servant girl

lying on the bed. There was so much blood I thought her throat was cut. I knew by her colour that she was dead.

Conran then went back to the kitchen and 'cried my fill'. He might have spent half an hour there before he went to his own room, put on his clothes and sat for a considerable amount of time. He then went to the kitchen door and found that it was still locked. He held the lamp down to the keyhole to see if the key was in the lock, but it wasn't there. 'I went to my own room window and stood there bewailing the women. For how long I don't know but it was a couple of hours or more. Then Michael Byrne arrived.'[5]

Dr William Langford Symes carried out the post mortem. He found fourteen shot wounds on the right side of Mary Farrell's neck and head. The direction of the shots went from the front of the ear to the back of her head. Her jugular vein was perforated and this wound alone was sufficient to cause death by haemorrhage. She would have to have been sitting on the bed facing the room door to account for the position of all the grains of shot, presuming they had come from the kitchen. Margaret Conran had no marks of injury to the front of her body. There were two bullet wounds in the back of her scalp. The right wound was large enough to admit an index finger; the left was somewhat smaller but passed directly into the brain. He found the bullet that caused this wound in the under-surface of the right side of her brain. She had been wearing a cap, or bonnet, when she was shot as it had a hole in the back and he found four portions of bullet matted in her hair. Dr Symes concluded that Margaret Conran's death was instantaneous. Dr John Alexander McDonnell, dispensary doctor at Baltinglass, County Wicklow, had assisted Dr Symes and agreed with the evidence given by him.

It emerged from the inquest that Margaret Conran was shot by pellets, or slugs, although none were found in the house nor were they common in that part of the country, and Mary Farrell was killed by shot only. The only immediate and logical conclusion to draw from this discovery was that two guns must have been used to commit the murders.[6] After a short deliberation, the jury returned a verdict of death from gunshot wounds 'inflicted by a person or persons unknown'.

When the two women were to be buried, none of the neighbours would wash, dress or coffin the bodies. In parts of the country, there would have been a reluctance to deal with the bodies of people who had died by violence and who had not received the last rites of the Church. Eventually, the constabulary had to prepare the bodies for burial.[7]

The police suspected from an early stage that John Conran had committed the crimes. Three days after the event, Detective Inspector McNamara, accompanied by Sergeant Moore, arrived at John Conran's home and took him into custody. 'He did not seem to be surprised and, apart from muttering something like "all right" he made no statement.' He was driven into Kiltegan village and was remanded by a magistrate to Wexford Gaol for eight days.[8]

At a special sessions in Hacketstown on 28 May 1893, John Conran was charged with the murders of his wife Margaret and Mary Farrell. Michael Byrne, the servant boy, was the first to testify and told the court that, on the day before the two women were murdered, he was standing outside the house with John Conran who told him to go inside and bring out the gun from the Conrans' bedroom. Conran took the gun, leaned backward and positioned his back against the wall of the cowhouse and aimed at some woodquests.[9] Shortly afterwards, Michael Byrne heard a shot. Then Conran told him to return the gun to the house and place it over the fireplace. In telling these events, he implied that this was a rare and unusual action. The farm worker William Dunne gave evidence of having been instructed by John Conran to fire a shot at woodquests in the cabbage garden. When he protested that there no woodquests in the garden he was told to fire a shot as the smell of the powder would keep the birds away.

Sergeant D'Alton was the next to testify. He told the court that, during his investigations, Conran told him about a deed of settlement which had been drawn up about thirty-four years earlier when he was marrying Margaret. Conran told Byrne that some woman 'had a claim' on him, which was usually taken to mean that he had fathered a child to a woman and there might be paternity claims against him or his estate. Alternatively, there might be a danger of a Breach of Promise case against him. Whether or not this was the full explanation for the drawing up of the deed is not clear but it was an unusual procedure to undertake in 1859. According to Conran, the deed specified that, on the death of either his wife or himself, the surviving partner would inherit the farm. Much was made of this deed in the court in an effort to prove it was a motive for the crime. The prosecution argued that, if Margaret Conran was the surviving partner, she would inherit the farm and it would pass out of the Conran family name to her relatives, who had no historical connection with the land. The loss of a long-established family name attached to a farm would have been a very emotional issue in nineteenth-century Ireland and this led to the inheritance issue being given as a possible motive for the killings.

A neighbour of the Conrans, Johanna O'Neill, added further to this line when she told the court that John Conran had told her that his brother, Pat, had offered to buy the farm and to build a separate house for Margaret and himself and maintain them for the rest of their lives. This offer came about when John told his brother that, because of his rheumatism, he could no longer carry on farming. But it seemed that Margaret Conran was not agreeable to this settlement with her brother-in-law. John Conran told Johanna O'Neill that he had not committed the two murders but that when the time came he 'would put the saddle on the right horse'. However, when the actual deed of settlement was produced in court there was, in fact, no mention of inheritance of succession. The document merely stated that, in the event of John Conran's, death a sum of £150 would be settled on his wife.

Following this disclosure, Conran's representative argued that the motive for the killings presented by the prosecutions was now 'dissipated' and, as a consequence, John Conran should not be put forward for trial. However, Conran was returned to the Leinster Winter Assizes in Wicklow town.[10] He was again sent back to Wexford Gaol where it seems that the enormity of his predicament overcame him, for the record states that: 'John Conran, unconvicted prisoner, attempted suicide. He inflicted a lacerated wound on the radial artery of the right forearm with the handle of a small tin.' But he survived the attempt.[11]

The Leinster Winter Assizes, under Mr Justice Johnston, opened on Wednesday, 6 December 1893, in Wicklow courthouse and the murder of Margaret Conran occupied the whole of the first day. John Conran was described as 'a decrepit old man' and was provided with a seat in the dock. He was indicted with having, on 16 May 1893, 'feloniously, wilfully and with malice aforethought murdered one, Margaret Conran'. Conran, who was defended by Dr Falconer and John Redmond, BL, MP, pleaded not guilty.[12]

In opening the case, the attorney-general concentrated on the crime of a husband murdering his wife, describing it as 'a domestic murder, a murder which set at defiance the law which governed the mind of every man, outside the law of the land, the law which bound a man to protect his wife, to guard her and ward off from her every peril, every danger, every foe'. He firmly set the motive for Conran's crime – he was too infirm to work the land and wanted to sell the farm to his brother Pat.

During the month of February 1893, Conran had told Pat of his condition and Pat had offered to buy the land at a good price and to build a house and look after them. However, Margaret Conran would not agree to that proposal. She was ten years younger than John and she was a healthy woman who was looking forward to surviving her husband. Consequently, she was anxious to retain her house and farm.

The attorney-general then analysed Conran's state of mind. 'Conran was under the impression that his wife had a claim to the land by survivorship and that that claim prevented his disposing of the land to his brother. What was the obstacle to carrying out that transaction? His wife.' He then spoke of the prisoner's infamous suggestion to a neighbour that he would 'put the saddle on the right horse'. Who was he referring to? There might have been some insinuation that his brother Pat had committed the crime to enable him to buy the land, and that Margaret Conran's objection to parting with the farm caused her death. Then he asked, 'Why was Mary Farrell killed? Because she would be a witness against the prisoner at the bar. The prisoner alone could have a motive for killing Mary Farrell.' It was reported in court that Margaret Conran had said to her husband on one occasion, 'John, for God's sake, stop or take down the gun and shoot us as you have often threatened to do.' Conran was supposed to have replied, 'God, look on me, ye would hang me.' The attorney-general concluded by stating 'there was the motive and there was the threat'.

Michael Byrne told again of the shooting of the woodquests on the evening before the murders confirming that he had never seen such birds about the place. He also stated that John Conran had removed the cap from the gun after firing it. Justice Johnston noted Michael Byrne's words, 'I never saw a cap on the gun'; 'I don't know was any cap on it' and 'I never saw woodquests'. Byrne seemed rather hostile towards John Conran though. When he was questioned about Conran's incapacity, Byrne said that he had seen him cover the ends of potato ridges with a shovel, though later he admitted that he aided John Conran in putting on his stockings two or three times.

When questioned about the relations between the Conrans, Byrne said that he heard John cursing his wife and Mary Farrell about three weeks before they were killed. He conceded that he only mentioned this fact at his fifth meeting with Sergeant Mullane, adding that he saw no baking on the evening before the murders but that 'baking always happened after I left'.

However, a close neighbour, Mrs Keating, said that she was a frequent visitor to the Conran household, sometimes milking the cows for them and that she had never seen any trouble between the couple. Two other neighbours, Mr J. Willoughby who visited the Conrans five or six times in the previous five years and

Henry Jackson, who was sent for on the morning after the murder, stated that the Conrans seemed to be on very good terms and had an amicable relationship.[13] A second cousin of Margaret Conran, Mrs Bridget Byrne, said that she visited the Conrans very often and always found them on good terms having only heard about one argument when John saw a light in an outhouse and complained that there were 'tin ware people there'. Constable Donnellan said that while he was searching the house he heard John Conran lamenting his wife and saying, 'What is to become of me in my latter days?' He then heard Conran say, 'Thank God, they were prepared. They were both recently attended by a priest.'

However, Mary Clifford, a travelling woman, had a different story. She was at the house on the Friday before the murders when John Conran told her that it would be the last night she would get a bed in his place while he was alive. His wife disagreed with him, telling him that Mary Clifford would always have a bed in the house while she [Margaret Conran] was alive. According to Mary Clifford, Conran replied, 'That won't be long.' According to local tradition, Mary then startled the court when she told the judge, 'My Lord, I was on the point of a fart of being shot myself.'

District Inspector McNamara added further speculation when he told the court that, on the day of the funeral, he asked John Conran to have a look at his wife before she was placed in the coffin but Conran replied, 'They may go to the devil. I'd sooner have a smoke.'[14] Sergeant McCarthy also added to these negative comments when he said that, in the course of a conversation he had had with the prisoner on 16 May, Conran cried out, 'O God, what brought her across me at all?' And later, after a pause, he uttered, 'What brought the devil into my house at all?'

Johanna O'Neill told the court that, on the day of the funeral, Conran had given her £3, which he had been given by his brother Pat, to bury the two women. When she remonstrated with him that £3 was hardly enough to get them coffined, he retorted that he would not spend a penny on them because Margaret would not agree to sell the place to Pat and 'that was what got her killed'. This evidence further added to the negative impression given of Conran.

However, John Redmond, for the defence, was not prepared to let these statements remain unchallenged and argued that, although in the days following the murders John Conran was physically in his own home, in a sense, it was no longer his home as he was constantly in the company of neighbours and policemen. Redmond tried to put the remarks in context, 'If, in these circumstances, he said blameworthy or contradictory things, who would dream of condemning him on evidence like that? When he said something like "they can go to the devil" it was more likely that he said it about policemen.'[15]

Constable Bollard produced a map and a model of the house to help demonstrate the prosecution case which was, as Justice Johnston noted, that the prisoner stood in his own room and fired across the kitchen into the servant's bedroom killing both women.

On the witness stand, Pat Conran stated that he lived thirteen miles from the house of his brother and that he was on friendly terms with Margaret Conran. The first time he heard that she would not agree to his purchase of the farm was on the day of her funeral. He then spoke of his conversation with his brother the previous February:

> I told him that if he was going to sell the place, I'd give him more than another. I said, 'I'd leave her and you in the place as long as you live and support you and if you don't like that, I'd build you a house in the sandpit.' I said I'd give them the grass of a cow and to let me know if she'd consent. I saw him no more and I have no idea how these people lost their lives.

During further questioning, Pat confided that, although he only lived thirteen miles from his brother, he had not stood in John and Margaret's house for twenty-seven years. The conversation about taking over the farm had taken place on the public road and John didn't invite his brother into his house. It was obvious that he had been communicating with John, therefore it would seem, that he and Margaret must have had a serious falling-out for such a depth of ill-feeling to last for so many years. John Conran had confirmed that he spoke to his brother about the sale and there was no substantial difference in their account.

Sergeant Byrne gave an interesting insight into Pat Conran's involvement when he told the court that he had heard Pat question his brother in the days after the murders about the money John had paid Mary Farrell. John replied that he had given her more than £50 but not all at once. The implication of this was that Pat Conran was trying to establish robbery as the motive for the crimes.

The court then learned that both bodies had been exhumed on 24 May and had undergone further tests by Dr Symes, Dr McDonald and Dr Lappen. They ascertained that Margaret Conran's death was caused exclusively by slugs while Mary Farrell died from shot alone – that no trace of shot was found on Margaret Conran and no trace of pellets on Mary Farrell. More astonishingly, no sign of either grain or shot was found on the pillow or bedclothes and there was no trace of shot on the papered wall behind the bed. Dr McDonald said that he had done some shooting in his time and it was his opinion that it was not possible that the two women were killed by a single gun firing two different types of missile. On Mary Farrell's body the extreme distance between the shot marks was ten inches.[16]

Sergeant Mullane told how he and other constables searched the ironwork and framework of the bed but found no trace of shot. They then removed the wallpaper and, despite intensive examination, did not find one grain of shot. In reply to Justice Johnston, Dr Symes said that there was no evidence that the women were shot at very close range.

At this point, Justice Johnston's mind was puzzled by events and he annotated, 'Tho [sic] both women are old and Mary Farrell delicate, there was no evidence that they were not active enough to have made some resistance against so infirm a person as the prisoner if he had been about to load the gun with two charges to shoot them with two discharges.' Later he noted that 'no evidence was given by anyone skilled in the use of firearms or having experience of firearms' and again 'there was no evidence to show that Mary Farrell was shot with shot corresponding to the shot found in the house'.[17]

A separate point that weighed heavily with both sides was the question of whether or not John Conran was wearing his socks on the morning of the discovery of the deaths. Because of his infirmity, he was unable to do this task himself so, if he had gone to bed in his usual way, as he had stated, his wife would have removed the stockings. If nobody conceded to having put the stockings on his feet during the morning of the discovery, the implication was that John Conran had not gone to bed in the usual way and had, therefore, lied about his movements. Michael Byrne had told the court that he had helped Conran on a number of occasions but not on that particular morning. However, in what seemed to have been a crucial bit of evidence, Margaret Byrne, Michael's mother, stated that she had put the stockings on John's feet on that particular morning, thereby resolving that point of argument.

Few, if any, forensic tests were carried out to test the various theories about the gun (or guns) used. No firearms expert examined the gun or the discharges in an effort to resolve the slugs and shot issue. Nor was there any evidence of blood spatter presented, although tradition has it in the area that there was much blood on the walls of the lower room where the bodies were found. However, this did not emerge at the trial though there was police evidence that the walls were minutely examined and no blood or shot were found.

The issue of the key being found seven or eight yards from the door did not become a tested issue in court either. Local tradition has it that the best and strongest policemen at the scene of the crime made various efforts to throw the key from John Conran's bedroom window but all failed to reach the spot where the key was found. But this information did not emerge in court. The only tests carried out at the scene to prove evidence was that provided by Sergeant Byrne. John Conran said he emerged from the room at eleven on the night of the murder and saw an intruder with the key of the front door in his hand. Sergeant Byrne experimented on 14 June at eleven o'clock. He stood at Conran's bedroom door while Constable Byrne stood at the kitchen door holding the key in his hand. The sergeant concluded, 'I could not see that the constable had a key in his hand or anything else, it was so dark.'

Having emphasised that Margaret Conran had no claim whatsoever to the farm, Dr Falconer, for the defendant, suggested to the jury that the witnesses were very hostile to John Conran, quoting from Shakespeare that 'trifles light as air are to the jealous mind confirmation strong as Holy Writ'. Michael Byrne and William Dunne had left the jury with the impression that there were no woodquests around the farm at all but later, under cross-examination, both admitted that there were plenty around the place. He then pointed out that, if John Conran had fired at Mary Farrell from his own bedroom, as the prosecution had claimed, the shot would have scattered but that was not found to have been the case.[18]

The evidence having been heard, Justice Johnston charged the jury in the normal way. However, he told them that they would have to consider that, if only one gun was used that was capable of firing only one shot, then the manner in which the different types of shot were drawn into each body 'could only be done by a juggler'. He then said that 'it was extraordinary that not a grain of shot was found in the bed or room, an extraordinary circumstance given that fourteen grains of shot were removed from the body of Mary Farrell'. Justice Johnston then introduced another curious factor into the case when he mentioned to the jurors that if, in their opinion, the crime was committed by the prisoner in complicity with another or if the crime was committed by Conran alone 'their duty was clear'. The introduction of another or others being involved had not been an issue before the court and there had been no evidence of conspiracy. The *Freeman's Journal* commented that Justice Johnston reviewed the case for the jury and his comments on various points were very favourable to the accused.[19]

The relevance of the deed of settlement, signed in 1859 by both John and Margaret Conran, is difficult to ascertain. There was great change in Irish landholding in the years following the 1870 Landlord and Tenant Act (when evictions were curbed and value for tenant improvement was secured) that continued with the Land Act (Ireland) 1881 (commonly called the Gladstone Act), which granted tenants the 'three Fs'– fair rent, fixity of tenure and free sale. By the time of the murders in 1893, John Conran could have left the land to whomsoever he pleased and could have disinherited his wife without any repercussions. His state of animation over the deed of settlement seems strange bearing in mind the circumstances prevailing at the time.

As the jury retired, there were strong indications that Conran would be found not guilty. John Redmond, the defence counsel, had stressed strongly that John Conran's original account of what happened on the fateful night did not vary in any material way during subsequent questioning. He did not change or deviate from his account throughout the whole of the ensuing period despite being interviewed at various times by policeman after policeman. The question of whether Conran was dressed and wearing his stockings was discounted when Mrs Byrne admitted that she had helped him dress. And, of course, the different types of shot which were found in each of the bodies perplexed everyone. There had been no evidence that two guns were used.

There were many questions arising from the suggestion that Conran had fired two different shots from the single gun found above his fireplace. Because of his infirmity, it was improbable that he was able to discharge the first shot, reload the gun with different ammunition and then shoot the second person dead. The preparation of the gun – a single-barrelled muzzle shotgun – for firing was a complicated process. To load it, it was necessary to pour a measured amount of powder into the barrel from a flask. This powder could not be put in haphazardly because the user could be in serious peril from explosion when the gun was discharged. The powder then had to be tamped down in the barrel with a tamper rod, which was attached to the gun. Then a wad made from paper or cotton had to be rolled by hand and inserted into the barrel and also tamped gently. When these tasks were satisfactorily completed, the shots or pellets could be inserted and tamped once again. With the ammunition properly in place, the firing mechanism had to be set. Under the hammer of the gun was the nipple to which a cap had to be fitted. A small hole in this nipple led into the part of the muzzle that contained the powder. To fire the shot the hammer had to be pulled back. When the trigger was pulled, the hammer struck the cap on the nipple, causing a spark that ignited the powder within the muzzle and the resulting explosion within the chamber expelled the shot.

Maybe, even with his crippling rheumatism, John Conran could have done all of these laborious tasks before the murders but was he capable of repeating the process to murder the second victim? If Conran had committed the murders, a further question arose about what the second victim was doing whilst Conran was reloading the gun. This latter query puzzled even Justice Johnston. In these circumstances, John Conran and his defence team must have been fairly confident of the jury's findings.

There was some shock when the jury returned within thirty minutes. Such a short sitting normally indicated that the members of the jury were so unimpressed by the weight of evidence that there were no topics worthy of serious consideration. To find a person guilty of murder in less than thirty minutes would require solid, overwhelming evidence. However, the eleven Protestants and one Catholic from County Wicklow who sat in judgment on John Conran did not conform to the norm. There was almost total disbelief when they pronounced John Conran guilty of murder – even Justice Johnston seemed totally unprepared for this eventuality and had not brought his black cap with him to court.

John Conran was sentenced to be hanged on 8 January 1894 but 'did not seem to be affected by the verdict'. As he was descending from the dock, Conran was reported to have looked up to Justice Johnston and said, 'I thank you, my Lord.' He also made an observation that he might also thank those that swore against him.[20] Like most aspects of this case there was another account of Conran's departure from the dock for he was also reported as saying, 'I may thank the bloody villains who swore against me.'

A letter from 'Concerned Citizen' appeared in the *Daily Express* on 28 December stating that the people were shocked at the verdict and saying that, although most people considered John Conran to be guilty at the beginning of the trial, as the evidence had unfolded, opinion had changed.

> *The two women were murdered, one by shot, the other by slugs or pellets. The Crown maintained, when it was proven that one shot could not have killed both women, that he first shot one woman, then the other. I am incredulous that the second woman sat quietly awaiting her fate. John Conran was so feeble that she could easily escape.[21]*

The writer continued: 'Ten of the jurors considered the case proven, the other two acquiesced.' The writer's bias then appeared. 'The sentence, if carried out, will do more to weaken the confidence of the public in the good sense and discrimination of the Protestant jurors of Wicklow[22] than a hundred disagreements like the Bradley murder in Mullingar.[23]

Immediately on his return to Wexford Gaol, two extra warders were employed to guard John Conran, specifically to ensure that he did not attempt suicide again.[24] A few days later, he requested a visit from the Sisters of Mercy and from Father David Bolger, the prison's assistant chaplain, which was approved by the Visiting Justice. The day following his meeting with the nuns and Father Bolger, John Conran requested permission to see his solicitor to resolve the disposition of his house and farm, which he left to his brother Pat.[25]

On 20 December 1893, in reply to a request from the undersecretary regarding information on Conran's health, Dr Woodehouse wrote that Conran was 'quite intelligent but very callous'. He then mentioned that because of his incapacity he would be unable to walk to the scaffold.[26]

The three solicitors involved in Conran's defence lost no time in organising memorials asking that the death penalty be commuted to life imprisonment. A memorial was organised in Wicklow, one in the Hacketstown/Kiltegan area, another in Naas and the final one in Wexford. Each had identical wording, with three written in the same calligraphy – the fourth was typed. They read:

> While it is true that after a fair and patient trial John Conran was found guilty of the murder of his wife, Margaret, the memorialists wish his Excellency, the Governor General, to order the commutation of the sentence of death ... It was said that the women were killed by one shot but one died by slugs or pellets and the other by shot alone. It was not proven that the lead used in the slugs or bullets was the same as the tea-lead found in the house nor was a single shot produced to show that the shot used in killing the other woman was the same as that found in the house ... The memorialists further state that the alleged motive, that the deceased Margaret Conran had an interest in the prisoner's farm, which rendered her consent to the sale necessary, was dispelled by the production of the marriage settlement.

It says much about the social structures of the time that the signatories were almost entirely composed of people of substance, such as bankers, solicitors, strong farmers, clergymen, military personnel and politicians. Fifteen members of Wexford Corporation signed it, together with a large number of hoteliers, ministers of religion and lawyers. In the Hacketstown area, it was reported that all members of the jury signed.

Dr Steward Woodehouse, the general medical officer of prisons, was asked to comment on the prisoner's health and on the case of the Wexford memorialists. He stated, 'I am informed that the memorial from Wexford in [sic] his behalf has been signed, not from any sympathy with him but from a general dislike to the execution in Wexford of a man who belongs to another county.' Therefore, it might have been the fear that the cost would have to be borne by Wexford ratepayers that created the basis for this petition.

Towards the end of December 1893, *The Irish Times* reported that no effort was being spared to have the death sentence of John Conran commuted. The report went on to say that the sight of an old man tottering towards the gallows would be a ghastly one and although there was a precedent for Conran being provided with a chair on the trap door, the authorities were anxious to avoid such a necessity.[27]

On 2 January 1894, the High Sheriff of Wicklow received a letter informing him that the death sentence had been commuted to penal servitude for life. From the time of his arrest until the death sentence was commuted John Conran had been incarcerated in Wexford Gaol but, when the commutation was announced, he was transferred to Maryboro Gaol in Queen's County (Portlaoise).

When Conran was brought to Maryboro Gaol on 13 January 1894, he was immediately placed in the invalid section. By 1895, he was unable to leave his cell, his hands were crippled from rheumatism and his legs and thighs were considerably swollen from dropsy.[28] The prison report stated that 'any attack of acute illness would carry him away'.[29] By 1896 he was unable to get into or out of bed without assistance and, by June 1897, the medical officers reported that he was subsiding quickly and that 'the inevitable can be at no very distant date'. Conran was bedridden and entirely helpless and there was no chance of any improvement in his condition. The prison authorities were satisfied that he was receiving all due care and Dr Woodehouse stated that nothing more could be done for him anywhere else.[30]

John Conran died in Maryboro Gaol at 5.15 p.m. on 20 July 1897, just over four years after the murders. An inquest, held on 23 July, found that 'death was caused by exhaustion supervening of gastric catarrh, weak heart and rheumatism'.[31]

The house, outbuildings and entrance lane of the farmstead where the tragedies occurred have now disappeared. Looking at the scene today, it is difficult to imagine that events that gripped the nation once took place there. From time to time, the murders are recalled locally and various versions of the 'truth' are proffered – some of the sympathy now lies in favour of John Conran for it seems very unlikely that he was the only person involved in the murders. However, nobody is certain about any potential accomplices. When all is debated and analysed, it seems a great pity that John Conran never did put the saddle on the right horse after all.

'But the stairs is not sound, sir!'
Friarstown, Tallaght, 1816

SEAN BAGNALL

ON 5 NOVEMBER 1997, a team of workmen opened a cable trench into a field situated between the River Dodder and the main road near the Old Bawn Crossroads in the townland of Killinniney, near Tallaght, County Dublin. As they were digging, they unearthed some bones which they initially thought were the remains of an animal. However, on closer inspection, they agreed that the bones might be human and sent for the gardaí who confirmed that the bones were indeed of an adult male. Not knowing anything more about them, the bones were sent to be dated – a process that would take some time.

Investigations and door-to-door enquiries started in the immediate area about missing persons or suspicious activities but nobody could remember anything that might lead to an identification of the deceased. After some weeks had passed, word reached the area that the bones were quite old and did not relate to a death within living memory. Consequently, the skeleton was boxed and taken into the care of the National Monument Service where it still remains.

In an area that has changed utterly in recent decades, the discovery of the bones and disclosure of their age created an opportunity for older people to revisit old memories and drag up recollections of old deaths, murders and shady happenings in the

Tallaght area. It enabled them to remember a time when Tallaght was still a village some distance outside Dublin and was totally rural in character. Barely remembered stories handed down from generation to generation were retold and this evocation of times past rekindled some of the spirit and memories of local folklore. The excitement of an old, local, unsolved murder sent many potential sleuths, young and old, into the libraries and archives in an effort to establish the true identity of the skeleton found in Killinniney and reveal the story of how the body came to be there. It was soon apparent that Tallaght had had its share of horror and of gruesome death in times when human life was not so sacred and justice was truly awful.

The focus of the community speculation narrowed on one particular crime. Ponsonby Shaw was a member of an old Kilkenny family with lands at Sandpits in that county. In County Dublin, Shaw owned lands at Friarstown just at the entrance to Glenasmole Valley in the Dublin Mountains. His father Robert of Terenure Manor was an original £5,000 subscriber to the capital of the Bank of Ireland and was one time controller of the post office. His brother, Sir Robert Shaw, married a Miss Wilkinson of Mount Jerome and it was through her that he inherited Bushy Park in Terenure. This Sir Robert was one time MP for New Ross and voted against the union. Their uncle, who remained in Kilkenny, was an ancestor of the playwright George Bernard Shaw.[1] The Shaws were a wealthy, landowning family in south County Dublin at a time when there was unrest and a proliferation of rural protest movements. The contemporary 'banditti' or 'Whiteboys' – also known as 'Shanavests', 'Hearts of Steel' or 'Hearts of Oak' – varied in name from one locality to the next but they expressed many of the grievances of the rural tenantry.[2] Opposition to tithes, rent demands and efforts to reduce rents after 1815 were all on the agenda of rural communities. In County Dublin, some land agents were nervous of these issues and also of the involvement of the peasantry in supporting the rebels of 1798 and Robert Emmet in 1803. Through his connection with Anne Devlin and the Currans in Rathfarnham, Robert Emmet was known in the area and had found support there.

Willie Kearney had a public house in Killinniney at the site now occupied by the Old Mill Pub at Old Bawn Crossroads. Anecdotal local evidence suggests that Kearney had Michael Dwyer, the rebel from County Wicklow, as a regular drinking guest in his pub.[3] Kearney had been friendly with Nicholas Stafford during the 1798 Rebellion and may have taken part in the fighting.[4] Before the rebellion, Stafford operated a pub at 131 James' Street and was one of 1,064 persons who received a conditional pardon for his part in the uprising. However, like many others who were involved, he soon learned that rebellion and business did not succeed side by side and, by 1803, was operating a bakery in Thomas Street.[5] Some sources suggest that the authorities moved to ruin the businesses of many of those involved in the rebellion in Dublin.[6]

Willie Kearney featured prominently in Emmet's rising on 3 July 1803. When Emmet discovered that there was no chance of success, he left Dublin to escape capture and tried to make contact with Dwyer and the Wicklow men. He spent the night of 26 July at the house of Mrs Rose Bagnall at Ballinascorney and, the following day, Emmet and thirteen of his rebels, including Nicholas Stafford, hid in the attic above Willie Kearney's pub, which was located on the main road from Rathfarnham to Ballinascorney and would have been on Emmet's route as he fled from Dublin to the hills.[7]

On two occasions Emmet and his group were almost discovered while they hid in Kearney's. During the afternoon of the 27 July, Baronial Constable Robinson called to Kearney's when he noticed strangers in the district. He stepped in among the men downstairs but saw nobody in uniform. The men he did see did not appear to be an unusual number to find in a public house at the time. Mrs Kearney, Willie's wife, came on the scene and her calm demeanour and assurances diverted him from further investigation. He soon left totally unaware that the men he sought were all up in the attic.[8]

However, he was only gone a short time when Kearney's was

again visited in search of rebels. This time the callers were the soldiers and the Rathfarnham yeomanry under the command of Captain La Touche and Sir Robert Shaw. Having searched down-stairs without success, Shaw started to climb the stairs to the attic. Mrs Kearney again came to the rescue and she persuaded Shaw that the stairs to the attic were unsafe and could not be used. She warned him, 'But the stairs is not sound, sir!' Luckily for Shaw, he accepted her protestations, as Arthur Devlin was waiting at the door of the attic with a loaded blunderbuss.[9]

Both Shaw and La Touche were men of the establishment, just as Emmet's family was.[10] Both families, including Shaw's father-in-law, Abraham Wilkinson, had been involved in the founda-tion of the Bank of Ireland in 1783. To these people position and respectability were paramount and no greater sins could be com-mitted than allowing oneself to sink into the ways of the peas-antry and rebellion against one's own class.

Emmet was eventually captured and executed. The years immediately after his death produced as many informers as any other period. Willie Kearney and the customers at his popular public house continued the ideals of 1798 and the spirit of Emmet in the following years and they were viewed by the Shaws, as well as other landlords and gentry of the area, as dangerous and corrupting enemies in their midst. Besides, they had also made fools of Constable Robinson and of La Touche and Sir Robert Shaw while these men were searching for Emmet, and had ob-structed the pursuit.

Emmet's consorting with Willie Kearney and others of trade and tenantry was not expected from someone of his background. As far as the gentry were concerned those of Kearney's class who consorted with Emmet in his rebellion, gave him shelter or encouragement or were otherwise implicated in his downfall and disgrace could only have been regarded with the greatest of suspicion thereafter.

This was the time of the French Wars and the ruling class' fear of the French and of the possibility of French invasion had reached paranoid proportions. The lord lieutenant, the Earl of

Hardwicke, is reported to have believed that Napoleon was scheming to conquer Ireland and install a Roman Catholic government. Many of the French politicians of the time were still openly described in newspaper reports as 'the regicides' and French forces had landed in Mayo in 1798. In addition, it was the period immediately after the union with Britain and the question of a repeal movement was linked with the question of Catholic Emancipation in many minds.[11] These were dangerous notions, particularly when espoused by what was described as 'the lower orders'.

However, the same wars against the French brought high prices for all farm output and the resulting prosperity brought a measure of serenity to the country. Both landlords and tenants benefited. However, 1815 and the Battle of Waterloo brought an end to all of this. Prices started to fall immediately and neither landlords nor tenants could adjust easily to the changing circumstances. Landlords found rents harder to collect and tenants demanded reductions and other concessions.

Ponsonby Shaw was not immune to these difficulties. His agent, John Kinlan, spent his days among the tenants listening to their pleas and demands. But folk memory paints Kinlan as an unyielding character. He was well known as a severe agent who took harsh measures against the tenants on the estate and also had a reputation as an informer.[12]

One night in 1816 Kinlan called to the house of one of Shaw's gamekeepers. He was under some sort of threat because the gamekeeper asked him strongly not to go home alone but to accept an armed escort of friends. Kinlan ridiculed the warning and set out alone. Just five minutes later a gunshot was heard. Despite immediate and extensive searching by the gamekeeper no body was located though signs of a struggle and part of a suspender were found. The suspender was later identified as belonging to Kinlan.[13] It was presumed he had been murdered but, despite subsequent exhaustive searches, no trace of Kinlan or of his body were found.

At the time of Kinlan's disappearance policing was largely the responsibility of each grand jury which appointed its own constables and paid them out of county funds which were raised from the 'cess' or rates. Policing varied from county to county and most areas only put a police force together as a reaction to an immediate threat of disturbance. Constables appointed under the Policing Acts of 1787 and 1792 wore no uniforms, were under no supervision, were subject to very little discipline and, when not acting as constables, followed their own occupations.[14] They were most often involved in searches for stolen goods but had no power to cope with disorder or riots.

Under an act in 1814 Robert Peel had formed the Peace Preservation Force. Under this act, resident magistrates were appointed together with chief constables and sub-constables. This force was formed in response to disturbances and could deal with disorder and riots but could be withdrawn or disbanded when the danger passed. This flexibility enabled the grand juries to minimise the cost of maintaining the peace.[15]

It was just two years after the formation of Peel's force when John Kinlan disappeared. The substantial landholders, such as Ponsonby Shaw, paid large amounts in cess contributions and, despite the changes brought about by the act, landholders still had much influence over the appointment of magistrates and constables and the conduct of investigations.

Because of the ongoing animosity, when the names of possible suspects in the disappearance of John Kinlan were being mentioned members of the Kearney family were high up on the list. They had been involved in protests going right back to 1798 and no doubt Shaw had learned of their involvement with Emmet during 1803. Kinlan himself may have conveyed some of this information.

It was also learned that, during Kinlan's dealings with some of the tenants, Peter Kearney, the father, and his two sons, Joe and Willie, were heard to say that they would finish him off if they ever got the chance.[16]

Just then, by diligent police work, a bloodied hatchet, which was marked with hair that resembled Kinlan's, was found quite close to the Kearney home.[17] As a consequence, Peter and his sons were arrested.

The trial was one of the first to be held under new legislation dealing with 'conspiracy to murder'. The effect of this legislation was that, to secure a conviction, it was not necessary to prove actual murder but merely to prove that the defendants conspired to commit a murder.

Lundy Foot, whose family owned a well-known tobacco and snuff shop in Westmoreland Street, was a local magistrate living in Orlagh, or Footmount as it was then called. He actively sought the conviction of the Kearneys and helped build the case against them.[18] He was friendly with both the neighbouring Shaws and with Daniel O'Connell and folklore has it that he sought O'Connell's advice as to whether or not the Kearneys could be tried under the new 'conspiracy to murder' legislation. O'Connell advised that they could.[19] Afterwards, Lundy Foot was the magistrate most active in bringing the Kearneys to trial and securing their conviction. Nineteen years later this same Lundy Foot was murdered on his estate in Rosbercon, County Kilkenny. It was not the first attempt on his life – he was shot not long after the Kearneys had been hanged – and nobody was ever brought to trial for the attempt or the murder, but local folklore has it that relatives of the Kearneys were involved in both incidents.[20]

The Kearneys' trial took place shortly after their arrest. Among the witnesses called was a man named Collins from Glassamucky, a townland adjacent to Friarstown. Collins was called by the defence to give alibi evidence for Peter Kearney, the father. Collins told the court that Kearney was in his house on the night that Kinlan disappeared and that, while there, they both heard a shot. They rushed out to discover what could be seen. The prosecution used this information as evidence of Peter Kearney's complicity in the crime by contending that he had gone specifically to Collins' home so that he would have a firm alibi at the time of the shooting. However, the judge ruled that Collins' testimony should be disallowed because there was no evidence before the court that Kinlan had been shot. As the trail progressed, the bloodied hatchet was instead proving a major part of the prosecution's case.

By the legal standards of the time, all three Kearneys were convicted of conspiracy to murder and were sentenced to hang.

At the time, hanging was the method used in all parts of Britain for capital offences. This was before Haughton's compassionate innovations and condemned prisoners were hung from a scaffold and strangled as their own weight caused the noose to tighten and choke them. It was a slow painful death. The condemned person did not lose consciousness immediately but struggled for air in considerable pain. During this struggle, his face turned purple, his eyes bulged, his tongue swelled and hung from his mouth and at a late stage in the process he lost control of his sphincter. At some stage he lost consciousness and his heart stopped. In some cases, the process could last for up to ten minutes with painful suffering by the unfortunate and considerable anguish among the watchers.[21] In these circumstances, it was not unusual for relatives to attach themselves to the legs of the hanging person as they hoped by adding extra weight to speed up the process and shorten the pain.[22]

On the day appointed for the hanging, the Kearneys were taken in an open cart from Kilmainham Gaol to the place of execution near their pub at Killinniney. Their route on the day took them past Bushy Park, the home of Sir Robert Shaw. At which point, they requested that the cart be stopped. The three convicts then knelt down in the cart and solemnly cursed the whole Shaw family through all their succeeding generations. It is reported that having thus relieved themselves of such depth of feelings, they went cheerfully on their way to the execution field on the banks of the River Dodder at Old Bawn, Tallaght.[23]

There were several reasons why hangings took place in the area in which the guilty party resided. First, the cost of the event would have to be borne by the people of the area. Thus this cost eventually devolved on the tenants who paid rents to the landlords. Second, the horrific event was staged as an example and warning to anybody who might be thinking of committing an outrage against the landlord or the state. Third, the attendance of family, kin and neighbours gave added intensity to the spectacle and left a cloud of significant mourning hanging over a townland for a long time afterwards.

Three gallows had been erected beside the River Dodder under the supervision of the hangman, Thomas Galvin, who had been functioning as executioner for some time.[24] He had carried out executions in 1798 and was credited (if that is the right word) with the executions of the Sheares brothers, William Michael Byrne and John McCann in July 1798. In 1803, he appeared again to execute Robert Emmet, when he allowed Emmet's body to hang for thirty minutes before cutting it down. Part of his function in the execution of a person convicted of treason was to sever the head from the body and, in Emmet's case, he did this on a borrowed butcher's block with a borrowed knife. Galvin then held the head aloft and carried it towards the excited crowd with the words, 'This is the head of a traitor, Robert Emmet.'[25] This ritual was designed to maximise the spectacle of the execution and add to the deterrent aspect of the hanging as the fate in store for those who would foment terrorism, treason and rebellion.

After their incantations in front of Bushy Park, the Kearneys eventually came to Old Bawn. From the chosen site, the River Dodder and Willie Kearney's pub at the crossroads were clearly visible as was Friarstown where Kinlan had worked and where Ponsonby Shaw still resided. Their home area of Piperstown and Glassamucky at the top of Friarstown Hill could just be seen.

Here the Kearneys were very much in their own space and surrounded by their own people. Reports indicate that thousands gathered to witness this major family catastrophe. A troop of dragoons that had escorted the tumbrel from Kilmainham now surrounded the place of execution to keep order and if necessary to quell trouble in so large a crowd.

The tumbrel drew up in front of the gallows and the Kearneys stepped down. One of the sons was the first to climb the ladder and turned to help his father up. At this point a third son, not implicated, interrupted to offer to take his father's place on the gallows, but his offer was refused.[26] The other son climbed to his place.

Galvin then did his business – but he had made an error.

One of the Kearney sons was unusually tall and when the support beneath his feet was removed he dropped but his feet just touched the ground. Galvin had given him too much rope. The gruesome struggle that followed greatly angered the crowd and the dragoons had to restrain them. Peter Kearney's wife, and mother to the unfortunate sons, was particularly angered and had to be restrained by a dragoon from attacking Galvin. The hangman was then handed a spade and dug out the soil from beneath the son's feet until the victim could find no further support.[27]

Eventually the Kearneys died, the spectacle ended, the crowd dispersed and the three bodies were cut down. They were thrown into the cart, covered with lime sacks, brought back to Dublin and buried within Kilmainham Gaol. As the gallows were taken down, a portion of the timbers almost fell on Galvin, a prospect that greatly amused the remaining crowd. At a later date, the three skeletons were exhumed from their resting place within Kilmainham and relatives arranged a more dignified resting place.[28]

Tallaght has changed utterly since the days of the Kearneys. It has left its green rural pastures and character behind and more than 100,000 people in urban development housing have crept over it during the last forty years. These people cannot be expected to know of the past history of the place. They have never heard the fireside stories of the disappearance of John Kinlan nor the hanging of the Kearneys. Indeed, many of the older people born and raised in Tallaght may have forgotten these stories as well. Through the finding of the skeleton in 1997, a ghost of a forgotten era has reached into modern Tallaght to remind us that the past should be remembered. It enhances all of our lives and gives us roots to bind us to the area.

Perhaps modern technology will confirm an identity for those bones. Perhaps evidence of a gunshot wound or of a severe blow to the head would complete part of the story. On the other hand, maybe Kinlan was not killed at all and made a new life for himself somewhere else.

'Every word stated by the prisoner may be taken *cum grano salis*'

Newtownstewart, County Tyrone, 1871

AUSTIN STEWART

IN THE MID-NINETEENTH CENTURY, Newtownstewart was a thriving market and post town in the parish of Ardstraw, in the barony of Strabane, County Tyrone. It was halfway between Omagh and Strabane and located at the foot of Bessy Bell, the most prominent mountain in the area. For centuries it was a place of much importance as it controlled the only pass through the mountainous terrain.[1] Such was its importance in the early seventeenth century that Sir Felim O'Neill, having captured the castle in the town in the 1641 Rising, found it necessary to raze the settlement to the ground, and didn't even spare the valuable church property in the ensuing destruction.[2] In 1689, almost fifty years later while on his way to the Siege of Derry, King James II enjoyed the hospitality of the town when he lodged for a night in the town castle. However, heading back south after the siege, he realised the strategic importance of the place and gave orders for the castle to be dismantled and the town burned.

The town remained a derelict place until 1722 when it was restored by one of the Stewart family. The town, then called Lislas, had originally taken its name from Sir William Stewart, who acquired the place through his marriage (*c.*1628) to a daughter of Sir Robert Newcomen, a plantation grantee.[3] After its restoration, the town became the centre of the great linen district and it thrived. By the mid-eighteenth century, it was the property of C. S. Gardiner and consisted of three principal and three smaller streets containing 346 houses. The main streets were well paved and there was an ample supply of water, with many houses in the town piped to access the water from a spring to the southwest of the town. As a measure of its status as an important thoroughfare, there were two 'good hotels' on the main street.[4]

By the early part of the nineteenth century, there was plenty of work and many were employed in the numerous limestone and freestone quarries around the town. The Ordnance Survey in 1831 commented on how the people lived in Ardstraw parish and noted:

> ... *the morals of the peasantry are not as good as might be wished. Drunkenness and party spirit still abound to a considerable extent, but cock-fighting and private distillation are on the decrease and almost wholly confined to the dregs of the people.*[5]

On the eve of the Famine, the population of Newtownstewart stood at an all-time high of 1,082 inhabitants. By 1871, it had dropped below 1,000, and a hundred years later it had crashed to an all-time low of 621 inhabitants, representing a decline of forty-three per cent since the Famine.[6] It was a population decline that was typical of that part of Tyrone in the late nineteenth and early twentieth centuries and it undoubtedly reflected 'a worsening situation in the domestic linen industry'.[7]

In the nineteenth century law and order in the town was upheld by a small constabulary force based in the main street and, close-by near the post office, a petty sessions room was hired to sort out any community miscreants. These were few, as the town of Newtownstewart was generally a peaceful community with the few misdemeanours there were being generally the result of too much drink. This became less of a problem as the century progressed with the establishment of a revenue police who waged constant war on illicit distilling.[8] Nearing the final quarter of the nineteenth century, Newtownstewart along with many Irish hamlets, was well positioned to benefit from the upturn in the Irish economy that followed the development of the world mass markets during the nineteenth century. As it happened, the inhabitants of Newtownstewart were not too concerned with economies of scale – they found themselves, dramatically and without warning, at the centre of a most audacious and puzzling occurrence that, over a century later, still excites interest and raises unanswered questions.

About March 1871, Sub-Inspector Thomas Montgomery arrived in Newtownstewart to take charge of the Royal Irish Constabulary in the town with Head Constable Thomas Hobson as his assistant. By June, their main concern was the threatened strike on the railway and they were expected to keep a twenty-four-hour guard in case any damage was done to the rails or rolling stock.

On 29 June 1871 Mr Strahan, the manager of the Northern Bank in Newtownstewart, visited a sub-office in Drumquin, a small village about ten miles away, where the bank held an out-office once a week. He left the bank's only other employee, twenty-eight-year-old William Glass, working in the branch on his own. The three-storeyed bank house still stands today, virtually unchanged – even the alignment of the main bank counter is the same today as it was then.

As was the custom, the bank manager and his family lived over the bank premises. There were three people in the bank house that day: Strahan's aunt, Miss Mary Thompson; Robert Cook, the gardener; and the domestic maid, Fanny McBride. Mrs Strahan and the family were away on holiday. At two o'clock, Robert Cook and Fanny McBride were eating their lunch together in the kitchen when Miss Thompson arrived back from her morning walk. Fanny immediately prepared some lunch for Miss Thompson and brought it up to the parlour. After this, Fanny went upstairs to a bedroom on the third floor to lead the fire grate. This room at the top of the house was the nursery and looked out onto the street. She then came down and cleaned up after lunch before going back upstairs to clean Mrs Strahan's bedroom. While there, she heard the cockle men from Donegal calling in the street below. She told Miss Thompson and went down to get the cockles and later joined Miss Thompson in the parlour.

Mary Thompson was a tall elegant lady and, as was her custom at this time of the year, she looked after the running of the house while the family was away on holiday. She knew few people in town but was acquainted with Sub-Inspector Montgomery. In fact, she had paid a visit to his wife at about one o'clock that same day. The Montgomerys, only in town four months themselves, were lodging in McClenaghan's Hotel. When she had called on Mrs Montgomery, Miss Thompson was taken into the back sitting-room to see 'a pretty view of the railway and the river'.[9] The policeman himself was there and very cordially offered her a glass of wine which she declined. She returned to the bank house around two o'clock to find the outer door of the bank open as usual – there was a spring bolt on the door and it was by all accounts very heavy indeed. The inner hall door leading to the residential quarters was shut and she had to knock on it so that Robert Cook could let her in.

It was a routine day in the bank, the same as any other. Several people did business during the last thirty minutes of business on that Thursday afternoon.[10] First, there was George McFarland, a cattle dealer in the town. He was in the bank at 2.30 p.m. and only stayed a few minutes – there was no other customer in the bank at the time. Next there was Mr Moncrieff, the local miller from Mill Street. He was there closer to three o'clock and James Coll and Mary Fulton were in the bank at the time. There were two offices in the bank, an outer office where the bank counter was and an inner office with an adjoining door in an archway. It was James Coll's recollection that the inner office door was shut. He got his money and started counting it at the window.

James Coll had spent two years in America and was in the bank with his girlfriend, Mary Fulton, daughter of the proprietor of Fulton's Hotel on Main Street, to cash a cheque. When he first produced the cheque, Glass refused to cash it unless Mary's mother signed the back. They both went back to the hotel where Mary signed it on her mother's behalf. They returned to the bank before three o'clock where an altercation arose between Coll and Mr Glass about whether Coll would have to pay 6d. for the encashment. Coll was very annoyed and said so to Glass, who retired to the inner office for further clarification. While he was in there, Mary Fulton thought she heard a whisper, as if Glass was talking to someone. Coll, who was closer to the door of the inner office, said subsequently that he heard nothing. Glass returned to the main office practically at once and he said he wasn't at all clear about the 6d. being due but said that Coll could fix up with Mr Strahan if need be the next time he was in. Mr Moncrieff, James Coll and Mary Fulton were the last people to do business in the bank on that day.

Upstairs in the bank house about this time, Mary Thompson retired to the drawing-room. Around 2.30 p.m., maybe slightly later, Sub-Inspector Montgomery came to the bank and came up to the drawing-room to ask when exactly Strahan was expected home that evening. He had a mind to go fishing with him. He was dressed in dark clothes and stayed only a few minutes. Some time later, Fanny asked Mary Thompson for permission to go into the garden but was refused and was told to prepare the vegetables for dinner at five o'clock when Mr Strahan would return.

As was her habit, Fanny went to view the clock in the bank office through the glass door in the hall, which is when she saw William Glass lying in a pool of blood, with more blood on the floor between the wall and the bank counter. Frightened, she ran upstairs to Mary Thompson who sent her to Mr McDowall, owner of a hardware shop across the street. He came over, pushed open the bank office door and found the young cashier dead on the floor.[11]

When Dr Todd, the local physician, arrived he found ten wounds on the dead man's head, any one of which he declared would have caused William Glass' death. The back of his skull was crushed completely and, most extraordinary of all, the prong of a bank file had been pushed through his ear into his brain.

The map on the wall of the bank office was spotted with blood and there was hair sticking to it. It was obvious that some money in notes and gold had been stolen from the safe. By any standards, it was a violent, horrific and savage murder. Although robbery appeared to be the motive so horrific were the wounds inflicted on the young cashier that, were it to happen today, the killing might be interpreted as having all the hall marks of a crime of passion, or at the very least the actions of a seriously deranged mind.

Sub-Inspector Thomas Hartley Montgomery was the most senior policeman in the town of Newtownstewart on the day of the murder. There were eight officers and men in the barracks who worked under him. His head constable, Hobson, was away on police business in Drumquin. When the alarm was raised, Montgomery was one of the first to arrive at the crime scene where he was joined by Commander Scott, a local magistrate. They examined the body and the bank premises but disagreed as to what was to happen next. Scott took grave exception to the police chief's first assessment of the situation that the cashier, William Glass, had committed suicide. However, Montgomery wasn't the only one to initially think this as it was also the impression of Francis Gordon, postmaster and local petty sessions clerk who arrived at the bank when the alarm was raised. Scott, who lived near Omagh, and Montgomery didn't know one another and there was an initial stand-off between them concerning what procedures to follow. Scott became troubled when he realised that Montgomery, though acting within his authority, intended to disturb the crime scene by removing the body from the bank premises.[12]

The head constable, Hobson, arrived back from Drumquin about 10.30 p.m. and stopped off at Sam Hood's public house for refreshment after a long day. While there, he learned of the murder and he set off straight for the bank, by which time Montgomery was back at the police barracks. Dr Todd was still at the bank and had extracted the file from the dead man's head and handed it over to Hobson, who hurried over to his police chief who was sitting in the day-room of the barracks. Montgomery appeared distraught and remarked to Hobson that it was all an unfortunate affair. He had just sent off two telegrams to RIC headquarters in Omagh, but Hobson's main concern was that it appeared that the five out-stations in the area had not been informed.

Just then Strahan, the bank manager, arrived in the station wondering if there had been any developments. He was questioned about who the last person in the bank might have been. Strahan said he didn't know. One of the constables suggested the last person in the bank was a man named Moncrieff. Hobson showed some annoyance when he learned that this lead had not been followed up. At this, Montgomery, together with Constable Shannon and the bank manager, set off for Moncrieff's house but he was asleep in bed and they decided not to waken him. They were back in the barracks within ten minutes. Hobson was a bit perplexed. He followed Montgomery into the office from the day-room where Montgomery told him that Commander Scott had taken a high profile during the early evening and had taken upon himself the task of interviewing people. At this Hobson suggested that the two of them should revisit the bank premises for another look.

On the way across the road, Montgomery was at pains to point out to Hobson that he had telegraphed Belfast and Derry, sent two telegrams to Omagh, one to Strabane and one to the inspector general of the RIC in Dublin Castle. He had indeed been busy and explained that he was in no way remiss. He explained to Hobson that Commander Scott was unhappy with Montgomery's first telegram sent to the police authorities in Omagh that had merely suggested that William Glass had died in 'suspicious circumstances'. He pointed out to Hobson that he could not have said any more at that time because the doctor had not then arrived.[13] His explanation for not immediately contacting the out-stations was that he was delayed by the officiousness of Commander Scott and that he had to carry out a search of Glass' lodgings.

At the bank, Hobson insisted on making his own search of

the office and discovered a piece of newspaper in the room between the corpse and the window. Montgomery was a little agitated that his constable was looking in places that he himself had already searched and was finding evidence he had missed. Hobson drew attention to a mark on the door post and a cut on the door. He pointed out that there was a large clump of hair on the door and some blood.

'I have already noted that,' Montgomery remarked testily. At his superior's comments, Hobson understood that he had done enough searching. Just then, the undertaker arrived with the coffin – the bank manager was keen to have the corpse removed from the premises as soon as possible. Hobson disagreed with moving the body and said so to Montgomery. In reply, the police chief pointed out that Commander Scott had been there earlier and had conceded that the body might be moved. The commander thought the body should be taken to the best room in the bank house. Dr Todd was present when the corpse was put in the coffin and he suggested that it be brought to the police station. The two policemen visibly winced at the thought – the day-room in the barracks was bleak enough without a corpse for company. Montgomery suggested that it be removed to Kerr's public house next door and Glass' body was taken to the outhouse of Kerr's public house.

Although subordinate to Montgomery, Hobson clearly had a mind of his own because before they left the bank premises, he had a discussion with Constable Shannon and Montgomery regarding the circumstances of the death. According to Hobson, it was obvious that no stranger had done the deed and that local knowledge had been needed to commit the crime. First, the fact that the bank manager was away at the fair in Drumquin and his wife and family were away on holiday were significant. The only people in the bank were William Glass and the three people above in the house, Robert Cook, Fanny McBride and Miss Mary Thompson. It was clear that, given the nature of the wounds inflicted on the dead cashier, there had been no chance of him surviving the onslaught. Putting the bank file through his ear into the brain was as wilful an execution that one could get. Dead men told no tales.

Hobson urged Montgomery to write up a communication to the out-stations immediately. In the presence of Hobson and Shannon the police chief took his pad and wrote up a communication, sealed it and gave it to Constable Shannon to post as soon as possible. It had been a long day for Hobson at the fair in Drumquin. There was always some aggravation over disgruntled traders and dealers, and the police had to be vigilant in the late evening when drink was in and sense was out. Hobson, ever meticulous in his duties, always found it a strain. This was compounded when, on his return, he was confronted with the vicious murder and found that his senior-in-command had failed to alert the out-stations. The failure to raise the alarm properly would surely reflect poorly on all incumbents in the Newtownstewart barracks when the full picture emerged at headquarters in Omagh and could damage his promotion prospects. Hobson had been stationed over a year in Newtownstewart and was ambitious to impress his new superiors.

Hobson was tired after his day at Drumquin and Montgomery, who complained of being sick in the stomach with the whole matter himself, encouraged him to go home and rest. Montgomery said he was also about to go home to bed. A message from the coroner conveyed to the policemen said that an inquest would be opened the following day. The two policemen agreed to retire, anticipating the long day ahead of them. Before they parted company, Montgomery emphasised to Hobson that he had received an order from the inspector general in Dublin regarding the ongoing dispute on the railway.

However, Montgomery did not return to the hotel where he and his wife had lodgings. His heart was heavy, as he had been on intimate terms with William Glass for some time. He needed to walk, no doubt to clear his head and take in the enormity of what had happened. As he had received instructions from Dublin the previous day to keep an eye on the railway lest the men strike and block the line, he headed out the Omagh road towards

Grangewood. He also knew that the Omagh police would be sending someone down and it was an opportunity to rendezvous with them on the way. Shortly after midnight, he met Sub-Inspector Willie Purcell coming by horse-drawn car from Omagh. With him were two constables. Purcell had received Montgomery's telegram that night which read: 'William Glass murdered. A large sum of money stolen. Please examine trains and lodging houses.' Purcell immediately had the telegram copied and forwarded to the out-stations in the district by mounted orderlies. Having done this, Purcell and the constables headed for Newtownstewart, where they met Montgomery near the poplar tree at the bottom of Moore's Field, which was located between the gravel pit and Newtownstewart.

Montgomery showed no surprise at Purcell's presence at such a late hour, about two in the morning, and saluted him warmly with the words, 'Purcell, I am glad to see you.' Purcell got out of the car and walked back into Newtownstewart with Montgomery, who took the opportunity to give Purcell a graphic account of what had happened at the bank that day. The two men then went to the bank premises where they found Strahan still in shock and not yet retired. He let the two men in and Purcell proceeded to do his own check of the murder scene. Strahan was able to confirm that £1,600 in cash and gold was missing.

Purcell noted that there were two pieces cut out of the carpet where there were stains and wondered whether they were bloodstains taken away for forensic investigation. Montgomery said he didn't know, but it prompted him to ask Purcell if the last person out of the bank could be accused of the murder if there were no bloodstains on their clothing. At this point, Purcell did not know that Montgomery was referring to himself, and summarily dismissed the suggestion as most unlikely that a person could be convicted of murder because of circumstantial evidence. Montgomery was much heartened by this reassurance and immediately conveyed to the bemused Purcell that he, Montgomery, had been in the bank after three o'clock that afternoon. Purcell made no comment but spent another couple of hours at the murder scene before departing. Montgomery, still obviously upset at the death of his friend walked part of the way out of Newtownstewart with Purcell. Outside the town, the horse and car picked up Purcell, who advised the sub-inspector to 'go home, and get some rest'. Montgomery replied that he preferred to be in the open air. He boarded the car with Purcell and went as far as the gravel pit where the men had met earlier. There Montgomery alighted and bade goodnight to Purcell who continued to Omagh where he arrived at 6.30 a.m.

Having parted with Purcell, Montgomery set off in the direction of Moyle Crossroads. He never returned home that night to his lodgings in McClenaghan's Hotel. He had been dining there earlier in the evening, when news of the murder broke and he had returned briefly to the hotel between ten and eleven o'clock. Then he left without giving any indication that he wouldn't return that night. Maggie McClenaghan, the proprietor's daughter, sensed his upset and waited up all night for him to return, but he did not come in until six the next morning. McClenaghan, the proprietor, was on hand then and scolded the sub-inspector on the matter complaining that his daughter had waited up very late for him. Montgomery apologised, though he did say that his wife knew that he would not be back that night. McClenaghan gave him some brandy as he retired to bed.

The following afternoon, Friday, the coroner's inquest opened in the hotel and almost immediately it was revealed that Sub-Inspector Montgomery was seen leaving the bank around the time of the murder and that he may have questions to answer.[14] This was the first time Hobson had learned of Montgomery's presence in the bank. This news stopped the proceedings. The inquest was adjourned and was to be resumed on the Saturday morning by which time Montgomery was advised to have a solicitor present to represent his interests and allay any untoward fears that he might have had something to do with the ghastly murder.

On the Saturday, the coroner examined witnesses who had been in the bank up to 3 p.m. the previous Thursday. Mary Thompson, the bank manager's aunt, told of the events of the day and Montgomery's arrival to enquire about the time Strahan would return. She was certain that he had come in at 2.30 p.m. She was the only person to see Montgomery in the bank house that day and her evidence was to become problematic because no one had opened the inner bank door to him, a door that during normal bank hours was kept shut. Was it possible that she became confused about the time of day?

A young boy, William McNamee, gave evidence. He lived in Newtownstewart and his father was a local auctioneer. He was not in school that day as the National School had a holiday, however, it was not a holiday for the pupils who attended the Model School. They were let home at three o'clock and young McNamee took a certain delight in them trooping past his house. He was upstairs looking out on Main Street. He knew William Glass, the bank clerk and saw him come out at that time, lift the weight that kept the heavy front door open and firmly shut the bank door. He then heard the cockle men at the end of the street and expected a bit of fun. He decided to go out on the street and left the house through the sloping door of the cellar. The cockle men from Donegal – Hugh Bonnar and Mickey Gallagher – stopped at the bank and Fanny McBride came out with a white delph basin. The cockle men stayed outside the bank for about ten minutes before moving on.

Bonnar and Gallagher had little to add when they were brought forward to testify. They had been so intent on selling their wares that they had no idea whether the bank door was open or shut. Gallagher said he saw a man come out of the bank but wouldn't know him again. Bonnar knew less, as he had just bought half-a-stone of oats from a neighbouring house and was busy feeding his mare. It was at this time that young William McNamee saw two of his school pals, ten-year-old Tom Stewart and eleven-year-old James Entrican. Stewart had followed the cockle men up the street from the bridge at the mill. McNamee went down the street then as the cockle men moved off and he sat at Ross Campbell's door.

Apart from the cockle men and schoolboys there were also

two other men outside the bank, Michael McLoughlin and Charles Haughey, who were unemployed labourers. Haughey made a statement at the inquest immediately following the killing. He admitted that he was loitering outside the bank from one o'clock onwards on the day of the murder. He did not move away and was there when the cockle men arrived two hours later.[15] He lived in the town with his sister in Methody Lane, couldn't read or write and offered no explanation as to why he was outside the bank for such a long period.[16] His evidence, along with that of McLoughlin and the young boys, was important because they alleged they heard noises in the bank around 3.15 p.m. when presumably the murder took place. Yet neither of the two men on hearing the unusual noises bothered to look through the large bank windows, and all four appeared to hear different kinds of noise. One described a moan, another a scream, a third the moaning of a cow and the fourth the moving of a body.[17] In one clear instance, Haughey failed to hear the closing of the hall door of the bank, when the servant girl, Fanny McBride, returned having dealt with the cockle men. Yet the shutting of the hall door made such a noise that it was heard in McDowell's shop across the street.[18]

Haughey was the only one of the four who saw Montgomery come out of the bank at the time, as McLoughlin and the two boys had already moved off. Haughey then went into James Moore's and sat on a bench inside the door. He wasn't there ten minutes when he heard the uproar and the news that William Glass had cut his throat. When he returned home, he did not tell his sister about the noises that he had heard in the bank – and strangely he was not called as a witness at the ensuing inquest on the first or second day. Over the weekend, Haughey spoke to a number of jurors from the coroner's court about what he had heard and seen. A reward of £300 had been offered by the bank for the recovery of the money and, by midweek, Haughey was called to give his account.

Another witness who was not in the bank, testified to having seen Montgomery leave the bank premises with a waterproof coat on his arm at the time the murder was committed. At this point, the coroner adjourned the inquest until the following Wednesday, 5 July. In the meantime, the body of William Glass was removed by train to Temple-Patrick in County Antrim. where his funeral was attended by a huge cortege.[19]

Back in Newtownstewart, rumour and counter-rumour freely circulated about what had actually happened at the bank on the fateful Thursday afternoon. The greatest excitement was generated by the possible implication of the town's chief law officer in the cashier's death, particularly when it was known that the two men were very close. By 4 July, more police had been drafted in to the area in an attempt to trace the stolen money and to find the murder weapon. The county police inspector, Alexander Heard, along with a detective officer named French and some more policemen, made a thorough search of Montgomery's lodgings in McClenaghan's Hotel. This was considered prudent in view of the apparent implication of the local police chief but they found nothing. However, the rumour factory in the town was already working overtime. The latest news was that Montgomery had received an unfranked letter with a Derry postmark stating a hatred of the young sub-inspector. Yet, despite the stated enmity, the letter went on to declare that Montgomery was innocent of the crime just committed, and that the real murderer had left the country. Sub-Inspector Purcell was in Newtownstewart on the day the letter was produced and immediately set off for Derry to make enquiries about its origin.

In the town itself at this time, there was a feeling of ill-ease that Montgomery was still at large and that the police appeared not to be actively pursuing the possibility of his involvement in the crime. In the following days, County Inspector Alexander Heard was accompanied to Newtownstewart by Cecil Moore, the crown sessional solicitor.[20] Montgomery was now feeling the heat of the situation and the strong possibility that he might be accused of the crime.

Up to this point, he had regarded such a possibility as absurd and said so to Cecil Moore. Moore agreed with him that it was a ridiculous charge, but he felt that the police chief was treating it too lightly in not fully grasping the significance that he was actually in the bank at the time of the murder. If he was the last person on the bank premises, he must be prepared to give some account of it. Montgomery asked Moore what he should do but Moore declined to give advice on the grounds that, as he was there in Newtownstewart officially, he was likely to be in the role of prosecutor the next day. He did advise Montgomery to seek professional help immediately and told him that he, Moore, would bring a letter to any solicitor in Omagh that he wished.

Montgomery was now somewhat agitated by Moore's concern and urged him to suggest what he, Montgomery, should do right then. Moore thought for a few seconds and then remarked that, if it was he that was involved, he would place himself under military arrest, if there were such a thing in the RIC force. Montgomery appeared a bit aghast at this, purporting that that would imply that he was guilty. Moore thought otherwise. Montgomery again reiterated to the lawyer that it would be ridiculous to bring a charge against him as he and the cashier had been the best of friends. He had no motive to do away with Glass.

Eventually, for Montgomery's own safety and to assuage local fears about a man only four months in the town, it was decided to put Montgomery under house arrest in the constabulary barracks on Main Street. Montgomery welcomed this as he was allowed to do his usual business in the barracks and he cashed an order in the bank where the murder took place, in order to pay the policemen under him.

Across in Belfast, the *News-Letter* published a full account of the proceeding at the adjourned inquest the previous Saturday and Montgomery was advised to retain the services of the Belfast solicitor, John Rea. On Wednesday, 5 July, the inquest resumed. The most important witness was Miss Mary Thompson who said that she was minding the house on the day of the murder while the family were on holiday by the seaside. She told the court that she was out of the house between twelve noon and two o'clock. She never saw Glass that day but she was certain that Montgomery had come to the bank house about 2.30 p.m. and that he had come up to the drawing-room to ask about the time of Mr Strahan's return from Drumquin Fair. He then disappeared and she had no idea where he went next.

At this point in the proceedings, the bank manager, J. G. Strahan, was called as a witness. He explained that, on the day of the murder, he was in Drumquin on bank business. It was normally a market day there but, on this particular day, it was a fair day and very busy. He was aware that Montgomery had called to the bank in the afternoon with the intention of going fishing with him. He himself was a keen fisherman but he had never gone fishing with Montgomery before. He agreed that the two families were close friends and visited each other's homes. In fact he was with Montgomery the night before. Strahan said that Montgomery knew William Glass well and that he would have been familiar with the workings of the bank as he had worked for over seven years in the Belfast Bank before he joined the police force. He would have known a good deal about the day-to-day running of a country bank office. In fact, Montgomery had previously pointed out to Strahan how easy it would be for the bank to be robbed and the cashier murdered. Strahan declared to the coroner that he read nothing sinister into this, other than it was perhaps a friendly interest in the well-being of his friend Glass that prompted the remark. Two months previous to this, a bank inspector pointed out to Strahan the very same possibility.

Strahan knew that Montgomery and Glass were close friends. Only a few weeks earlier, when Strahan was away in Drumquin, Montgomery called to the bank and Glass, having imbibed some brandy 'on the job', went with Montgomery at the close of business to McClenaghan's Hotel. Normally, Glass would have come back to the bank about five o'clock when Strahan would have returned from Drumquin, and they would go over the money together to do the daily cash return. On 11 May, Glass did not return to the bank and Strahan sent a messenger for him. The messenger brought back the key to the outer office and, ten minutes later, Montgomery turned up with the key to Glass' desk. The police chief was all apologetic and admitted giving Glass a sup of brandy while he was in his office. The police chief always carried brandy with him when he was out and about. Strahan was very annoyed and felt he would have to report Glass for dereliction of duty. Montgomery pleaded with him not to do so as no doubt there would be implications for him if word got out that he had intoxicated the young bank clerk. Strahan agreed not to report him on that occasion.[21]

Numerous other witnesses were called at the inquest, one of whom gave a new twist to the case when he gave evidence that he saw a man with full black whiskers, washing blood off his arms in a wood near the town. Constable Thompson then escorted this witness to the wood in question but, when he went out with him, he noticed that the man wore military boots. On further investigation the constable discovered that the man had the letter D branded on his chest. Further enquiries regarding this witness showed that the man had been detained in custody on the charge of being an army deserter.[22]

With no sign of murderer or murderers being apprehended, the finger of suspicion increasingly pointed at Montgomery. The inquest lasted for four weeks and, at the final sitting which lasted for just thirty minutes, the members gave the following verdict: 'That Montgomery with malice aforethought murdered William Glass on Thursday 29 June 1871.'

Almost unbelievably, Montgomery was to find himself marched under a strong escort of police, bayonets drawn, through the streets of Omagh to the barracks. Crowds collected to hoot and hiss with shouts of 'murderer', and Montgomery was removed to Omagh Gaol in handcuffs.[23]

Montgomery was to stand trial initially in August 1871 but the date was put back as no murder weapon had been found and the crown lawyers were having difficulty producing witnesses to secure a conviction. Most of the money had been recovered a fortnight after the murder by three men, Andrew Hamilton, Samuel Hood Jr and Charles Marley in Grangewood,[24] though money was still being found in different places as late as December

1871.[25] When the money was first found, it was hidden under a heavy stone. Marley came into town to get Inspector Heard and the policeman, French, to come out before the money was removed. Yet, despite this precaution on the part of the three men, there were strong rumours consequently in the town that 'hiders are finders'. A farmer in the area, Edward Armstrong, said that he had searched under the stone where the money was found a week before and had found nothing. He was present when Mr French found the money under the stone by turning it over with a crowbar and he made it clear to those present then that he had searched that spot before.[26]

Andrew Hamilton told the court that the three of them went out to search Grangewood because the bank had offered a reward if the money was found and that he would not have gone if it weren't for Samuel Hood Jr. The advertisement of the £300 reward first appeared in his public house window at the time of the inquest.[27]

Then, at the end of December 1871, the murder weapon was also discovered in the Grangewood area. It was a billhook with a sharp blade, twelve inches long. There were stains of blood and hair on it, and the handle was loaded with lead to make it more deadly. The weight of the lead was nineteen ounces, which was less than a quantity bought by Montgomery some time previously to make bullets for a musketry course he was pursuing. In any event, it was to prove impossible to ascertain that the two lead deposits came from the same source. Glass' body was exhumed and Dr Todd and two other medical men confirmed that the weapon corresponded with the gashes on the skull of the dead man.

The crown felt it had sufficient evidence to proceed with the case. All the witnesses in the murder were unexpectedly summoned to appear in Omagh courthouse for the assizes in February 1872.[28] The case was then, inexplicably, adjourned for a further five months. When it resumed in July, it was considered 'the most exciting *cause célèbre* in modern Irish crime'.[29] People travelled from near and far to be in court and it was reported that English literati were in Omagh with a view to writing a book on the proceedings. When the courthouse opened, there were quite a few ladies clamouring to get a seat, so many in fact that the Tyrone High Sheriff opened the galleries especially for them, though many disappointed people still failed to get admittance. Inside the courthouse, there were several large and neatly executed models of the Northern Bank at Newtownstewart.

When Montgomery appeared in court, there was a huge stir. He cut a handsome figure – his hair was close cut, he looked fresh and, as becomes a man who believes in his innocence, he projected a sense of personal strength and firmness of character. His face was composed and he never looked to right or left. He was a man fully focused and managed to project in court a sense of his own invincibility. In prison, he had spent a lot of time reading, making a special study of algebra and *Euclid*. He was still on full policeman's pay and was allowed access to the newspapers. As a consequence, he was fully aware of the state of public opinion regarding his trial.

Away from the Omagh courthouse, it was reported that people hoped that Montgomery would be convicted. The first anniversary of the death of Glass had passed a couple of weeks earlier and a Belfast paper reported that most of the shopkeepers in Newtownstewart had put up the shutters on the windows of their shops. A large black flag hung from the upper window of Stewart's (one of the jurors at the original inquest) draper shop. On the flag in large white letters was written 'Justice'. The bell of the Episcopalian church in the town kept tolling for two hours in commemoration of the day.[30]

Mr McDonagh, who led Montgomery's legal team, swiftly applied to have the trial postponed. He produced three affidavits – one from Montgomery, one from his attorney and a third from Revd Charters, chaplain at Omagh Gaol. Montgomery's affidavit dealt with the long time it had taken to get the case to court. As a result, there was huge speculation on the matter in the public mind, all to his detriment and huge prejudice had been stirred up against him. He thought that, in the present circumstances, his hopes of a fair trial were greatly diminished. Montgomery also alleged that there was an attempt by the press to prejudice his defence and create an unfounded belief in his guilt. The trial should be taken away from County Tyrone to another county. Revd Charters also signed an affidavit affirming his conviction that the class of people usually serving on juries were so far biased as to render a fair trial unlikely. It was a view not borne out as the trial developed but there was enough truth in Charters' concern to question the competence of jurors in a complex murder case.

The crown solicitors, Henry McGrath and Cecil Moore, opposed the affidavits, saying they were too late coming from the defence. It had already been decided that no juror would be taken from within a five-mile radius of Newtownstewart. The panel of jurors had comprised 152 names and many of these lived twenty or thirty miles from the murder scene. In reply, Mr McDonagh, the chief defence lawyer, pointed out that they were told at the last assizes that the crown did not intend proceeding against Montgomery at all. Why, consequently, would they make representation regarding jurors, if the case was never going to be brought to trial? Furthermore, the five-mile exclusion radius was purely cosmetic, as Glass' hometown of Strabane was not excluded, and Omagh, where feelings were resolute, was only a mere seven miles from Newtownstewart. He added that there was at least a strong case for postponement.

At this point, Judge Lawson intervened. It was his view that, even if the trial were postponed, there wasn't the slightest possibility that the venue could be changed. At this Montgomery and his defence challenged some twenty jurors. A number of others claimed exemption from serving as they had already formed an opinion on the case. Eventually, the following jury was sworn in: Robert Andrews (foreman), Joseph Alexander, Daniel Buchanan, George Bullock, James O'Brien, Guy Clements, David Crawford, Thomas Cross, John C. Donnelly, Hugh Graham, John Hueson Jr and Robert McCoy. The court then adjourned to resume the following day.

Dr Todd gave his considered assessment of the full extent of the attack on Glass. The attack took place in the inner office of the bank but, after the first vicious blow, the doctor reckoned Glass had sufficient strength to try and escape to the outer office. In doing so, he hit his head off the door post of the outer office and he was thrown back against the wall. His attacker followed him, striking blow after blow to his head, every one a mortal wound. One of these blows missed the head and made an impression on the door itself. There was hair found there indicating that one of the blows was so violent it severed a section of scalp from the skull. There was blood on the door threshold where the body was dragged from the inner office to the outer.[31] Doctors Thompson and Porter were to give further evidence in court when a plaster cast of a skull was produced scored with marks made in appropriate red, representing the wounds that killed Glass. Three of the marks made a 'three-quarter circuit of the entire head'. The doctors proceeded to apply the billhook to the crimson lines on the skull model and in the process described in detail the manner in which Glass was murdered.

Three witnesses, who claimed to have seen Montgomery leave the bank around 3.30 p.m., were called. The first was Mary Ann Cameron, who lived at Grange, a mile from Newtownstewart and was married to a labourer there. She maintained that, while she was in McDowell's shop directly across from the bank, she saw Montgomery come out of the bank. She did not know who he was but recognised him in the coroner's court a year previously. She had offered her services in court because she had heard that there was a reward of £300 for the apprehension and conviction of the murderer. However, under cross-examination her testimony beggared belief. She said she only saw the colour of Montgomery's beard, whiskers and hair on the particular day and that she was not close enough to see anything else. She told the court that, prior to appearing at the inquest, Detective Crawford brought her to Fulton's Hotel and sat with her inside the window. There they waited until Montgomery came from his lodgings. As he passed by, Crawford tapped the window attracting the momentary attention of the police chief, thus affording a clear view to Mrs Cameron of what Montgomery looked like.[32] On other points her evidence was not consistent with her original deposition to the coroner's court, so much so that Judge Lawson advised the court that 'no juror ought to find a verdict of guilty against Montgomery resting on the evidence of that woman, Mary Ann Cameron'.[33] Perhaps now, the tide was about to turn in favour of the police chief, Montgomery.

The second witness to see the police chief leave the bank on the day of the murder was Mrs McDowell, whose husband, James, owned the shop situated directly across from the bank. The shop was separate from their dwelling-place, which was further up the street. She came from there about 3.20 p.m. and saw Montgomery leave the open door of the bank. He was wearing a round hat, dark clothes and had a waterproof coat on his arm and a stick in one hand. She told the court that she had attended the inquest but was not called to give evidence and made no deposition regarding the matter until 15 January 1872, six months after the murder.[34] Mrs McDowell said that she had told her husband what she had seen but his advice to her was not to mention it, as it 'might end in nothing'. It was not an insignificant thing that McDowell himself had been an ex-policemen and a member of the mounted constabulary. He knew that Mary Ann Cameron had allegedly seen the same thing as his wife and, in order to keep his wife out of the picture, he apparently went with Detective Crawford to get Cameron to serve as witness.

When examined, Mr McDowell corroborated his wife's story. He said he was standing at a desk in his shop, close to the window inside the counter. There was nothing in the window to obstruct his view and he saw the police chief come out of the bank at the time his wife said. He looked up from his desk when he heard the shutting of the bank door. He further confirmed that, a couple of weeks previous to the murder, Montgomery had come to him for a few pounds of lead to make bullets and complained afterwards that the lead was not much good to him as he had spilled most of it into the fire.[35] When the McDowells had finished giving their evidence, Judge Lawson remarked how Mc-

Dowell's wife appeared to be 'intelligent and truthful and a woman of considerable sharpness'. He asked why she had not been brought forward as a witness at the inquest a year previously as she 'undoubtedly ought to have been'. If her observations were known (and by all accounts they were) the persons conducting the inquest were 'subject to a very grave and serious responsibility for not having brought her forward at the inquest'.[36] Clearly, the judge was unhappy that Mary Ann Cameron had been given precedence over Mrs McDowell.

On the final day of the trial, excitement was everywhere. The courthouse was full an hour before the judge took his seat. Apparently, all kinds of theories were abroad as to what actually happened in Newtownstewart and at least a dozen versions of how Glass died existed. In Omagh, the trial had filled the hotels and lodging houses and there was an unreal air of festivity about. Every day police and bailiffs escorted the jury to the principal hotel where they dined and slept in rooms under guard. They were described as twelve inoffensive ratepayers who 'shamble about like guilty beings in the constant custody of their regular keepers'.[37]

The jurors were not the only people who may have felt under threat. Montgomery himself had perceptibly altered in appearance from the first day. He wore the same well-cut clothes, which showed off his fine manly physique, but his face had become pale and haggard with anxiety. He was obviously attempting to maintain an unconcerned demeanour but he started suddenly when the judge appeared, and listened attentively to the summing up.

There was a huge stir in the court when the judge declared that Montgomery must have been in the bank when the murder took place. The key question was what did he do when he was in the bank house, and where did he go when he left Mary Thompson in the drawing-room. He said that he left to walk on Peter's Bank and observe the railway. If that was the truth, there was no case for him to answer. He said he entered the bank when both doors were ajar after three o'clock. Miss Thompson's recollection was that it was about 2.30 p.m. If he did enter the bank at 2.30

p.m. how did he get up to the residential quarters when the inner door was shut during bank hours? The judge agreed with the defence that witnesses could not be relied upon when they were speaking about time. As regards one of the chief witnesses, Mary Ann Cameron, her evidence should be disregarded. She may not have seen the police chief at all that day. Sixty-two witnesses had been examined at the trial but hers was the only testimony about which there was doubt.

The trial had shown that the evidence of Fanny McBride and particularly of Miss Thompson was of vital significance. Mary Thompson maintained that Montgomery came to visit her at 2.30 p.m. She always maintained this was the time and never varied in her account. Furthermore, she maintained that when Fanny McBride went out to fetch cockles she had a clear view of the hall door and maintained that no one entered the bank when the cockle men were there. In researching this story, I stood at the same window where Miss Thompson allegedly stood, but would not have the same certainty that someone could not have entered the bank premises unseen. Yet, everyone involved agreed that it was the practice that the inner door to the bank house was kept shut until the bank officially closed at three o'clock. If this was true, Montgomery could not have visited Miss Thompson at 2.30 p.m. Cook, the gardener, had opened the inner door to let Mary Thompson in at two o'clock and had shut it after her. Fanny, the housemaid, opened this door twice after three o'clock – first to let the sand woman in and, second, when the cockle men came she went out through this door and on through the hall door of the bank.[38] Significantly, when she had ascertained that the cockle men had indeed arrived at the bank door, Fanny went back into the kitchen to fetch a basin, leaving both doors ajar. Was it at this point that Montgomery arrived at the bank, found both the outer and inner doors to the bank ajar and went up to Miss Thompson to enquire when Mr Strahan would be back that evening? Having consulted Miss Thompson, Montgomery immediately left the bank, shutting the door behind him. The shutting of the door made a noise that attracted the attention of

Mr McDowell across the road. The police chief never shut the door like a guilty person not wanting to attract attention to himself. He continued out along the railway as part of routine duty. At no time did he ever attempt to hide the fact that he left the bank at the time he did.

The jury went out to consider the evidence at 1.50 p.m. and, over three hours later, came back and told Judge Lawson that they could not agree on a verdict. The judge asked them to retire again, which they did. At ten o'clock that evening, the judge sent for them. The foreman told the judge that there was no way they could agree. Reluctantly, the judge dismissed and thanked them for their services and Montgomery was put back for trial at the next assizes. The *Freeman's Journal* of 23 July 1872 remarked that while the court was densely crowded there was 'not the slightest demonstration made at the result'.

In March 1873, Montgomery was again brought before the assizes in Omagh for his second trial. No new evidence had come to light and the case stood where it had nine months earlier. The failure of the crown prosecution to establish a motive for the killing was a primary factor in not getting a result at the first trial. Along with that, there were huge questions about the evidence of one of the key prosecution witnesses, Mary Ann Cameron, because it appeared that she was set up by Detective Crawford into giving evidence against Montgomery. If this new trial was to get a conviction, a clear motive had to be established. Mr McDonagh, QC, and Mr Keys were retained for the defence. For the crown Sergeant Armstrong, one of the leading lawyers of the day, was drafted in to lead a formidable team, which included Mr Greer, Mr McLoughlin and Mr Fay. Given the status of the two leading counsel, the case had all the hallmarks of the cut and thrust of a modern *Rumpole of the Bailey*.

When the trial opened and Montgomery appeared, a huge hush descended on the court. He advanced to the centre of the bar, rested his hands, and surveyed the court audience with a steady but respectful gaze and an air of great self-possession.[39] He was dressed in a pea jacket and grey trousers and the only visible change in his physical appearance from that of nine months previously was that his beard was longer and 'silver o'er'. He folded his arms and in answer to the charge declared himself not guilty. The jury was then sworn in and the case began.

Almost unbelievably, the crown again introduced Mary Ann Cameron as a witness. Even though, in the previous trial, the judge had described her evidence as opportunistic and coloured by the prospect of monetary reward and had only just stopped short of calling her a liar.

The main thrust of the crown prosecution was to establish motive. It was very soon clear to the court that Sergeant Armstrong intended to prove that the motive for the killing of William Glass was linked to Montgomery's clandestine financial situation. At the first trial, Judge Lawson had ruled out of order the introduction of Montgomery's pecuniary affairs. At this second trial, Judge Barry ruled the matter admissible. Now the prosecution argued that Montgomery was in serious financial trouble at the time of the murder and needed money in a hurry, even if it meant killing his close friend William Glass.

By the third day of the trial, huge crowds, larger that any seen before, were clamouring to get into the courthouse. There was a sense of impending high drama as the case progressed fuelled by the unusual interaction of this jury with both the defence counsel and the prosecution. Two points were to be argued in depth. For the prosecution, it was Montgomery's financial situation; for the defence it was the possibility that the real murderer or murderers entered the bank via a rear entrance when the cockle men were causing a diversion at the front of the bank.

During a ten-hour address to the court, McDonagh, for the defence, came back again and again to the fact that there was not an iota of evidence to directly link Montgomery with the murder. Many people had seen Montgomery on the road after the murder. They all gave the same description of how he was dressed. If he were the murderer he had to have the bloody billhook on his person and the stolen £1,600 secreted in his clothes.[40] After such a savage attack, he would have to be spattered with blood from the dead man, yet no blood was ever found on his garments even though they had been sent off to Belfast for forensic examination. Where were these clothes now? Why were they never produced in court? Was it that there were no pockets in the coat to hide the stolen bank notes, some of which were bloodstained? No one who saw the police chief on the day observed anything strange in his appearance. If he were the murderer, he was also the thief. If he was the thief why would he put the money in more than one place? It was strange that a £100 had remained in a furze bush till December 1871, even though the police had conducted a thorough search of the area since the murder. Was there an accomplice? At this point, Mr Farnan from the jury jumped up and demanded that the crown produce Montgomery's clothes or give a reason why they could not.

In an attempt to put the juror's mind at rest Sergeant Armstrong said that the clothes had been in court all the time but he accepted that, since they were not bloodstained, there was no point in producing them as evidence. But the juror now insisted that the clothes be produced to ascertain whether or not such a large amount of money could have been concealed within them. Constable Quilter then produced Montgomery's clothing – an ordinary reversible coat, which had been cut to pieces during forensic examination; a light summer pea jacket that had two outside pockets; a pair of lightly lined trousers; and a dark-coloured felt hat. Inspector Heard confirmed that they were the clothes Montgomery wore on the day. At the request of the jury, four of the Newtownstewart constabulary were called to confirm that these were the defendant's clothes on the day.

McDonagh then proceeded to analyse the evidence, demonstrating that the demeanour and conduct of Montgomery at the time of the murder were the movements of an innocent man. He never concealed the fact that he was in the bank house that fateful afternoon. The absence of blood on his clothes was a vital fact in the case. On the question of monetary embarrassment, the motive alleged by the crown, McDonagh pointed out that the police chief's salary was £250 a year. His wife's uncle and his own uncle intended to help him, as he was shortly to leave the police force to pursue a career in commerce. That he was in distress for money was 'grossly unfounded'.[41]

McDonagh spoke for a full ten hours. During his address, the jury frequently interrupted him asking numerous questions and commenting freely on the conduct of the police chief after the murder. They also felt free to comment on the conduct of some of the witnesses, but their major intervention came the following day when Sergeant Armstrong put the case for the crown. McDonagh was not there to hear it as he was exhausted by his exertions in court the previous day and had been told by his doctor to stay in bed. Armstrong began his address, weaving the facts of the case with consummate skill only to be stopped in his tracks by the interruptions of the jury. He rebuked one of them because of an observation he made about a key witness, Miss Mary Thompson, while Judge Barry had to intervene to avoid further interruptions.[42]

Armstrong concentrated on setting out a clear motive for the crime by emphasising that, at the time of the murder, Montgomery's career in the police was about to come to an abrupt end. He had taken money from two subordinate officers in the force to invest for them but he had not invested the money. He failed to produce proof of investment in court even though he apparently had paid some dividends to the officers arising from the investment. While he had been employed in the bank, he had speculated in bank shares and lost all his money, including a sum of money left to him by his mother. It was after this that he disposed of £200 from a policeman called Kelly and £30 from a policeman called Kenny. While in this state of pecuniary embarrassment, he had married a niece of the late Revd Bradshaw and afterwards revealed to him the dire state of his finances. Bradshaw promised to help him. Because he had married a local girl, he had to be relocated to another barracks, as was the custom in the RIC. He was transferred to Newtownstewart but left a number of shop debts behind him, which, as a member of the constabulary, he was expected to pay. Bradshaw paid these debts for him but a balance was still owed to the bank. After the murder, Montgomery wrote to Bradshaw to clear the balance at the bank so that it wouldn't be used against him at the trial.

Armstrong then dismissed the theory that other men had entered the bank when the cockle men were at the front. Apparently, this was a pet theory of Mr Hackett, the foreman of the jury, who now took exception to Armstrong's comment that it was the 'grossest absurdity'. Somewhat miffed, Hackett wanted to know if Armstrong was referring to him by such comment. Mr Farnan, another juror, spoke up, pointing out to Armstrong that the foreman of the jury held it as a theory before the defence put it forward. Armstrong then thought that the jury might need some direction and cautioned them that they 'were not at liberty to imagine matters for which there [was] not a tittle of evidence'.

Armstrong was now bent on showing that not only had Montgomery motive, he also had knowledge. He knew that the bank manager would be away at the fair in Drumquin; he knew the ordering of the local bank office and had free access there, due to his close relationship with William Glass. At this, the foreman of the jury interrupted saying that everyone knew that there was a fair in Drumquin that day. Again, the foreman questioned whether Miss Thompson had a clear view of the hall door from the drawing-room when the cockle men were out at the front of the bank. The foreman said he would like to see the view from the window to the hall door. Armstrong replied this was not possible. Then Farnan came back at Armstrong asking why did Fanny McBride and Mary Thompson not look in to see the body of Glass, implying that somehow they had something to do with the murder. Armstrong thought this was absurd and again thought that the jurors were concerning themselves with evidence that was not before them. Farnan immediately responded and addressed Judge Barry saying that, if Armstrong were referring to him in his last comment, he would seek permission to defend himself.

The court proceedings were on the point of deteriorating into farce because of the interventions of the jury many of whom were exhausted, and the court adjourned. The judge in summing up, justified the latitude he had given to the jury because many of them had not served before. Ten days later, the trial recommenced, but it then transpired that Montgomery had no legal team because his means were exhausted. He requested that Mr McDonagh be reinstated with the help from the attorney-general. Judge Barry took all the circumstances of the trial into consideration – the exhausted state of the present jury, the great number of general objections from the jury itself and Montgomery's objection to continuing at this point without proper counsel – and decided that the trial should once again be postponed. The jury was dismissed and a date for the new court hearing was set for the next assizes. Montgomery was left to ponder whether it was all a further step to deliverance or one step nearer his Armageddon.

Four months later, on 21 July 1873, the third trial opened. The case was still talked about up and down the country but commentators and observers alike were becoming more and more confused regarding the true order of events on the day of the murder. Judge Barry was again the presiding judge. Many potential jurors stepped aside because they admitted to having already formed an opinion in the case. The new jury comprised the following members: Thomas Thompson (foreman), Robert Scott, James Watson, Robert Barnes, Robert Gibson, Benjamin Marshall, David Hamilton, James Orr, Jas Marshall, Robert Orr, William Johnston and John Waters.

The courthouse was not as crowded as in the former two trials but the ladies still managed to fill the galleries. There was no change in Montgomery's appearance, he was still firm and composed.[43] It was understood from the outset that the crown would produce no new evidence but it soon emerged that Mary Fulton was now unclear whether the whisper she heard from the inner bank office was of one person or two. She admitted that Coll and Moncrieff, both in the bank at the same time, had as good an opportunity of hearing the whisper as she had. In fact, Coll was nearer the archway leading to the inner office than she was. Both men heard nothing. William McNamee, the schoolboy across the road who saw Glass shut the door at three o'clock, now confirmed to the court that, when Fanny McBride came out through the hall door to the cockle men, she had no basin. She left both inner and outer doors ajar to go back in to fetch the basin.[44] All this boded well for the besieged police chief.

Two days later, Montgomery's body language in court indicated a growing sense of optimism. He continually surveyed the court and jotted down notes from time to time with an 'air of nonchalance'. Outside the courthouse, interest in the proceedings was increasing, as there was a clear expectation that the case was coming to a close. It was at this point that the prosecution produced its trump card. They had already established a motive, the defendant's monetary embarrassment, and now, in dramatic fashion, they set out to show how Montgomery had made off with the money after he murdered William Glass.

Constable O'Neill was called and asked to hop up onto the main table in the courtroom. There were gasps of surprise as he stood there. Sergeant Armstrong pointed out that he was wearing the clothes that Montgomery said he was wearing on the day of the murder, down to the detail of a waterproof coat slung over his arm. There was nothing remarkable in his appearance except that his coat was buttoned in front. Armstrong then told the mesmerised courtroom that O'Neill had on his person all the banknotes found in Grangewood, as well as the nefarious billhook. To a hushed courthouse, he explained that the handle was in one of his trouser pockets and the blade was wrapped in a newspaper, between his shirt and waistcoat. It was not noticeable. After the fashion of a male model, O'Neill walked from one end of the table to another – he apparently had no difficulty walking, only stooping. To large gasps from the captive audience, he then produced £1,500 from the five pockets of his clothes and from under his shirt. He said it took him about five minutes to hide and place the notes and weapon and that, before removing the notes or billhook, he put on and took off the waterproof coat with total ease.[45] Newspapermen with telegraph deadlines to meet in London and Dublin made early exits from the courtroom convinced that the end was in sight.

But the trial dragged on for another three days before the summing up by both sides. Before asking the jury to retire to consider its verdict, Judge Barry pointed out how exceptional and unparalleled a case it was due to the horrendous nature of the murder, the robbery and the position of trust occupied by the prisoner, Thomas Montgomery. The jury retired but were back fifteen minutes later having found the police chief guilty of the murder of William Glass on 29 June 1871.

What happened next was extraordinary and probably unprecedented. When Judge Barry asked Montgomery if he had anything to say, the once self-possessed prisoner delivered a statement that was totally out of character. To a shocked courtroom, Montgomery stated that for twelve months before the murder he had been insane. The insanity was induced by a drug administered by his future uncle-in-law, Mr Bradshaw, who tricked him into marrying his niece. He explained that, six months later, he got a craving for 'foolish and ridiculous' speculations and developed a mania for attacking banks. He alleged that he had told colleagues of his obsession.

He went on to say that, when he had taken up duty in Newtownstewart, he was completely deranged. He couldn't sleep and he had to keep towels on his head. It was a terrible murder but he was demented and his reason was gone.[46] The judge, somewhat moved at this unexpected outburst, pointed out that this excuse for the crime was never presented to the jury and he had no choice but to pass judgment. Assuming the black cap, the judge declared that on the 28 August 1873, Thomas Hartley Montgomery should be hanged until dead.

However, the police chief had one more throw of the dice. Intrigued by this outburst some of the Dublin press reporters sought an interview with the prisoner in his condemned cell. When the reporters crowded into the cell with their pencils and pads they found Montgomery languishing 'pale and wasted' on his prison bed. He proceeded to give his account of how he carried out the murder whilst insane and how the prosecution had got it wrong on detail. He maintained that, when he saw

Miss Thompson, he had the money and weapon on his person and the deed was already done. He struck one blow in the inner office and the rest of the blows in the outer office into which Glass had stumbled. Then he sat down in the chair and read the newspaper. He maintained that the money and the murder weapon were not found in the place where he had left them. When asked by the press the obvious question of why he had not built his defence around a plea of insanity, he maintained that he wanted to do so, but his legal team argued that no jury could find him guilty on the crown evidence presented. The press visitors, having got their death-cell interview, withdrew, bolstered in their belief 'that every word stated by the prisoner should be taken *cum grano salis* (with a grain of salt)'.[47]

But Montgomery had no further surprises for the public. He was not granted a reprieve and on the day set for his execution, 28 August 1873, he was hanged. Prior to the event, many local people believed that he would never see the scaffold and that a way out would be found for him to evade death. However, he was hung but not without an initial hitch. No local tradesmen could be induced to build the scaffold, and the authorities had to bring in men from Cavan to do the job for the sum of £20.[48]

When the old gaol in Omagh was closed in 1904, Montgomery's skeleton was discovered in a rough coffin. For some, the intrigue of morbidity is yet another fashion and some well-to-do people divided up the bones between them. Carson, the local crown solicitor, put the skull on a shelf in his office until a sister of his business partner, a Miss Dickie, decided that it wasn't right that such a skull was preserved in this manner. She took the skull and buried it in a wood.[49]

What of the extraordinary feelings that the case aroused around the area? We are told that the two young men, Glass and Montgomery, were very close and intimate friends. What does this mean? Were they lovers? Three or four blows of the lethal bill-hook would have been enough to finish off Glass. Why did Montgomery continue the frenzied attack? Why was the bank file pushed into the Glass' brain when it was clear he was dead? Was it a valedictory gesture of a lover scorned? Hardly. Was robbery the real motive for the murder? Probably.

If Montgomery was indeed mad, what do we make of the pathetic insanity plea in the courtroom and prison cell? Surely, the place for this was in the first trial when the prosecution had no motive and there was an unreliable key witness? More outlandish still, in the bizarre unfolding of the case in its final stages, did the real killer or killers walk away? Did a demented man, under pressure for so long, finally break and confess to a murder he never committed? Maybe, Montgomery was unlucky. A defence built around an insanity plea, which was commonplace and successful by the end of the nineteenth century, arrived too late to save him.[50]

All the evidence relating to Montgomery's involvement in this crime was circumstantial. It took the inquest six weeks and three further court trials to bring a guilty verdict – in itself a unique occurence in the history of Irish nineteenth-century jurisprudence.

'It's not fit for you to be keeping company with that unfortunate fellow'

Ballyforan Bridge, County Galway, 1879

JOE CLARKE

BALLYFORAN PARISH, FORMERLY KNOWN as Taghboy, is divided by the River Suck. The greater, eastern portion lies within the barony of Athlone, County Roscommon, leaving the remainder to the west in the barony of Killian, County Galway. Just as the river's course determines the line of administrative boundaries, the physical landscape too is dominated by its powerful presence. At Ballyforan Bridge, it meanders slowly south towards its confluence with the Shannon beyond Ballinasloe. Along its banks on either side are extensive low-lying callows that flood in any season after spells of heavy rainfall. Stretching further from the river are tracts of raised bog that have been exploited for fuel over many generations by the local population. Béal Átha Feorainne has been of strategic importance as a fording point on the river from time immemorial. On the night of 16 October 1879, its picturesque eighteenth-century bridge, spanning thirteen arches, became the stage for an incident that was to bring the village into national prominence.

The timing of the incident coincided with a period of unrest known as the Land War, when an agricultural depression roused the indignation of Ireland's rural population to its highest pitch since the Great Famine. Prices had tumbled and the effect on tenant farmers was most acutely felt in western counties. At the benchmark sale of Connacht, the great October fair in Ballinasloe, the price of cattle was down £3 a head on the previous year. Demand was so sluggish that 'not a tail was sold till Tuesday morning'.[1] Nevertheless, sellers had to accept what was offered because rents fell due on 1 November. Tenants who had already fallen into arrears were now threatened with eviction because of their inability to pay. Hardship was widespread and the finger of accusation pointed to the landowning class as the architects of the country's misfortune. The archbishop of Tuam added his voice to those calling on the 'landocracy' to 'display their sympathy to their wretched serfs in these gloomy days'.[2]

Michael Davitt couldn't have chosen a better time to return from England and establish the Land League in his native Mayo. The country was ripe for protest. As the movement gathered momentum, crowds flocked to mass demonstrations where they heard a fiery rhetoric of defiance. At a south Roscommon rally in Dysart, to establish the Dysart and Taghboy branch of the Land League, the people were urged to carry on a 'constitutional struggle until Irish landlordism is swept clean from the fair face of your country'.[3] Though the movement's leadership openly condemned violence, calls for acts of disobedience in pursuit of its aims drove the populace to the limits of what was legal. In every province, agrarian secret societies and tenant 'combinations' were ready to carry their protests into the realm of outrage and criminality. Throughout the nineteenth century, counties Roscommon and Galway witnessed spasmodic outbursts of unrest. A confidential police report confirmed that Ribbonism (a term used by the authorities to describe various forms of violent agrarian protest) continued to linger in east Galway into the 1850s and needed only 'an exciting cause' to reactivate a campaign.[4] The events at Ballyforan and elsewhere ensured that Ribbonism continued to be a force in east Connacht right into the 1880s.

Even though the rumblings among the masses were a cause for concern, the gentry class strove to preserve at least the appearance of normality. One of their favoured traditions was hunting – although opposition from landholding tenants was growing. Given the variety of terrain in the vicinity of Ballyforan, there can be no doubt that the hunting and game rights to these lands were a prized acquisition by John Ross Mahon, a land agent who lived at Weston House, approximately six miles from the village. The Suck provided a habitat for salmon, trout, pike, rudd, bream, roach and the occasional otter, and the plantations, wetland and farmland were host to deer, rabbit, fox, hare and red squirrel. There were birds in abundance – pheasant, grouse, woodcock, snipe, pigeon, moorhen, mallard – as well as a host of other native and migrant species.

John Ross Mahon employed William [Will] Mahon as gamekeeper in the district. The jealously guarded store was viewed with envy by the tenants who were willing to risk the wrath of landlord, and statutes of the land, to share in the bounty that nature provided. It was inevitable that the battle of wits between the enthusiastic gamekeeper and the daring poachers would lead to feelings of acrimony within the community. When Will Mahon failed to arrive home on Thursday night, 16 October 1879, his family's anxieties were raised.

The Mahon family had real reasons for concern on two counts. First, there was the possibility that Will's disappearance was the result of an act of retaliation – within the immediate locality, feelings were running high because of court proceedings against a neighbour involved in poaching. Second, in the climate of hostility pervading rural Ireland, it was possible that a landlord's employee might fall victim to agrarian outrage. The previous twelve months had seen a steady increase in such crimes in counties Galway and Roscommon. Incidents reported to the police numbered 214 in 1879 and rose to 438 the following year.[5]

After dinner on 16 October, Will Mahon left home to go to the house of John Cox, a neighbour who often wrote letters for those who were unable to do so themselves. Mahon wished to correspond with one of his sons who, like many in the parish, had emigrated to England. On occasions such as this, it was normal for Will not to have returned by nightfall because he was regarded as a man 'whose usual habits were eccentric'.[6] Since a poacher does not work regular hours, and typically prefers the cloak of darkness, the gamekeeper's devotion to duty often detained him at some outpost into the small hours. On the other hand, Will's fondness for alcohol was another reason why he might be gone from the house for some hours. These explanations were not sufficient on this occasion and there was some unease in the Mahon household because Will's absence was a departure from the routine he had adopted of late. Recently, his two small children had heard some people in the area threaten their father. As a result, the gamekeeper had stopped going out at night and appeared less often at John Burke's public house in Ballyforan village.[7]

By Friday morning, there was still no sign of the missing man, so his eight-year-old son, William Jr, initiated the first search. From the information available, it would seem the youngster was burdened with responsibilities beyond his years, because at no point in the records or reported details of this case is there any mention of Will Mahon's wife – it would appear she had either deserted the family or, more likely, had died. So it fell to the little boy to despatch his younger sister, Mary Anne, in search of their father. He himself was due to spend the day working with a nearby farmer to bring in the harvest (at the time it was common for children to help out in this way rather than attending school).

The place for Mary Anne to begin her search was the home of the letter-writer John Cox, where she was told that her father had spent Thursday evening in Burke's public house. Will had not met John Cox at home because Cox had been engaged in bringing home hay for John Burke, the publican.[8] The gamekeeper had walked to Ballyforan and waited until the hayrick was completed at about four o'clock in the afternoon. Cox told Mary Anne he went into Burke's kitchen to light his pipe and, as he emerged, her father was standing in the hallway with a candle, paper, pen and ink in hand. He explained that he wished to have a letter transcribed, so the two adjourned to a sitting-room upstairs. By way of payment, a pint of porter was ordered. John Cox knew that the drink was obtained 'on strap' because the game-keeper was reckless with his money and 'generally under the influence of drink, any time he could get a shilling'.[9] It was probably out of sympathy for Will's plight that Cox did not take the porter.

The letter was only five or six lines in length and, just as the envelope was being addressed, Thomas Kennedy, a neighbour from Derryfadda, appeared in the doorway. 'Beg pardon, maybe it would be any harm to go in?' enquired Kennedy.

'Sorra bit! The letter is finished, and it was no importance,' replied Cox.

Since the pint still stood on the table, Kennedy and Will Mahon shared it between them. The men rose then and headed downstairs with the intention of going home together. Kennedy blocked the doorway to prevent their departure. 'Come on here till we have a drink!'

'Devil a tint can I take,' declared Cox.

'Come here till I show you this wheat I have in my pocket!'

Kennedy said he wanted help at reaping and he brought a sample to show that the corn was ripe enough to harvest. Eventually, he convinced the pair to join him in the tap-room, where they were served by Emily Burke, the proprietor's daughter. Kennedy ordered a half-gallon and a quart of porter. While they sipped, the conversation turned to matters of the moment and became so animated that three other men in the tap-room could overhear what was being said. Kennedy asked Cox if he would assist with his harvest the following day and the letter writer replied, 'I will if I possibly can.'

'Damn it, I'll go with you too, so long as there is no one there I do not like!' added Mahon.

'I'll have none of the Tanseys there, so it's up to yourself,' replied Kennedy.

The thinly veiled reference to a subject of controversy stung Mahon. He had been on friendly terms with the Tanseys, a neighbouring family, until about three years earlier when relations began to sour as poaching grew more prevalent and the game-keeper felt compelled to take action. Apart from the Tanseys,

Thomas Kennedy himself and John Nolan, the tailor from Bally-foran, were also known to be involved. At the recent petty sessions in nearby Ballinamore, Roger Tansey was summoned to appear on a charge of 'shooting and killing a grouse'.[10] His father, Michael, told the court that the youth had absconded, so the case was adjourned to the next sitting on 28 October. Will Mahon realised that feelings in the village were running high and admitted to his drinking companions, 'That's a thing I did, to summon one of the Tanseys – but I could not help it.'

The gamekeeper left the room 'to kindle his pipe' in the kitchen and, in his absence, Kennedy's manner became darker and more aggressive. Although several hints had been dropped earlier in the evening, John Cox was now left in no doubt that it would be better for him to leave the pub and go on home alone. Kennedy pressed him against the wall and blurted, 'It's not fit for you to be keeping company with that unfortunate fellow!'

'I never knew the poor fellow to do any harm to any one except what he could not help doing,' Cox replied.

Kennedy was determined, 'Damn it, sure you can be going home when you are not drinking!'

After the gamekeeper returned to join their company, John Cox excused himself and left the pair in the tap-room. That was between 6.30 and 7.00 p.m.

Will Mahon's girl hurried to tell her brother of what she had learned during her search for their father. Young William rushed to Ballyforan where John Burke confirmed to him that Will Mahon and Kennedy had indeed spent the evening in the company of his neighbour and that they left together at about eight o'clock. William then went in search of Kennedy, whom he met on the boreen to his own house. Kennedy told him that he had accompanied Will Mahon as far as the road turning towards Ballygar where they went separate ways. Kennedy himself had gone to the house of Pat Morris in search of men to help with drawing in the hay. Tom Kennedy speculated that, after they parted, the gamekeeper had either gone home or on business and he suggested that the missing man might have reached home by now – about five o'clock on Friday afternoon.[11] The children waited a second night but their father failed to return.

On Saturday morning, the police were alerted and the search for Will Mahon intensified. William Mahon Jr was joined by his uncle, Edward Hickey, and during their search they met Tom Kennedy on the road near Ballyforan Bridge. When Hickey enquired about the mysterious disappearance, Kennedy declared that, having parted ways with Will Mahon, he went to look for men and met Pat Morris on the road. Hickey challenged him that this account was different from that given on Friday. Kennedy said no more and walked away.[12]

Constable Patrick Lawless came upon evidence of a scuffle on the 'high road' to Ahascragh, not far from the bridge.[13] He traced the marks which indicated that a person in bare feet and wearing corduroy trousers had been dragged about 400 yards through the soft mud to the edge of the river where a boat could come to the bank. Though the circumstantial evidence was compelling, there was no conclusive proof that Will Mahon had been the victim of assault or had met an untimely end. In this, the Mahon children and their relatives saw enough hope to continue the search for the gamekeeper over several months. The police made no progress either, but theirs was a more pessimistic outlook. Believing the missing man to have been drowned in the River Suck, they dragged the river using boats and diving bells but had no success.[14] The resident magistrate at Ballinasloe offered a reward of £10 to the person who discovered what the RIC believed would certainly be the body of murder victim, William Mahon.

Early in the day of 19 May 1880, Winnie Gately, from the townland of Cloonagh, south-east of Ballyforan, was out fishing on the river. Winnie was a widow who, along with her children, had been evicted some time previously from their holding near Athlone. Fleeing westward, they found a marshy place in Cloonagh beside the river where they built a house of sods. Always on the lookout for fear that she would be pursued and arrested, the mother became known as 'Winnie the Watch'.[15] Evidently, she was left undisturbed and felt free to supplement her family's food supplies with whatever could be caught in the Suck.

Because the spring had been drier than usual, the level of the river was low and an object floating in the water caught her attention. She steered the boat a little closer to get a better view. The oarswoman was shocked to discover that it was a sack from which a human hand protruded. The contents had attracted a shoal of eels and other fish. Realising its significance, she reported immediately to Sergeant Lawless at Ballyforan Barracks. When the sack was retrieved, the policeman concluded that it had not been afloat for very long because the rope by which it was fastened to a weight had snapped, due to its being frayed from constant movement of the current. The body was well preserved and it was identified immediately as that of the missing gamekeeper.[16]

Doctors Healey, O'Kelly and Shanley conducted a post-mortem and found that five of the dead man's ribs had been broken and his right lung had been punctured, while he was still alive.[17] They concluded that Will Mahon had died as a result of the injuries inflicted – which now left the police with a murder case on their hands. Despite the furore that followed, Winnie Gately was not forgotten and she received the magistrate's £10 reward before the end of the month.[18]

From the outset, Sergeant Lawless was convinced that he knew who was responsible for the attack on the gamekeeper. Shortly before his disappearance, Will Mahon had lodged a complaint that threats were being made against him. An early indication that the RIC suspected the involvement of local men was apparent when the arms licence of Michael Tansey was revoked in November 1879 and that of John Nolan early in 1880.[19] Within days of the discovery of the body, the police assembled a large force and made a surprise raid on the limekiln in Caltraghduff where a consignment of lime worth £50 was being burned.[20]

The villages around Ballyforan were renowned for lime burning. They had the advantages of a plentiful supply of good quality turf to fire the kilns, and every townland was dotted with small limestone quarries. Once the fire was lit, it was essential to maintain a high temperature in the kiln and, therefore, lime burning was a labour-intensive, round-the-clock operation. Since every member of the family would have a role to play during this process, the swoop on Caltraghduff was timed to perfection. The lime burner, Michael Tansey, was arrested along with his four sons – Bernard, John, William and Roger. The five Tanseys were taken before the magistrates at Ballinamore petty sessions. Since Tom Kennedy was the last known person to have seen Will Mahon alive, the police thought it fit to arrest him too.[21] Another taken into custody on suspicion of being involved in the murder was John Nolan, the tailor from Ballyforan.[22]

The prosecution case was not very robust and charges were restricted to 'suspicion of being concerned in the murder of William Mahon'. Its argument relied on testimony such as that of eight-year-old William Mahon Jr who had overheard the threat against his father issued by ten-year-old John Tansey. Sub-Inspector Smith of Moylough, conducting the prosecution side, was unable to produce Mary Anne Mahon, another 'important witness', because she was ill. The nightmare for the two children was compounded by their separation from each other – the boy was lodged at the industrial school in Galway, while the girl was sent to a convent in Loughrea. Proceedings halted and the accused were remanded in custody at Galway Gaol.[23]

If the crown wished to secure a conviction, investigators would need the co-operation of the local community in gathering incriminating evidence. But the silence of the people proved a major stumbling block. This must have come as no surprise to the police, because the attitude in Ballyforan was no different from other districts. Official statistics revealed that, of the 445 agrarian offences reported to the RIC in counties Galway and Roscommon in 1880, no offenders were brought to justice in 397 instances.[24] Presiding at the opening of the 1880 Winter Assizes in Galway, Baron Dowse gave vent to the frustration caused by the reticence of the population in general. He complained that many persons injured in attacks had declined to give assistance so that the guilty could be brought to justice.[25] One reason for this may have been a sense of tribal loyalty among the tenantry who were reluctant to give the authorities any information that might be used in court against a neighbour or friend.

Another reason for lack of co-operation was fear. In this period of intensive agrarian activity, the police files were swollen with unsolved crimes and incomplete prosecution cases.[26] One of these was an attack on the eel weir at Ballyforan in 1879 for which John Cornwall, the proprietor, received £60 in compensation.[27] Another incident was the posting of a threatening notice in Brideswell village, eight miles from Ballyforan, during October 1879. It warned tenants that anyone who paid rent would be shot.[28] Understandably, intimidation of this sort deterred potential witnesses.

In an effort to breach the wall of silence, the government issued a proclamation on 27 May 1880, offering £300 'to the person who would, within six months from this date, give information leading to a conviction' in the case of the murder of William Mahon.[29] A sum of £100 was offered 'for such private information as would lead to the same result'. Copies of the proclamation were posted in the East Riding of County Galway. They appeared at the villages of Ballinamore and Ahascragh, four and six miles respectively from the scene of the crime. Curiously, no notice was displayed at the police barracks in Ballyforan itself – because the village lay in County Roscommon. However, the attractions of a substantial reward were not enough to bring forward any informant with the crucial evidence required. The magistrates' inquiry dragged on but no credible case could be constructed against the accused men and they were released after two months in custody.[30]

The dust might have settled over police files on the killing of William Mahon except that some of the suspects became involved in another outrage. On the night of 25 March 1882, two and a half years after Will Mahon's disappearance, there was a dynamite attack on Weston House, near Ahascragh, the home of John Ross Mahon, the land agent who had employed the murdered gamekeeper. At an early stage in their investigation the police achieved a breakthrough that helped to solve this crime and, more importantly, provided a key to unlocking the Bally-foran mystery.

John Ross Mahon had angered tenants in Ahascragh by evicting the vice-president of the local branch of the Land League for non-payment of rent. The tenants decided to seek revenge and made overtures to a secret society which they knew was active in the Ballyforan area. Ignatius Kelly, who lived in Cloonshee, acted as intermediary. He approached William Tansey with an offer of £500 for an attack on Weston House and the promise of more money if any lives were taken. The proposal was attractive, and the society's members busied themselves with preparations. One of the group, Patrick Rogerson, found employment with James Jones, a well-sinker from Dublin, who was working in the neighbourhood. Dynamite was part of his stock in trade and Rogerson had secured a position that gave the conspirators access to whatever would be required for the attack on Weston. By mid-March, Rogerson had obtained two sticks of the explosive. He buried them in a garden at the house of Bernard Geraghty, who had been sworn into the society the previous Christmas by William Tansey.

Early on Easter Sunday, 25 March 1882, James Jones packed twelve sticks of dynamite in a sack and left them in his bedroom. When Rogerson, Tansey, Kelly and Patrick Naughton dropped in later that evening, the well-sinker handed over the explosives. For a share of the £500, he consented to join the escapade, offering his expertise to prepare the material for detonation. During that day, the attackers' movements attracted attention. Some of them had met in Cassidy's pub, Four Roads, during the afternoon and after a few drinks departed for Ballyforan. There, they were joined by Jones and the others in Burke's pub at around six o'clock. At about 9.30 p.m., RIC Constable O'Brien noted that people were slipping quietly out of Burke's in twos and threes.

The party setting out for Weston House was a formidable force of about eighteen men. As well as the explosives, they carried firearms – four had revolvers and three were armed with shotguns. The group made its way to a clump of trees near the target via a circuitous route and there the crude bomb was assembled. The sticks of dynamite were placed in a canvas sack, which was then packed with clay and some fragments of a broken iron pot, which were added for a more lethal effect. Patrick Rogerson and William Tansey were chosen to plant the device against the house. Jones was excused because he feared that he would not be able to escape since he'd sprained his foot.

The blast rang out at 3.20 a.m. and was heard a mile away by Constable Edward Hayden who was out on night patrol. Remarkably, James Paye, the butler at Weston House, slept soundly through the whole commotion. As it happened, John Ross Mahon was away in Dublin and none of the occupants upstairs was hurt. The damage caused was limited to smashing the window, glass, fittings and furniture in the drawing-room. The device would certainly have had more devastating effects if deployed by an expert, such as Jones. As the attackers fled, they took turns at carrying the hobbling Jones as far as an old house where he remained until dawn.

Within minutes of the explosion, Constable Hayden (disparagingly known locally as 'Old Hat') was on the scene. Later in the day, Lord Clonbrock, whose family was connected to Mahon by marriage, visited Weston House in a show of solidarity. Father Healy, the Catholic parish priest of Ahascragh, also came to sympathise and aired his view that the outrage was not the work of his parishioners. The trail of footprints leading away from the scene pointed north towards Ballyforan.[31] In a follow-up operation by the RIC, Michael Tansey was found in possession of explosives 'in a proclaimed district' on 6 April, for which he received a custodial sentence of one calendar month. Traces still probably remained in his house since the night of the attack because that was where the dynamite had been 'softened'.[32]

James Jones was in the constabulary's sights from the beginning – he was familiar with the use of the explosive and had been spotted on the road to Ahascragh by a policeman early on Easter Monday morning. Evidence at the trial supports the local story that he and William Tansey entered a house on the journey home where they boasted of the deed – which led to their being reported to the RIC.[33] Within two days of the attack, Jones accompanied Constable Hayden to the scene and pointed out the escape route to Ballyforan. Eventually, the well-sinker was brought to the barracks in Ballinasloe, where he formally 'gave information' on 2 July.[34] A week later the police came in force to arrest three men in the Ballyforan area – William Tansey, Patrick Naughton and Bryan Cormican – they would be held for the next twelve months.[35]

During that time, two separate magistrates' inquiries were conducted and their trial was twice postponed at the assizes. All the while, the police were following leads on those of the perpetrators who had absconded to England. In June 1883, John Rogerson, who had assumed the alias 'John Smith', was arrested in the street at Widnes in Lancashire. Soon afterwards, Bernard Geraghty was apprehended in a wood near Handsworth after 'an exciting chase' through the fields. When the captives were returned to Ireland, Geraghty gave way under questioning and made statements to the police at Ballinasloe on 2 July 1883 – one year to the day after Jones had done likewise.[36]

When the four prisoners were put on trial at the Sligo Summer Assizes for the dynamite attack on Weston House, the prosecution case was built around the independent evidence of the two 'approvers' who had actually participated in the crime. The judge, summing up for the jury, was scathing in his criticism of the 'hirelings who had come secretly at night to destroy an innocent family by dynamite … and those were the men who were to found nations and create an Irish Republic'. Unsurprisingly, the accused were found guilty. William Tansey, 'the leader in this terrible proceeding', was sentenced to fourteen years' penal servitude and Patrick Rogerson to twelve years. As they were led away, Tansey proclaimed, 'Three cheers for old Ireland', while Rogerson cried, 'God save Ireland!' Patrick Naughton received eight years' penal servitude and James Kelly was sentenced to two years' imprisonment.

The crown's success in prosecuting the Weston House case was achieved by bringing pressure to bear on the weakest links in the conspiracy. Jones was obviously an outsider from Dublin, whose only interest in the deed was a share of the £500 bounty. There was no logical reason for such an individual to become entangled in local agrarian activism when his journeyman occupation offered so many legitimate and profitable opportunities elsewhere. The scenario presented by the constabulary left Jones with a stark choice. They had sufficient evidence to find him guilty of charges up to and including attempted murder, so his only means of avoiding imprisonment, for an exploit in which his only interest was mercenary, was to 'turn approver'.

Bernard Geraghty had already been at the centre of controversy before he became a key 'witness for the crown'. On 6 December 1880, he was the target of an intimidatory notice posted in Taghboy. It ordered him to 'give up working for the Revd Mr O'Rorke who has been "boycotted" on account of disputes with his tenants about their rent'.[37] Geraghty was an outsider in the townland of Taghboy, his family having moved to the Roscommon side of the parish. He did not have the same reservations as his new neighbours about taking up employment with the Revd John O'Rorke, a Church of Ireland clergymen. However, the timing and style of the warning may have been prompted by another agency: less than a week earlier, the meeting to establish the Dysart-Taghboy branch of the Land League was given this advice on the enrolment of members: 'Take down the names of those who refuse to join the League. If they hold back, publish a list of their names on every chapel gate in the district, so that the people may know their friends from their enemies.'[38] The anonymous notice indicated that Bernard Geraghty was neither well liked nor integrated into his new neighbourhood.

Considering this unconventional background, the recruitment of Geraghty for the Weston House conspiracy two years later is mystifying. Surely it was inviting disaster to accept a 'landlord's man' into a group that was plotting a deadly attack on another landlord? What convinced William Tansey that the new recruit would 'do everything [he] was ordered to do and be true to the society'?[39] Bernard Geraghty's commitment to the cause must have been less than whole-hearted because of the treatment he had received in the area. This was confirmed when, under cross-examination at the Mahon murder trial in 1884, Geraghty stated openly that he could be tempted with money, '[I] did say I'd act as Casey did if I got a good consideration for it.'[40] Geraghty's escape to England in the wake of the explosion might have been a genuine dash for freedom but the police seemed to have had no difficulty in convincing him that the game was up. He made a deposition in Ballinasloe within two days of his arrest and, a fortnight later, was freely giving evidence in the Weston House case at the Sligo assizes. That sworn testimony sent his wife's brother, James Kelly, to jail. No matter what their feelings towards him had been, local people must have then felt that in the future they definitely could not trust Bernard Geraghty, 'the dynamite informer of '83'.[41]

Ominously, for the men suspected of Will Mahon's murder, the 'approver' employed by the police to solve the Weston House case might also supply damning evidence of the Ballyforan atrocity. Geraghty would have preferred not to stand alone, so he made attempts to convince one of his neighbours to become another witness for the crown. In conversation with John Rogerson, he mentioned the rewards offered by the government and John Ross Mahon in the murder investigation.[42] Even though this strategy failed, it appears that the police were able to build successfully on their coup. They enticed other witnesses to overcome their fears and to be more forthcoming with information. When sufficient evidence was accumulated, the RIC raided again. At four o'clock on the morning of Sunday, 27 January 1884, a large force arrested Michael Tansey, Thomas Kennedy, John Nolan and Laurence Hannon. The four men were taken to the Bridewell in Ballinasloe and charged with murder.

A magistrates inquiry was conducted by P. T. Lyster and W. J. Paul in the grand jury room of the county courthouse in Galway. The charges laid against Tansey, Hannon and Kennedy were of conspiracy and murder, while Nolan was charged with being an accessory. George Bowler, a Ballinasloe solicitor, represented the four prisoners and acting for the attorney-general was the imposing George Bolton, who had steered the prosecution through the controversial Maamtrasna murder trial two years earlier.

Shades of Bolton's obstructionist tactics in that case re-emerged at the commencement of the Mahon Inquiry. As *The Galway Vindicator* reported on the opening day's proceedings, Bowler complained that, when he sought to meet his clients in Ballinasloe on the Sunday before the hearing, he was prevented from doing so by the policemen guarding them.[43] He met Bolton at Hayden's Hotel in Ballinasloe on Monday and was given assurances that an interview would be allowed at the earliest opportunity. The solicitor called to the barracks but was denied access several times throughout the day. In frustration, he penned a letter of complaint, which infuriated Bolton when it appeared later in the *Freeman's Journal* and in the *Western News*. Not until 5.30 p.m. did the authorisation from the attorney-general's office arrive through Bolton, and even then Bowler was only admitted to the barracks with reluctance. To his surprise, Hannon and Tansey were not in Ballinasloe – they had earlier been removed to gaol in Galway city. The solicitor interviewed Nolan and Kennedy on Monday, but was forced to travel to Galway to visit the other men on Tuesday – fully two days after their arrest.

Many of the witnesses had been examined before the magistrates at the public proceedings in Ballinamore three years previously, so their evidence was mainly routine. Nevertheless, since 1880, the prosecution had strengthened the case against the men with new testimony, especially that delivered by Bernard Geraghty.[44] Because of his supposedly close association with the Tanseys and others in the Weston House explosion, Geraghty was in a position to provide crucial information. He was a witness to fulfil all expectations on two counts – he told the inquiry that he was privy to another conspiracy, against the life of the gamekeeper and he delivered an account of the deed itself because he claimed to have actually seen the murder being committed.

Geraghty said that, about a fortnight before 16 October 1879, he was at the limekiln where he heard Tansey say that they 'would have satisfaction out of William Mahon' for summonsing his son, Roger, on the poaching charge. On the night of Will Mahon's murder, Geraghty said that he was walking across Bally-foran Bridge towards Muckloon when he heard a scream further along the road. Running in that direction, he came upon a cluster of four or five men beating Mahon wickedly. He watched as the gamekeeper's life was brought to a violent end over the following ten minutes. He was 'positively certain' that the three men charged – Tansey, Hannon and Kennedy – were at the scene and were participants in the crime.

Although George Bowler claimed that five persons would swear that Laurence Hannon was not at the scene at the time of the murder, Geraghty insisted that it would be false for them to do so. In support of this line, Timothy Geraghty was later called before the inquiry to verify that his son had been absent all night from the house.[45] This established that he was likely to have been at the scene and was, therefore, in a position to identify the assailants. Bernard Geraghty added that, after the body had been taken off the road and into a field in the direction of the River Suck, he simply continued on his way towards the house of his father-in-law, John Kelly. Under cross-examination he denied involvement in the assault.

The defence solicitor expressed incredulity that someone would stand idly by, without remonstrating with the attackers and watch 'an unfortunate man done to death'. Bowler next sought to undermine the integrity of Bernard Geraghty by recalling his part in the Weston House case. Geraghty acknowledged that his role initially was as conspirator and perpetrator of the attack on the home of John Ross Mahon. Then Bowler pressed Geraghty to admit that he had turned informer in the trial, but Bolton objected. The defence solicitor found a different way to make the point by asking what his occupation was: the witness professed to having none but said he was being 'supported by the crown'.

Bowler pressed home the advantage with the seemingly innocuous, 'Where do you live at present?' There was another interjection by the prosecution, presumably because this question, probing the private life of the witness, could be deemed inappropriate. His wife, Mary, must surely have reacted with indignation to the jailing of her brother, James Kelly, on the word of her husband. His latest revelations posed a further threat to Mary's kinship network in Muckloon – Laurence Hannon was her second cousin and his sister was married to Thomas Kennedy. Feelings of family solidarity outweighed any sense of loyalty to a husband turned informer. The deposition made by Geraghty's father to the magistrates' inquiry confirmed that, wherever he was he was being maintained by the crown, Bernard was living apart from his wife at this time. Bowler's provocative query, therefore, touched on a host of sensitive issues both for the witness himself and the prosecution side. Little wonder, therefore, that Bolton intervened.

The defence solicitor continued to harry his quarry and now elicited that the first time Geraghty's account of the Will Mahon murder had been given to the authorities was a mere six months prior to the present inquiry. Assessing the evidence before the trial proper in July, Andrew Reed, the district magistrate, drew attention to this as a significant detail.[46] In a memorandum to the attorney-general, he noted the difficulties pertaining to Geraghty's testimony and was particularly concerned that the informant only came forward in December 1883, more than four years after the murder was committed. There were reasonable grounds to question his motives and cast doubt on his version of events. The legal teams were conscious of this and, while one side sought to exploit weaknesses in his deposition, the other strove to protect it and limit the damage to their argument.

Apart from producing a witness at the scene, the prosecution's other major advance at this inquiry was to extend the conspiracy beyond the Tansey family. Collusion against Will Mahon was consistent with what had already been proven in the Weston House incident: a secret society, which organised agrarian attacks, was based in the Ballyforan area and was using the home of one particular family as its headquarters. The Tanseys were ideally situated to take on a leadership role. Their limekiln was a focal point for the community – its supplies of lime for fertiliser, building and whitewash were in constant demand; their skill as carpenters was another service that brought a steady trickle of customers to their cottage. Traffic to and fro was the perfect cover for co-ordinating the activities of a covert organisation. William Tansey was a ringleader in the Weston House affair – and his father was being portrayed as a chief organiser of the William Mahon attack.

Another house was equally accommodating to conspiracy – the local tailor had his customers too. The prosecution produced a witness who had, by sheer chance, tumbled on a secret conclave at John Nolan's home.[47] Martin Lally was uncertain about the date but claimed to have heard the conspirators discussing plans some time between one and three years before the murder was committed. Lally worked as a herd for Mr Kelly of Claremount House, Ballyforan. One evening, on returning from a fair, he strolled into Nolan's house to light his pipe. The tailor lived in a two-roomed gate lodge close to Ballyforan Bridge. Lally found the kitchen empty but 'waited longer than was necessary to light [his] pipe, tempted by the conversation' coming from the back-room:

> You have good boys of sons. If you got it out on the annagh choke it and put it into a bag and throw it into the River Suck … throw it in Mr Bayley's place as it would give a great deal of trouble if it rose.[48]

The speaker, allegedly the tailor, favoured putting the sack in the Roscommon side of the river because it would deflect attention in that direction if the body were found – and the Galway men would evade the extra taxation levied by the grand jury to defray any police expenses incurred as a consequence.

A little girl then peered into the kitchen and called to those in conversation that there was a stranger lighting his pipe. Lally was convinced that the first to emerge from the back-room was Michael Tansey. The herdsman left and, proceeding towards Ballyforan, saw another individual, whom he presumed was John Nolan, staring after him. Thinking that the subject under discussion was nothing more than a dog, Lally regarded it as harmless until the disappearance of Will Mahon. Then, as the search for the gamekeeper was being conducted, he informed his employer, Mr Kelly, of the conversation he'd overheard.

In his deposition, John Cox, the letter-writer, described an incident less than three months before the murder, which indicated that another of the accused was implicated in the murder conspiracy.[49] He stated that, about the beginning of August 1879, he was bringing a donkey load of turf along the high road to his daughter in County Roscommon when he saw the gamekeeper emerge from a plantation near Tansey's house. Thomas Kennedy, whom he met a little further on, enquired, 'Who is that man up there?' When told it was William Mahon he declared, 'Ha! I'll nib that fellow!' The direct threat against the gamekeeper was made within sight of the location where the actual murder was committed.

Given his central role in the events of 16 October 1879, Kennedy was being cast as the villain of the piece. On being cross-examined, Cox conceded that he had not considered this encounter to be of any significance until Sergeant Finn queried him about the relationship between Kennedy and Mahon. The interview with the policeman had taken place in Galway less than three weeks before the start of the magistrates' hearing.

With the conspiracy net closing about them, the accused men's movements on the evening of 16 October 1879 appeared to seal their destiny. Thomas Gately worked as a letter-carrier between the post offices at Muckloon and Ahascragh. He told the inquiry that he had collected the mailbags from Muckloon about six o'clock in the evening.[50] A short distance from the bridge, he met Thomas Kennedy who requested him to convey a message to Dr Kearns in Ahascragh, probably concerning a consignment of hay that was to be delivered the following day. Soon they were joined by Michael Tansey and the postman hurried on, leaving the two men together at a spot very close to the scene of the attack on Will Mahon.

Details of the men's movements later in the evening were disclosed by another villager, Thomas MacDonnell – the information was also to result in a dramatic development in the case.[51] At around seven o'clock that evening, MacDonnell decided to go down to Burke's pub for a drink having finished his duties at Claremount House. Thomas Kennedy was standing in the roadway, looking into the public house for a few minutes. Then he walked towards the bridge to hold a brief conversation with Tansey and John Nolan before returning to enter Burke's. The other two men walked back in the direction of the bridge. Mac-Donnell himself now strolled into the tap-room where Kennedy was in company with Cox and Will Mahon. Upon leaving a short time later, the witness saw the tailor's son, Thomas Nolan, standing opposite Burke's yard gate. On the following morning, when MacDonnell learned of the gamekeeper's disappearance, he told his employer, Mr Kelly, that it came as no surprise on account of 'the way parties were going about all night'.

MacDonnell admitted that he had not given as full an account of the goings-on to any previous investigation because he had been too frightened to do so. The chairman of the inquiry, W. J. Paul, interjected, 'At that time everybody was afraid to give evidence in Ireland!' The witness told Bowler that his fears had now dissipated. This was probably because, since the murder occurred, he had emigrated to Handsworth – where, coincidentally, Bernard Geraghty was captured. MacDonnell's statements confirmed that the threat from the conspirators was seriously regarded within the local community. Seven months previously at the Weston House trial, Justice Murphy drew attention to the effects of intimidation by commenting on the demeanour of those giving evidence in the courtroom, 'One could not fail to observe during the progress of the case that some of the witnesses trembled, apparently from terror, when they came to the witness-box.'[52]

After his deposition was completed, there was a brief exchange between MacDonnell and Thomas Nolan, who was in the courtroom and called out, 'Well, MacDonnell, I never did anything to you, at all events.'

MacDonnell replied, 'Well, Mr Nolan, I am telling the truth, and no one can say anything to me!'

George Bowler, anticipating the next move by the constabulary, asked Inspector Joyce what action was to be taken on foot of the day's revelations. The policeman refused to divulge his intentions, but a constable was already in possession of a warrant, and Thomas Nolan, principal of the local school, was arrested as he left the hearing.[53] Thomas Nolan declined the services of Bowler, declaring that he would act in his own defence. The prosecution team must have viewed the outcome of the day's business with some satisfaction – it was proven that a second member of the tailor's family was implicated in the conspiracy against Will Mahon.

There was some surprise when John Cox was sworn in to make a second deposition at the next session, but there was good reason, and the inquiry was treated to more dramatic evidence that had not been heard before.[54] Cox described a terrifying ordeal that he had suffered, walking home from Burke's public house on the night of the killing:

> Cox: 'When I was coming to the foot of the bridge on the County Roscommon side, a man came behind and threw a cloth or a handkerchief over my face. I started immediately and asked what was this for and turned round asking who that was. Michael Tansey, the prisoner, was close to me. The same as if they were in a tuft, there were two or three other men by the wall. I could not know who they were. I went my way home in a hurry.'
>
> Mr Lyster, RM: 'What was done with the handkerchief?'
>
> Cox: 'Pulled away.'
> Bolton: 'It was taken away, sir, when they saw it was the wrong man!'
>
> Bowler (seeking an explanation for the sudden revelation of this sensational information): 'When did you tell it to anyone?'
>
> Cox: 'About nine or ten days ago.'

Bowler: 'Why did you not tell this story here the last day you were examined?'

Cox: 'Because I was afraid to tell it then, and often before it. I might often have thought of it before, but was afraid to tell it!'

The fear of reprisal that gripped the countryside ensured the silence of witnesses during investigations into crime and was powerful enough to hold sway over sworn testimony inside the courtroom itself. John Cox was not the only individual who admitted to being afraid. He was not reprimanded by either the magistrates or the legal teams for his failure to make a full disclosure during his first appearance on the witness stand. All sides accepted that being subject to intimidation by persons known or unknown was a legitimate excuse for reticence, even when under oath. Michael Tansey claimed that coercion of a different dimension forced John Cox to break his silence at the Galway inquiry. In a petition for release, Tansey stated that: 'Cox swore that Mr Bolton, crown prosecutor, and the district inspector, Mr Joyce, told him it would be worse for him if he did not swear what he was told by them.'[55] Regardless of what explanation is given for his reappearance on the stand, John Cox's graphic account was another piece of circumstantial evidence that made a significant impression on the magistrates.

The sub-headline above *The Galway Vindicator* report of the magistrates' inquiry on 22 March proclaimed another step forward for the prosecution: 'A National Teacher turned informer.' One month in jail was enough to convince Thomas Nolan that he should seek a convenient way out of his predicament. Because he had given information, he was not brought before the magistrates with the other accused. As a footnote to this episode, the press also reported the manner of Thomas Nolan's interrogation by the authorities, which was raised in the British Parliament by Mr Sexton, MP.[56] He queried whether the schoolteacher had been terrified into giving false evidence by Mr Bolton and the constabulary during his time in custody, but the solicitor-general refused to discuss any suggestion of impropriety by crown officials in the case.

On 28 March, the closing day of the Galway inquiry, the twenty-two depositions were read over to the four remaining prisoners.[57] Then the chairman, Mr Lyster, announced that they were to be committed for trial at the next assizes. The charge against Tansey, Hannon and Kennedy was that they did each 'with others conspire to murder, and did feloniously murder, one William Mahon'. In reply, each man protested his innocence. John Nolan was charged with being an accessory prior to the commission of the murder. He refused to say anything in response to the charge, unless through a lawyer. The four were placed in Galway Gaol to await trial.

Thomas Nolan was brought before the next Friday sitting of the magistrates.[58] Bolton, the crown solicitor, stated that although there was sufficient evidence to make a strong case, there was no wish to bring him to trial on account of having accepted the deposition he had made. In addition, the prosecutor did not favour reopening the inquiry because the magistrates had 'so much trouble with it', and the evidence against the four already sent for trial was 'so complete'. Bolton then told the magistrates that any further action to be adopted was left to their discretion after which the chairman proposed that they 'had best discharge him!'

With that, the schoolteacher was a free man. The price of liberty was declared in the courtroom to consist of statements that corroborated evidence previously given to the inquiry. Thomas Nolan did not remain long in Ballyforan thereafter, nor did he resume his post at the local school. Judging by the report of the inspector, there were feelings of animosity towards him within the community even before he turned informer: an investigation in May 1883 concluded that an allegation of drunkenness was 'unfounded and malicious'. What caused him to make his next move is unclear. Was he already being subjected to a campaign of social ostracisation? Was it shame at betrayal of his fellow conspirators? Or was it fear of reprisal from friends of the accused?

Regardless of these local considerations, the board of education would not employ a teacher in such disgrace and, within a few months of his release from custody, Thomas Nolan emigrated to America.[59]

The next major development in the William Mahon murder case was a tragedy within the walls of Galway Gaol.[60] At six o'clock on the morning of 30 June 1884, a warder discovered that Thomas Kennedy had committed suicide in his cell during the night. A key figure in events surrounding the gamekeeper's murder, the thirty-two-year-old farmer had followed the example set a few weeks earlier by another untried prisoner and 'forestalled the work of the public executioner'. Since his arrest, Kennedy had spent five months in captivity and had shown himself to be 'of perfectly sound mind … and fit for punishment' up to the final day of confinement. But anxiety at an imminent trial on a charge of murder had its effect. In what he must have felt was the last throw of the dice, Kennedy had bargained for his life by becoming a witness for the crown at some time during his last weeks. So, perhaps it was remorse at having betrayed neighbours, his fellow-accused, that drove him to take a final desperate step. A coroner's inquest found that death was self-inflicted. The end for Tom Kennedy was ignominious. No person claimed his body because the burial of a suicide victim in consecrated ground was prohibited – instead he was laid to rest in an anonymous prison plot.[61]

Days later, the gamekeeper's murder was back in the national spotlight. The decision was made to try the three remaining men – Tansey, Hannon and Nolan, in that order – at the Summer Assizes in Carrick-on-Shannon, County Leitrim. The solicitor-general explained that transferring these proceedings to Leitrim, outside the county in which the murder was committed, had been done in the interest of finding an impartial jury whose verdict was less likely to be tainted by local prejudice. The trial began on Tuesday, 8 July before Judge Johnson. The prosecution team included the solicitor general, Sergeant Robinson, The MacDermott, QC, Mr Nolan, QC, and Mr Le Poer Trench, instructed by George Bolton, crown solicitor. The defence team was led by George Orme Malley, QC, who was assisted by Mr Taylor, instructed by George Bowler. The first to be arraigned was Michael Tansey.

Sergeant Robinson outlined the sequence of events, dating from March 1877 (when the conspirators were first overheard by the herdsman Lally) to May 1880 (when the body of William Mahon was taken from the River Suck). The facts had previously been gathered by police detective work and in depositions to the magistrates' inquiry in Galway. Now, the sixteen witnesses for the prosecution and four for the defence, presented the evidence in the heightened atmosphere of theatricality that attended the process of deciding whether another man was to die by the hangman's noose.[62] The prosecution, in pursuit of a guilty verdict, sought to impress the jurors with the most damning pieces of evidence.

Colourful and emotive phrases that would linger might be decisive in the jury-room. When Bridget Gately, wife of the postman, was examined she recalled a visit by Michael Tansey to her house shortly after the body was discovered. Tansey had warned her husband not to tell the police what had transpired. On another occasion, according to Bridget, Tansey threatened that 'if she did not hold her tongue, he would kick all the talk out of her'. Thomas Gately also told the court of another death threat early in the summer of 1880. On the way home from Ballyforan chapel, Larry Garvey had said, 'There is a man and woman to be shot in the village!' The postman answered, 'Perhaps it is myself.'[63]

According to *The Galway Vindicator*, the star witness was 'a well-dressed, intelligent-looking young man, named Bernard Geraghty'. His evidence was crucial because he was the only person who claimed to have seen the murder being committed. Furthermore, in claiming that Tansey had reprimanded him for being late at the scene, Geraghty suggested to the court that he himself was involved in the plot to attack the gamekeeper. The defence strategy was to attack the credibility of the crown's principal witness, concentrating on his ambiguous role throughout the Weston House affair – it was pointed out that having joined in a criminal outrage he betrayed his companions by turning police informer. The jurors were being made to ponder whether they could rely on the word of a man of such character.

Under cross-examination, Geraghty's involvement with the secret society was further scrutinised.[64] The portrait of the conspirators that emerged was less like an agrarian tenant 'combination' and more closely resembled a cell of the revolutionary Fenian Brotherhood. Geraghty stated that, after he was sworn in, they 'planned several crimes', one of which was the Weston House attack. He admitted that he continued to mix with those in the conspiracy while in England and there they had drawn up 'several dynamite plans [including] some in England'. The defence counsel challenged by asking Geraghty if he was 'in the swim'. To which Geraghty replied, 'Yes.'

Mr George Malley, for the defence, condemned Geraghty as a man 'who thought nothing of taking away the life of a fellow-creature, whether by dynamite or by perjury'. Witnesses were then produced to prove that Geraghty could not have been at the scene of the crime on the night of 16 October 1879. One of them was Mary, his wife. Under questioning, Mary revealed that she and Michael Tansey were friends of long standing and it also emerged that the accused man had arranged the match between herself and Bernard Geraghty. The woman swore that her husband had remained at home on the night of the murder with nobody but herself and his father. A poorly co-ordinated defence allowed this alibi to be wrecked by two other witnesses, both named John Rogerson (they were cousins). Each claimed to have been in Geraghty's house on the fateful night – contradicting Mary's evidence. The first (a brother of Patrick, convicted in the Weston House case) had emigrated some time after October 1879. He travelled from England for the trial to swear that he had been in Geraghty's between seven and ten o'clock on the night of the supposed murder. He had not seen Bernard leave home in that time. The other John Rogerson, Geraghty's neighbour, told the court that he too had stayed until ten o'clock and left as Mary was preparing supper.

Further testimony from the second John Rogerson was disputed – which was to have a dramatic impact on the trial. Rogerson told the court that Geraghty had spoken to him, after the body was found, about the reward on offer for information leading to a conviction in the Will Mahon murder case. The prosecution wanted an immediate rebuttal of Rogerson's evidence.[65] When a 'private inquiry' was made among the Ballyforan policemen, none of them could remember anything other than the £10 for finding the body. So Constable Thomas Keegan, who was in charge of Ballyforan station in the summer of 1880, was put forward to contradict the defence witness – but he was in error. He admitted later, 'I quite forgot when giving my evidence that a reward was offered in the "Hue and Cry".'[66] His lapse of memory was also probably due, in some part, to the fact that notice of the proclamation (advertising sums of £300 and £100 for information) was not on display in Ballyforan station – because it lay outside the East Riding of County Galway. The policeman's inadvertent mistake discredited John Rogerson's claim that he had heard Geraghty mention the money.

As the hearing had lasted for two days, Judge Johnson decided to defer charging the jury until the following morning.[67] As a press correspondent reported, his final admonition was 'to find a verdict, regardless of consequences'. At 1.30 p.m. on Thursday, 10 July, the jury retired for a mere forty-five minutes before returning a guilty verdict. The foreman added that they wished to recommend Michael Tansey to mercy, on the grounds that the crime was committed so long ago and that the country was now returned to a peaceful state. Judge Johnson, however, was in no mood for appeasement. Before sentence was pronounced, Michael Tansey addressed the court. He denied involvement in the killing, or that he had seen his fellow-accused on that evening. Then he declared himself willing to die. The judge donned the black cap and sentenced Michael Tansey to death by hanging in Galway Gaol on 11 August. The condemned man's only request was 'to let me shake hands with my wife before I die'. He then saluted judge and jury saying, 'Well, good-bye gentlemen', and left the dock. There was an emotional farewell from his wife before he was led away from the courtroom.

The prosecution asked the judge to fix the trial of the second accused, Laurence Hannon, for the following morning. Mr Malley, the defence counsel, requested a delay because he was not keen to proceed with what would essentially be a rerun of Michael Tansey's trial – hearing the same evidence, and the awful prospect of the same guilty verdict. Counsel for the prosecution acquiesced, so the judge agreed to postpone the Hannon and Nolan hearings until the next assizes.

In Galway Gaol, special arrangements were made to place the condemned man in a separate cell from his fellow-accused. The government agreed to the employment of warders on a temporary basis, to be paid at the rate of one guinea per week, and four police pensioners were appointed to supervise Michael Tansey in his final days. A special diet was approved for the prisoner and arrangements made to allow visits by the chaplain.[68]

Outside the prison walls, the condemned man's plight was a source of continuing disquiet. Michael Tansey had won the sympathy of people in his native place, including Joseph M. Kelly of Claremount House, who organised a petition to the lord lieutenant, Earl Spenser, for a reprieve.[69] The 'humble memorial of the inhabitants of Muckloon and adjacent districts, and others interested in the peace and welfare of this country' begged for clemency on several grounds, including the 'slight extent to which the prisoner was proved by reliable evidence to have participated' in the crime. Almost fifty men from the neighbourhood of Ballyforan signed the document. The appeal was greatly strengthened by the additional signatures of forty-seven MPs, including the most influential Irish political figures of the day – Charles Stewart Parnell, Tim Harrington, Tim Healy, Edward Shiel, T. P. O'Connor and John Redmond.

George Bowler, the defence solicitor, worked tirelessly on behalf of his client. He contended that the conviction was unsound because Constable Keegan gave false evidence regarding the reward offered for information. Bowler wrote to the inspector general of constabulary seeking clarification on the matter. As a result, Thomas Keegan was questioned and admitted his mistake. Robinson and Trench, from the prosecution team, attempted to dismiss the commotion over the RIC man's inaccuracy, claiming that he had sworn 'to his belief' that there was no reward.[70] Of course, this line of argument was an attempt to remove the blame resting on their shoulders for the flaw in the prosecution case. Although there was no way of measuring the precise extent to which the jury was swayed by his evidence, the crown side had to concede that, if the policeman had given the correct information, the verdict might have been different.

The condemned man had another advocate – of whom he probably never heard. Marian Hawkes of Ashgrove, Newry, County Down also wrote a memorial to Earl Spenser. Her certainty that Providence would exact retribution three-hundredfold for the hanging of one man was founded more on religious zeal and nationalist sentiment than on orthodox theology. Yet the lord lieutenant had to be struck by her fervent opposition to the impending execution: 'If Orange bigotry must have a victim, give me Michael Tansey's place in Galway jail now, and his doom on August 11th.' That her memorials were attached to the prisoner's file is an indication that the pleas were not totally disregarded.[71]

Another factor that must have weighed heavily on the minds of crown counsel was the pressure being exerted on the authorities to revisit another controversial murder trial – Maamtrasna. Convictions in that case, resulting in three executions, had also been secured on the word of informers. A call for an inquiry was made in the British parliament just before the 1884 summer recess. A sensational development of more immediate concern to Dublin Castle was that the 'approver' Tom Casey had recently contradicted statements given in 1882.[72] The crown could not avoid comparison between Maamtrasna and Ballyforan because, in both, it had bought testimony that helped to bring in a guilty verdict. There was another striking parallel – the crown prosecutor at the two trials was the same person, George Bolton.

Reservations at the conviction of Michael Tansey were reflected in the advice offered by one officer in the Law Room at Dublin Castle, 'I do not think it would be safe to carry out the capital sentence in this case. It is better for the administration of the law that the sentence should be commuted to penal servitude for life.'[73] The declaration made by Tansey himself two days later reawakened memories of the nightmarish execution of Myles Joyce and its aftermath, 'I solemnly declare that I did not commit the murder for which I have been accused and condemned and that, furthermore, I know nothing whatever about it … The evidence of those that swore against me was false. I forgive them.'[74] The seeds of doubt were being sown in the minds of those who would determine whether it was to be life or death for Michael Tansey.

Judge Johnson steadfastly represented the alternative voice of the establishment, and sections of the population at large, who believed in the ruthless application of the force of the law in order to suppress insurrection. Ignoring the recommendation of the jury at Carrick-on-Shannon, he pronounced a death sentence. Credit is due, nonetheless, to the judge for immediately conveying the jury's concern to the lord lieutenant and more so for his conscientiousness in preparing, at the request of Dublin Castle, a detailed forty-six page report on the trial. His analysis did not omit the points of contention – discrepancies in four depositions of the letter-writer John Cox, confusion caused by the herdsman Lally's two accounts, criticism of Bernard Geraghty's testimony as 'concocting a story for the police to fit in with [well known] facts', and the disputed evidence regarding the rewards offered. Yet, the report concluded, 'I regret to be obliged to say that there are not, in my opinion, any circumstances which would render the prisoner a proper object of mercy.'

When an appeal was presented, the lord lieutenant had to weigh these arguments in considering whether or not clemency should be granted. Time was running out – Michael Tansey was within three days of execution and the hangman, who had arrived in Galway on Thursday, was busily preparing the gallows for the following Monday morning, 11 August. On Friday, the governor of Galway Gaol received a telegram from Dublin Castle. Preferring the more cautious option, the lord lieutenant had decided to grant a reprieve. Michael Tansey's capital sentence was commuted to penal servitude for life.

Crowds gathered in Ballyforan to celebrate the good tidings. Bonfires were lit and loud cheers raised to hail the work of George Bowler and Joseph M. Kelly. The press welcomed Earl Spenser's decision, 'the reprieve has given the greatest satisfaction'.[75] If the public in general were heartened, what relief must the condemned man have felt? The intensity of emotion may be gleaned from the words of Michael Tansey, written more than a decade later: 'The magistrates and the gentlemen of my neighbourhood petition[ed] for my reprieve and got it. Thanks to them and the Lord that granted it to me.'[76] Evading the hangman's noose brought some comfort, but it would mean a life spent following a daily routine of monotonous, dreary labour such as picking oakum, breaking stones or sewing sacks. Tansey was escorted from Galway Gaol to the railway station and left for Mountjoy on the 11.30 a.m. train the following Thursday.

At the Winter Assizes in Carrick-on-Shannon, the jury failed to agree on a verdict in the trial of John Nolan. Laurence Hannon was released on bail and informed, on 14 February 1885, that the crown intended to drop the charge against him. The procedure was formally concluded at the Spring Assizes in 1885, when a *nolle prosequi* was entered in the cases of both Hannon and Nolan.[77] With one of the conspirators behind bars, it might be perceived that the scales of justice were neatly balanced: Michael Tansey's freedom was forfeit for the life of William Mahon. Just as the declaration at the close of his trial of his readiness to die marked him out as assuming the responsibility of leadership, the condemned man seems to have been resigned to spending the remainder of his life in prison and accepting the burden of reparation for those involved in the affair.

Prison life, with its poor living conditions, less than ideal sanitary facilities and minimal food provisions, took its toll. Combined with the psychological oppressiveness of incarceration and physical demands of penal labour, they were sufficient to weaken the most resilient. Inmates fell victim to a range of gastrointestinal, respiratory and febrile diseases – ulcers, rheumatism, debility, tonsillitis and jaundice were common afflictions.[78] Michael Tansey adapted to the severe regime in Mountjoy and earned commendation for years of good behaviour and proficiency at carpentry. No protest was issued until his health came under strain. Gradually, a combination of afflictions was becoming more acute and debilitating – he suffered with heart disease, liver condition, a double hernia and bronchitis. The decline was exaggerated by age – he was sixty-five when the prison authorities conceded that he was no longer 'fit for ordinary prison labour' from 2 November 1899.[79]

Imprisonment had also eroded the defiance of his stance at Carrick-on-Shannon. Michael Tansey's first petition for release in 1895 was turned down by the lord lieutenant. It was an emotional plea to 'let me die a free man with my family', although it might be adjudged that he did little for his cause by stating where they were – 'seven of them in the city of Boston, two in Yorkshire and two and the mother at home'.[80] A second plea was made in 1899, fifteen years after his conviction. On this occasion, the prisoner's submission was more substantive, dwelling on the flaws in evidence given at his trial and alluding to the crown's inconsistency in discharging his fellow-accused, allowing them to go free while he languished in a cell. A public petition was also organised by Father P. J. Shanagher, the parish priest of Ballyforan, in support of his application for release.[81] It was signed by twenty-six priests from surrounding parishes, the chairmen of Roscommon and Mayo county councils, several councillors, businessmen and two MPs – James O'Kelly, North Roscommon and Jasper Tully, South Leitrim – but the lord lieutenant was not swayed by their appeal.

Eventually, the chief secretary's office decided to grant a discharge, on health grounds, following Michael Tansey's hospitalisation on 17 March 1901 with bronchitis. His son William, released having served the sentence for his part in the Weston

House affair, travelled to Dublin to meet the governor and medical officer of Mountjoy, requesting them to intercede on behalf of his father. The old man was set free in December 1902, and returned to his fourteen-acre farm in Muckloon. A condition of release was that he had to report to the RIC station once a month, a duty he carried out faithfully until 1907, when he sought a dispensation. The sands of time were slipping and one can sense that the tragedy of Will Mahon had finally worn Michael Tansey: 'I am now 77 years of age, weighed down with infirmity and weakness and tottering fast to the grave. I am feeble and unable to walk from my long incarceration.'[82] Early in 1909, 'Mike' Tansey died and, with him, many secrets of the previous thirty years were laid to rest.[83]

Probing the background to the murder of William Mahon at Ballyforan in 1879, two motives emerge: one is political in nature; the other more personal. The crime was committed the year that Michael Davitt founded the Land League, an organisation that mobilised the tenantry and pressed for radical reform of land tenure practices. Coupled with the restive agrarianism that this movement engendered in rural society, the glowing ember of violent nationalism stirred the peasantry into a continual state of agitation. Across County Galway, and part of Roscommon, the proclamations issued in 1866 under the Peace Preservation acts to counter Fenian rebelliousness were still in effect thirteen years later.[84] Among the population in general, there was a simmering hostility towards authority. Consequently, in Ballyforan, Will Mahon was regarded not merely as another next-door neighbour but as a figure who represented the long arm of the law reaching into the heart of the community. Resentment towards him grew to outright hatred when he pressed trespass charges against a local youth. In their anger, the perpetrators of Will Mahon's murder were driven by a belief that the deed would serve their immediate purposes of expediency and personal revenge.

A potent cocktail of political and personal grievance had given rise to a deed that brought Ballyforan under the national spotlight. The parish priest described that time as one 'of great excitement [with] a wave of turbulence passing over the land'.[85] Though it occurred in 1879, a milestone year in Irish history because of Michael Davitt and the setting up of the Land League, the murder was consigned to oblivion – probably the gentlest way to heal the wounds opened by such a traumatic event. Desirable as this may be within a local community, the story of William Mahon's killing fits into greater schema and deserves its place in piecing together the picture of social upheaval throughout Ireland at the end of the nineteenth century.

The intriguing tale of a Galway gamekeeper's murder is a parable of late nineteenth-century Irish life. It provides an intimate, localised view of an archetypal conflict between the governing authorities and a hard-pressed peasantry. Enforcement of strict legislation, such as the Coercion Act and the proclamation of districts, was the reaction of the authorities to the widespread discontent that was vented in an outburst of agrarian crime. In this struggle, individual identities were subsumed, with the result that the protagonists assume a symbolic role in one of history's inglorious dramas. Yet, analysis of this murder illustrates that the reality of human suffering and sadness are necessary ingredients of what took place. The story of these men and women is a personal tragedy. The context in which the Ballyforan murder unfolded, and the concerns it raised, provide an insight into the conflict between officialdom and private interests in the administration of life in post-Famine Ireland. The police were often frustrated in their efforts to hold the internal world of a small community up to scrutiny. Their difficulty is reflected in the words of John Cox, the neighbour who was loathe to give evidence against Michael Tansey, 'He was a friend, and I didn't want to be hard on him.'[86]

'Oh! Good God, is there no one to assist me?'
Osberstown, County Kildare, 1799

SUSAN DURACK

THE SIGHT OF THE Sutton and Lidwell families entering the courthouse at Naas, County Kildare, to take part in a bitter trial was unusual. It was described in some of the newspapers of the day as a trial which 'excited extraordinary attention'[1] and as 'a most interesting and *nouvelle* trial'.[2] Mr Plunket's opening prosecution speech reiterated the point that: '...the present case is not a common one. It is aggravated by every breach of honour and of hospitality and accompanied by circumstances of peculiar depravity.'[3] The sexual context only added further frenzy and inquisitiveness.

In the second half of the eighteenth century, most reported sexual assaults were from vulnerable sections of female society – children, elderly women, servants and unaccompanied women – but only a small number of these reported rapes involved gentlemen from the upper end of the social spectrum.[4] The majority of sexual attacks on married women were perpetrated by individuals known to the victim and only a small number came to public notice as the victims were advised against pursuing their case by members of the family.[5] However, when the Suttons and Lidwells entered the courthouse there was no turning back for they were in the grip of status, honour and position. Their fall from grace could be ruinous.

Both families had been long-standing friends and were connected by marriage, living near each other in Portarlington,
Queen's County [County Laois], where they socialised together
and with other members of the local gentry, such as the Warburton and the Ogle families. The Lidwell and Sutton families had
considerable property, with the Lidwells holding extensive
property in counties Carlow and Tipperary.[6] In the late eighteenth
century, the patriarch of the family was Thomas Lidwell who had
married Jemima Cowley.[7] Their eldest son, John, was married at
the age of eighteen to Ann Fitzpatrick. He was 'unluckily en-
snared to marry into an artful designing family in Queens County
near Durrow'.[8] His father disapproved of the marriage and encouraged his wife to disinherit John in favour of the youngest of
their four sons, Thomas (the family also had four daughters).
Thomas Lidwell had married Elizabeth Julia O'Grady in 1773
when he was twenty-three years old.[9] (She was a second half-
cousin to Standish O'Grady who was prosecutor during Robert
Emmet's trial.)[10] They had only one child, a daughter called Mary
Margaret who married Henry Grove Grady in 1799.

The Lidwells lived in Portarlington but, in September 1799,
they took a lease on Osberstown House near Sallins, County
Kildare, which had formerly belonged to Dr Esmonde who was
hanged for his part in the 1798 Rebellion.[11] They moved there
shortly afterwards.

Their close friends, the Sutton family had lived at Glasshouse
in Portarlington since 1798. In 1793, Jacob Sutton[12] had married
nineteen-year-old Sarah Reade, whose mother was Naomi Reade,
a widow of property from County Wexford, who was living with
her daughter in 1799.[13] They had four children living by 1800.
Mrs Julia Lidwell's mother was married to Sarah Sutton's uncle
and Thomas Lidwell and Jacob Sutton were both yeomen of the
Portnahinch Cavalry. The Lidwells and Suttons had been family
friends for many years and Jacob's mother had known Sarah
Reade since she was a young child.

On Saturday, 28 September, the day after the Lidwell's move
to their new home, Sarah Sutton travelled in the company of

Mary Grady, Thomas Lidwell's daughter, from Portarlington to Osberstown House 'with the approbation of her husband' on foot of an invitation from Mrs Julia Lidwell. Some time after her arrival on the Saturday evening, Thomas Lidwell, his daughter Mary and Sarah went out for a walk. Mary got her feet wet and went home for fear of cold. Sarah Sutton said she had 'no idea of any ill-intention' from Thomas Lidwell but he proceeded to 'press [her] to his bosom several times'. This happened about seven o'clock, as dusk was falling and within view of the house. Sarah Sutton said later that she resisted these approaches and told Thomas to stop his behaviour. They were on the road, having come out of the field in which Mary Grady had left them. But Thomas Lidwell did not stop. He then '… dragged her along the road into the same field, against her will, and he still repeated pressing her to his bosom which she resisted … he then threw her down against her will. She got up immediately and he did not effect any criminal purpose at that time.' After this incident, they walked home to the house during which time she 'admonished him both by looks and words and manner'. She avoided him for the remainder of the evening but did not mention the incident to any member of the Lidwell family, as she did not wish to cause any upset.

On the following day, Sunday, Mary Grady, Mrs Julia Lidwell and Sarah went to church in Thomas Lidwell's gig after which they did a tour of the countryside. Sarah Sutton later said that she tried to avoid Thomas Lidwell all day and told Thomas and Mrs Lidwell on the Sunday evening that she would go home the following day. They pressed her very much to stay but she said she would prefer to go home.

At the start of her visit to Osberstown, Sarah had mentioned that she wanted to take some flour from the local Montgomery's Mill home with her, so it was arranged to go there early the following day. On the Monday morning, Thomas Lidwell, Mrs Lidwell, Mary and Sarah started out to walk to the mill which was about a half-mile away. After a short while, Mrs Lidwell did not want to continue the walk as she was wearing a yellow petticoat and the road was dirty. Thomas Lidwell proposed going in the gig but Sarah Sutton declined the offer and said she would not go with him. He replied, 'I don't want you to go with me. Mary will go with you.' They returned home and Sarah Sutton stayed upstairs until the gig was brought to the front door. When she came downstairs Mary Grady said she had a headache and that her father would go with her instead. Sarah went with him.

Sarah Sutton and Thomas Lidwell went to Montgomery's Mill and bought the flour which was to be delivered to the house later that day. Thomas Lidwell then proposed that he take Sarah on a tour of the local countryside. Sarah later said that, to the best of her knowledge, she thought she told Thomas Lidwell that she wished to go back to the house but she did not recollect whether or not he made any answer. Later, Sarah Sutton also said that she was unsure where Thomas had taken her but she thought that they were about a mile from the Lidwell house though she was not certain.

Near the top of a hill on the road, Thomas Lidwell turned his horse down off the road into a gravel pit. She attempted to take the reins to stop him but he stopped the horse after about thirty or forty yards and then got down from the carriage and asked her to get out and walk with him. She refused. He repeatedly begged her to get out of the carriage but she persistently refused. He then got up on the carriage to get her out but she held on to the carriage for as long as she was able. There was no one about and she called out, 'Oh! Good God, is there no one to assist me?' Lidwell finally pulled her roughly from the carriage – the marks he inflicted on her arms remained for about three or four days – and threw her to the ground. She said she didn't have any strength left to resist him. She said she was ready to faint with weakness and did not know what she said or did but knew that 'he did effect his purpose and committed a rape on her and that it was committed by force and against her will'. Afterwards, she did not know what to do. She considered walking back to Osberstown House on her own but thought of the disturbance it would cause. Thomas Lidwell put her in the carriage and spoke to her several times but she would not answer him. However, she remembered him saying, 'I wish to God, my Sally, you would consent to live with me for ever.' She told him that she had a good husband and that he (Lidwell) 'was a most desperate man to want to seduce her from the family' to which he replied that she was a poor little whiner. She said she would never step inside his house again. About one hour after they returned to Osberstown House, Sarah Sutton and Mary Grady set off for Portarlington, about twenty miles away where they arrived about eight o'clock on Monday evening.

On the following morning, Sarah told her mother what Thomas Lidwell had done to her. Her mother advised her to say nothing to her husband 'as he was so determined a man that he might leave her and her children forever or lose his life'. Sarah held the secret from her husband, Jacob, for almost a fortnight but she felt in the end that she could no longer conceal what had happened 'from so good a husband'. On 13 October 1799, without her mother's knowledge or agreement, she informed Jacob Sutton what had happened between herself and Thomas Lidwell.

Sarah Sutton had given birth the previous January and after-wards had a complaint known as 'the whites' (*Leucorrhoea*). She went to the salt water at Booterstown in Dublin to be cured and her health was restored. She thought the rape had brought about this complaint again and, when she told her husband of the attack, she didn't suspect she had anything other than a return of 'the whites'. After she had mentioned the attack to her husband he said Lidwell had 'destroyed you too, for I never had any communication with any woman but you since I was married and I have got an extraordinary complaint', referring to a venereal complaint.

Jacob Sutton then took advice from friends in Wexford and soon afterwards instituted legal proceedings against Thomas Lidwell. Whether to bring the charge of rape or that of criminal conversation against Thomas Lidwell must have exercised Jacob and his advisors. Many cases of rape and criminal conversation were reported in eighteenth and nineteenth-century newspapers in Ireland but it appears from the published accounts that criminal conversation cases were much more common. In his *Bibliography of Irish Trials and Other Legal Proceedings*, Paul O'Higgins cites four rape cases and fifteen criminal conversations cases that were published between 1790 and 1818.[14]

Criminal conversation cases made for more salacious reading and, therefore, there was more demand for this type of material. This should be borne in mind when thinking about this case. The defence alluded to the Sutton's consideration of a case of criminal conversation, although it was denied. Jacob would have been compensated for damages, of up to £10,000, if he had pursued that route – some cases earned even higher damages. The case of *Massy v. Headfort* heard at Ennis Summer Assizes in 1804 earned £40,000 for the aggrieved party.[15] However, Jacob also had a lot to lose if he pursued a criminal conversation case. The family unit could be severely damaged and might even be destroyed with Sarah Sutton's position as a wife and mother completely compromised. The question of family position and dignity would not be fully addressed because compensation alone could not replace lost honour. Jacob Sutton was to make it clear during the trial that he was not pursuing damages. A case of criminal conversation might have put the property of Sarah's mother, Mrs Naomi Reade, and any subsequent inheritance issue at risk, although unwittingly her property might have helped Sarah Sutton and her family. In any case, the Suttons decided that the protection of honour and family dignity should prevail rather than the pursuit of damages. To bring a case of rape was risky but, if won, would restore their honour and the Suttons were probably aware that young affluent women of respectable backgrounds were more than likely to win a rape case whereas the outcome of a criminal conversation case had too many negative possibilities.

In this atmosphere, Sarah Sutton made a statement on 21 October 1799 on foot of which Judge Downs granted a warrant. Thomas Lidwell was arrested and brought before the judge on the evening of the 28 October. Sarah Sutton also attended and was sworn and examined by the judge in the presence of Thomas

Lidwell who was allowed to take notes of her deposition and to suggest questions.

At three o'clock on Tuesday, 22 April 1800, Thomas Lidwell was arraigned at Naas Court on the charge that he 'feloniously did ravish and carnally did know, contrary to the peace of our said Lord the King, his crown and dignity and contrary to the form of the statute in such case made and provided'. Thomas Lidwell pleaded not guilty to the charge, which was a capital crime.

The legal teams consisted of eminent, high-profile people of differing political backgrounds, most of whom were later connected to Robert Emmet and the rebellion of 1803. The counsel for the prosecution included W. C. Plunket,[16] A. Moore, W. Johnson, W. Ridgeway[17] and the agent was Mr R. Waddy. Representing the prisoner were John Philpot Curran,[18] Standish O'Grady, Jonah Barrington,[19] R. Espinasse, Leonard McNally[20] and J. Montgomery and their agent was Mr Henry Grove Grady. On Wednesday, 23 April at ten o'clock in the morning, with Lord Viscount Carleton sitting as judge, the jury was sworn in.[21]

Mr Plunket for the prosecution opened the proceedings and made a persuasive and convincing address to the court regarding any suspicions of Sarah Sutton being an adulteress. She was a woman of family respectability, liberal education and virtuous sentiments. He also highlighted the points from her statement that Lidwell's defence team would make use of. These included her return to the house after the first assault on the Saturday evening, going alone with Thomas Lidwell in the gig, returning with him after the attack was committed and her composure in front of Lidwell's family, her taking refreshment, permitting Thomas Lidwell to salute her at parting and the subsequent concealment of the attack from her husband. Mr Plunket stated that, if these areas of doubt were not satisfactorily cleared up, then the case for Thomas Lidwell was strengthened.

He continued that Sarah Sutton had changed the day for returning home from Wednesday to Monday and that she was betrayed into accompanying Thomas Lidwell in an accidental and unexpected manner on Monday. Then he asked the court to whom could she turn to tell what happened. He stated that: 'a woman of a strong and determined disposition would ... burst into a passionate declaration of her injuries to the first stranger'. Sarah Sutton '...was a woman, gentle, timid, retiring ... She had two lines of conduct to chuse [sic] between ... One was to tell the whole transaction; the other was to assume composure and endeavour to return home without exciting suspicion as to what she meant to do.' As for not telling her husband, she took the advice of her mother not to inform him because of the detrimental effect on the family. She told him after ten days when she heard that Thomas Lidwell was back near her home in Portarlington and that there was every chance that the families would meet again.

Mr Plunket ably tackled the question of adultery. He asked the court 'would an adulteress choose a gravel pit as the scene of her gratification; would an adulteress return home and communicate everything to her mother; would she droop and weep under the recollections of the enjoyments and, finally, to make a discovery to her husband?' He got to the core of the issue when he asked:

> If the jury believed that this lady, whose life had been marked by delicacy and virtue, had at once become profligate in her morals and engaged in criminal commerce with an old man, the intimate friend of her husband; if they believed that, on her suspecting that she had communicated infection to her husband, to screen her own guilt, she told the story of the rape; if they believed that Sarah's mother perjured herself by swearing to the immediate disclosure; if they believed that Sarah perjured herself for the purpose of effecting an atrocious murder under the form and colour of the law; if they believed all this in favour of a man whose defence was that he had debauched the mind and polluted the body of the wife of his intimate friend ... then they ought to acquit the prisoner ... but if they found the testimony of witnesses, whose character was above impeachment, reconcilable with every circumstance arising in the case ... were satisfied that an act of brutal violence had been offered to this lady, they were bound ... to bring in a verdict of guilty.

John Philpot Curran began Thomas Lidwell's defence by acknowledging the 'able address' of the prosecution and asked the judge if his client would be given the same opportunity to state his case. The judge refused, stating that it was the privilege of the crown to have the case stated for the prosecution but that the law did not confer such rights on the prisoner in cases such as this. Philpot Curran and his team could only make their case on the questions put to the various witnesses. The defence case was not that the incident never happened but that it occurred with the consent of Sarah Sutton. In their questioning, certain issues were implied and some were established. The examination focused on three points: the decision to prosecute; Sarah Sutton's return journey to Portarlington; and the circumstances around the timing and sequence of telling her husband of the venereal disease and the attack.

In their examination of Sarah Sutton, the defence team for Thomas Lidwell implied that a relationship already existed between her and Thomas Lidwell. When questioned about being in Lidwell's bedchamber alone with him, Sarah denied it, saying that there were always other people present when she was there. The defence indicated that Thomas Lidwell called her by a more familiar name than Sarah but she replied that this had happened only once. They established that she had always found Lidwell a pleasing man and, if her husband had not been at home, there would have been no other man to whom she would have gone to for advice.

The defence then focused on a trip to Dublin in 1798 taken by Jacob and Sarah Sutton, Thomas Lidwell and a Mr Carey when they lodged together in a house on Grafton Street for the duration of the visit. Jacob Sutton was in town to buy clothes for the Portnahinch Cavalry and Sarah Sutton had a tooth problem that she wished to have seen to but could not receive treatment for it because she was pregnant. In May 1799, Sarah went to Booterstown, County Dublin, to take the salt water. Booterstown was a fashionable place in the early nineteenth-century 'situated on the road from Dublin to Kingstown [Dún Laoghaire] and Bray, and on the southern coast of Dublin Bay, the shores of which here assume a most interesting and beautifully picturesque appearance ... numerous handsome seats and villas ... much frequented during the summer season on account of its facilities for sea-bathing ... numerous lodging-houses have been prepared for the accommodation of visitors'.[22] Under examination, Sarah admitted that Thomas Lidwell visited her in Booterstown on one occasion when her husband was at home in Portarlington.

The defence questioned Sarah about the amount of clothing she brought to Osberstown House for her visit and established that she had not brought enough linen to stay until Wednesday. Philpot Curran focused on her lack of objection when Thomas Lidwell was familiar with her on her first night in Osberstown which included putting his arm about her waist, kissing her and throwing her to the ground twice. Philpot Curran commented, 'You did not seem much surprised at Mr Lidwell's conduct. It might be a matter of curiosity to know how far a man might proceed without exciting alarm.' He then suggested that Sarah Sutton helped Thomas Lidwell in and out of the gig and implied that Lidwell had made advances to her before they arrived at the mill on the Monday morning, expressing surprise that this did not raise any suspicion on her part.

Sarah Sutton told Philpot Curran that she first thought of prosecuting Thomas Lidwell as soon as she told her husband, who had suggested that course of action and said he would punish Lidwell with her assistance. Sarah said she was very willing to do so. Philpot Curran pressed the point that it would become a public matter once she told her husband, she replied that she did not care. Curran then asked her why she did not complain while she was at Osberstown House and she said that she was afraid that Thomas Lidwell might run off with her. She explained that the fear of abduction was the only reason for not informing his family.

Viewed from our present day perspective this excuse may appear rather weak, but 200 years ago such an explanation had to be carefully considered. Thomas Lidwell did want Sarah to go away with him and he even pleaded with her according to her own testimony. Abduction was a capital crime and most offences were committed on single women of fortune or widows. The practice was dying out by the beginning of the nineteenth century, but it was slower to do so in Munster and in south Leinster. Between 1802 and 1816 there were fifty-two abductions in County Tipperary.[23] The memory of the infamous case of Henry Grady's abduction of Susanna Grove in the 1750s was still fresh in the minds of people involved in the present case, especially as a descendant of the abductor, Henry Grove Grady had just married Mary Lidwell. Sarah Sutton's presentation of Lidwell as a possible abductor gave credence to his reckless character in the eyes of the court. On the other side, Lid-well as abductor might be seen by the jury as evidence for the existence of a passionate relationship. However, the question must be raised in this case of the feasibility of abduction being a real threat given that both parties had spouses and children and their own property rights that had to be protected.

Sarah's journey home after the rape then came under scrutiny. Thomas Lidwell's daughter, Mary Grady, and David Fitzgerald, a servant on horseback who accompanied Sarah on her journey home to Portarlington, stated that her disposition during the journey was cheerful and that she sang and joked with the servants. However, Sarah denied all of this.

Philpot Curran then brought the court's attention to the issue of which came first in informing Jacob Sutton – the story of Thomas Lidwell's attack or the question of venereal disease? Sarah Sutton said she had thought that she was suffering from a return of her old complaint of 'the whites' five days after the attack and that the reason for telling her husband of the attack was because he had agreed to dine with Thomas Lidwell later that day. Philpot Curran strongly presented his own belief that Jacob Sutton questioned his wife about the venereal complaint. It was only then that she told him about Lidwell's attack. Curran asked her, 'Had not Mr Sutton found himself disordered before you told him?'

Sarah replied, 'I can't answer to that.'

He suggested that Jacob Sutton might have contracted the disorder by 'his own libertinism' to which Sarah replied, 'I believed he was conscious he had not.' Sarah Sutton denied that she heard any talk of criminal conversation. Philpot Curran asked her directly if she felt this was a struggle between Lidwell's life and her own character to which she replied that Lidwell's behaviour towards her was against her will and, therefore, it was more just that he should suffer rather than herself. In court, it was overheard and reported to the defence team that someone said to Sarah Sutton 'go through with it; all depends upon it'. When questioned about this, Sarah said that her interpretation of the comment was that she was to tell the truth.

Mrs Naomi Reade, Sarah's mother, was the next to be examined by Mr Johnson for the prosecution and was questioned as to how her daughter appeared when she came home to Portarlington after her trip to Osberstown House. Mrs Reade described her as quiet and sad and was upset and crying while in her company. Mr Grady cross-examined and questioned her as to whether or not Jacob Sutton would leave his wife if he thought she had agreed to the intercourse with Thomas Lidwell. Mrs Reade believed he would but would continue to live with her if he thought it was committed by force. Mr Grady highlighted the fact that in the midst of her unhappiness, Sarah Sutton had invited company to Portarlington. Mrs Reade pointed out that this was at Jacob Sutton's request as it was just before he was leaving the country. Mrs Reade's view of Lidwell before the rape was that he would not be guilty of anything improper. She told the court that her daughter told her that Thomas Lidwell 'used her so ill and she was so shocked that she would not care if she lost her life'.

Mr Ridgeway, for the prosecution, then questioned Jacob Sutton who stated that he and Sarah were married for almost seven years and they had lived happily. They moved to Portarlington in February 1798 and became friends with the Lidwells. He would consider Thomas Lidwell as the 'best protector with whom to leave my wife and children' if the need arose. Jacob was then questioned about the trip that he, Sarah, Thomas Lidwell and Mr Carey made to Dublin in July 1798. He confirmed the details of

Sarah Sutton's account. Next, Sarah's stay at Booterstown was raised. Jacob told how she went to take the salt water at Booterstown on 15 May 1799 for the same illness she had had three years previously and for which she found the salt water an effective treatment. Jacob said he went up every two to three weeks to see her and knew that Thomas Lidwell visited her once while she was there.

Jacob Sutton was questioned about his contact with Dr Blair the family doctor. Jacob Sutton had dined with Dr Blair and Mr Richard Clarke, an apothecary, on the evening of 12 October, about two weeks after the attack. He asked the doctor to come and see to his mother-in-law, Mrs Reade, because he believed that she was not well. Sarah told him previously that the reason she was upset was because she thought that her mother was dying. During the course of the evening Jacob Sutton said he discovered 'very extraordinary symptoms' and he said to Dr Blair and Mr Clarke 'if I had connexion [sic] with womankind, except my wife, I would swear I was disordered'. Dr Blair assured him that it was nothing but the effect of some strain.

On the following morning, Dr Blair came to see both women as Jacob Sutton had requested. After breakfast, Jacob Sutton told Dr Blair that he would meet him in town later as he intended to dine with Thomas Lidwell that day. It was after Dr Blair's departure from the house that Sarah Sutton came to him in an agitated state. He told how she had made him promise not to leave her before she told him what had occurred. His initial reaction was confusion and he walked up and down the garden for some time. He then told her that he would like her better than ever for telling him. He later informed her that he would be 'satisfied' with her assistance in taking action against Lidwell. Sarah's reply was, 'There's nothing to do but to punish him, but I will do. Think of the villain wanting me to forsake you and my four children and my mother to go live with him.' Jacob Sutton said it was then that he asked her did she notice anything different about her health. She replied that there was nothing extraordinary, except that she had a return of 'the whites' from the stress she was under.

Sutton told her that she did not have 'the whites' at all but that she was 'disordered' and that she had also 'disordered' him.

Ridgeway's further examination focused on the location of the attack. Jacob Sutton had gone there with his wife to see the place on the Thursday before the court case but Sarah Sutton had difficulty in finding the place at first. Sutton described it as being 'on the road from Johnston to Sallins, on the hill, about a half a mile from Mr Hendrick's house on the left hand side of the road' and, when Sutton stood in the sandpit he could not see any house or even the paper mills.

Mr Barrington, representing Lidwell, cross-examined Jacob Sutton who confirmed that he knew Thomas Lidwell had been confined with gout for about five or six weeks before Sarah Sutton went to Osberstown House. Barrington then asked Sutton if he had 'indulged in gallantry'. Sutton replied that he never knew anyone in the previous five years. When Barrington brought up a statement taken from Dr Blair that Jacob Sutton had been involved with a harvest woman, he denied it. Significantly, Barrington suggested to Sutton that Mrs Reade's death 'would not be an unpleasant circumstance in a pecuniary way as she had a comfortable jointure'. He agreed but pointed out that she had other children and would be dividing her property. Strangely, it was confirmed that Jacob Sutton had been asked to dine with Lidwell which he did on the day after the informations were sworn. He stated that he did not issue the warrants because he wanted to wait for the arrival of his brother, Joshua.

Joshua Sutton guarded Lidwell in a room after he was arrested. When questioned Joshua said that Lidwell pleaded with him, 'Sir, if you and your brother would listen to me dispassionately, I would prove to you, in a few minutes, by the testimony of physicians, that it was impossible for me to commit the act.' Lidwell also said he had had no relations with his wife for several years and that he had physicians attending him for a dreadful 'gleet' which debilitated him. Joshua Sutton stated that this information convinced him even more that Lidwell was a villain.

Character witnesses were called on behalf of Sarah Sutton.

Mrs Ogle, wife of the Rt Hon. George Ogle, said she had known Sarah Sutton since she was an infant and described her as 'a most innocent girl and the best conducted in every particular way'. When pressed further, she confirmed that she had no contact with Sarah since her marriage to Jacob. A similar report came from Richard Neville Esq. and Mrs Elizabeth Sutton, Jacob's mother, said she knew Sarah Sutton from the time she was eight years old and that she was a delightful, innocent, character and did not 'indulge in any kind of levity with men'. However, she added that she had not been in the company of Sarah Sutton in the last two years as she had been living in England.

The judge asked Thomas Lidwell if he wished to say anything. He declined, leaving the defence to his counsel. Under questioning from Philpot Curran, Lidwell's daughter, Mary Grady, outlined that her father had been very ill with gout and had been confined from 8 August until towards the end of September. Sarah Sutton had been invited by Mrs Lidwell because she expressed a wish to see Osbertown House even though they had only moved in the day before Sarah's visit and had scarcely any furniture.

Mary reported that Sarah definitely said that she would return home on the Monday. She told the court that her father was so weak that he needed the assistance of herself and Sarah Sutton in order to walk about. When they had gone out for the walk on the Saturday evening, Mary had wet her feet when she helped her father over a stream and returned home at Sarah Sutton's request. She did not see anything unusual in Sarah Sutton's appearance or demeanour when they returned from the walk. Contrary to Sarah's account, she said she had left her father and Sarah Sutton alone together in the parlour as she had some domestic business to attend to. She said that Sarah told them on Sunday that she would return on Monday according to the original plan but, the next day, Sarah said she wished to buy a half stone of flour at Montgomery's Mill. It was proposed to walk to the mill, but Sarah feared she would get her feet wet. Her father proposed to go in the gig but Mary declined because she had a journey of twenty miles to do later that day.

When her father and Sarah returned they had no flour with them as her father would not give her the trouble of standing up in the gig. Sarah and a servant assisted Thomas Lidwell out of the carriage. Mary Grady did not see the 'smallest alteration in her dress nor the smallest change in her countenance' and when asked, Sarah Sutton reported that she had a pleasant journey, although she did not know the roads. Mary said Sarah partook of a healthy snack and drank three or four glasses of wine and that, on leaving Osberstown House, she shook hands with and kissed Thomas Lidwell. Mary continued saying that the journey home to Portarlington had been cheerful. David Fitzgerald, the servant, was in attendance on horseback, and Sarah had sung several songs in the course of the trip. Mary asked Sarah to join her for dinner at her residence in Portarlington but she declined, stating that it was too late.

The next evening, Mary met Jacob and Sarah Sutton and Mrs Reade at Glasshouse. She was cordially received and the family was as friendly as usual. Mary remembered that Sarah said she was glad she had come as she had already written an invitation to them to come and dine and they arranged to dine on the following Saturday. Jacob confided in Mary that the party was Sarah's idea. At the gathering, Sarah was as cheerful as ever. She 'came out to me and brought me into the dining-room to adjust my dress and walked with me to the drawing-room, leaning on my arm'. She said Jacob Sutton, as usual, borrowed everything from Thomas Lidwell such as plate for the party as well as a servant to attend. Mary concluded her testimony for the defence by saying that she hadn't noticed anything amiss with Sarah Sutton.

Mr Plunket's cross-examination of Mary Grady established that she made notes the morning after her father was taken prisoner. She said that it was Mrs Lidwell who pressed Sarah Sutton to stay longer than Monday. He questioned her as to the level of her friendship with Sarah Sutton to which she replied, 'I was intimate with her so far as visiting.' Mary Grady said she would never have considered or suspected that there might have been any relationship between her father and Sarah. Mr Plunket then returned to her story about her getting her feet wet and questioned how her father had got over the stream if he was as feeble as described. Mary's explanation was rather unconvincing and, when she had finished, Plunket sardonically described Lidwell as a 'poor decrepit old gentleman'. When she again described her father's feebleness and his need for assistance to alight from the gig, Plunket asked why, if her father was so feeble, had he originally intended to walk the half a mile to the mill to get the flour? Mary Grady's unconvincing reply was that he might have been able to walk halfway and would have waited in one of the cabins for the return of the rest of the party to which Plunket replied pointedly 'very probable indeed, Madame'. Most importantly, when asked on her oath if she believed that criminal intercourse had taken place between her father and Sarah Sutton, Mary answered, 'I do not know, Sir … It is difficult to say … I cannot form a belief.' A juror asked whether Sarah Sutton expressed any desire to see Thomas and Mrs Lidwell among the company at the party. Mary's answer was significant in that she conceded that Jacob Sutton did but Sarah did not.

Dr Blair was called for the defence and questioned by Mr Espinasse. It was established that Dr Blair had attended Thomas Lidwell and his family over a ten-year period. When he was asked if he knew that Thomas Lidwell was afflicted with a venereal disease during his confinement with gout, the doctor replied that he never heard mention of any venereal complaint during that illness. He said that he was sent for by Thomas while he was in prison to inspect him but he found no venereal disease. Asked if Jacob Sutton had ever said anything in respect of Sarah Sutton, Blair said that he recalled meeting Jacob at Thomas Lidwell's house when he had told him that 'he [Sutton] had gone up for Mrs Sutton; that she had gone to the salt water for her health, but was in Dublin, instead of being there [Booterstown] and he could not get her back; but he would bring back the children'. When Jacob Sutton's fidelity was called into question, Dr Blair revealed that Jacob told him 'in a joking way, as a man over a bottle, that he had fun with the girls who were picking bark off the trees ... that he had a connexion [sic] with them ... he had a bedfellow in Mrs Sutton's absence'. Dr Blair said he believed him. Mr Moore then questioned him on the nature of gonorrhoea and established for the court that it could not be concealed.

It was confirmed by Dr Blair that Thomas Lidwell had attended Mr Smith (a practitioner in branches of medicine) but not for a venereal complaint. Mr Smith had absconded a the month prior to the trial because he 'was embarrassed in his circumstances; he had been soliciting a surgeonry from Sir Ralph Abercrombie'. Dr Blair was asked if there was a similarity in the symptoms for 'the whites' and gonorrhoea to which he replied there was not except for the discharge. Dr Blair was asked his opinion if the prisoner was capable of committing the offence he was charged with to which he replied, 'His general character is that of a man not capable of forcing a woman against her will.'

A witness named A. Hardinge Giffard was the next to be called to the stand. He was brought to the attention of the defence team as he claimed that he overheard a gentleman who was with Sarah Sutton say, 'Be determined, and go through with the business. Everything depends upon it.' The prosecution berated the witness, stressing Sarah Sutton's agitation and got him to admit that he did not believe Mrs Sutton spoke falsely during the court trial. However, the gentleman who was talking to Sarah was produced in court. His name was Joseph Daly and he was in the court when Sarah Sutton came in. He said he never saw a woman more completely embarrassed and agitated and that he gave her assistance by sending out for water and also sent to an apothecary for drops. All he had said to her was, 'Summon up fortitude; you are going to do justice; tell the truth, that is all you have to do.'

Mr Richard Clarke, an apothecary who had lived for twenty-five years in Portarlington and who had furnished Thomas Lidwell with medicines for about ten years, said he never supplied medicine for a venereal complaint. He recalled having a meal with Jacob Sutton on 12 October during which Dr Blair came in. Clarke said that Sutton had asked him since that date, if he remembered him asking about a venereal complaint. Clarke said he could not recall. Sutton suggested that Dr Blair might recollect it. Clarke had then asked Dr Blair if he heard it on the night and he said he did not. Mr Plunket suggested that there might have been a lot of conversation on the night that might be forgotten the next day to which Clarke agreed. Plunket remarked that Clarke looked 'like a gentleman who took more port than rhubarb'. Clarke could not swear positively if Jacob Sutton told him that he came to know of his disorder before or after Sarah Sutton told her husband. It was suggested by Plunket that Jacob Sutton tried to 'bring a fact out from Clarke on his oath which he was not willing to give'. Clarke agreed with Plunket on this point.

David Fitzgerald, a servant in the Lidwell household, was questioned and he confirmed that Sarah Sutton was cheerful and sang on the return journey to Portarlington. Asked under cross-examination if he heard Thomas Lidwell press Sarah Sutton on the Sunday to stay longer, he said he heard them ask but that she had said she had to return on the Monday as she had promised her husband that she would be home.

Jacob Sutton was recalled to the stand and questioned by Mr Ridgeway about Sarah's return journey from Osberstown House. Sutton informed the court that he did not expect them home on the Monday to which Mary Grady was heard to utter, 'I declare to God, I never met so obstinate a woman; all entreaties of my father and mother could not keep her.' As to the plate that was borrowed for the party, Jacob said Mary Grady offered them and, two hours before dinner, he asked the servant to attend. He stated upon questioning that Mr Clarke was a worthy man but that he was mistaken.

The case was then closed for both sides. There were certain procedures laid down in the conduct of rape cases. Shani D'Cruze refers to the research of Anna Clarke, who has done much research into rape cases, which found that a high degree of credibility was required from the victim and certain stock criteria had to be satisfied by the court.[24] One of the most important conditions was the immediate disclosure of the assault to a third party, which Sarah Sutton did not do at Osberstown but did as soon as she could the next morning. As to evidence of physical injury, Sarah Sutton said she had marks on her arms for about four days and, although this could have been corroborated by her mother, there was no mention of it. To be able to prove her efforts to resist was another important point. Sarah Sutton had no witnesses and said, 'Oh! Good God, is there no one to help me?', but she did not cry out or scream.

As all the testimonies had been heard, Judge Carleton proceeded with his summing up. He reminded the jury of their responsibility and went over the main points of the case and advised the jurors that they were to weigh carefully the testimony of the witnesses and to decide upon the degree of credit and to consider any contradictions that appeared. He recalled the different periods which deserved consideration: Sarah Sutton's visit to Dublin; her lying in; her visit to Booterstown; her return home; the visit to Osberstown; the day of the alleged crime; the disclosure to her mother; the first appearance of the venereal complaint; the disclosure to her husband; the swearing of the informations; and the arrest of the prisoner. He pointed out that the visits to Dublin and Booterstown drew inference that Sarah Sutton had had criminal conversation during those visits, either with Thomas Lidwell or with somebody else, and that, in the latter of those visits, she had contracted the venereal disease. However, he said that the circumstances were too slight to warrant such inference. If she had done this, Jacob Sutton should have known about the venereal complaint earlier than 12 October.

He referred to the conduct of the prisoner on 28 September and left it to the jury to decide if this was an indication of more serious conduct later or whether they were satisfied with Sarah Sutton's evidence and if that evidence explained sufficiently in accounting for her conduct. The determination to return home on the Monday and not the Wednesday was raised. Sarah Sutton, Mrs Reade and Jacob Sutton agreed that Wednesday was the date set for her return while Mary Grady and David Fitzgerald agreed that she was to return home on Monday. The shortage of clean linens for Sarah Sutton was also taken into account.

The circumstances of the crime were then considered. The judge gave a summation of Sarah Sutton's evidence which the jury were to reflect upon carefully: that she did not cry out; the distance of the pit from any habitation; the weakness of her bodily frame; the depth of the sandpit; her return to Osberstown with the prisoner; and her appearance and conduct there and the journey home. As to the extreme frailty of Mr Lidwell, the judge stated that this was not easy to credit given other circumstances disclosed in the evidence.

Judge Carleton made some observations on the parts of Mrs Reade's testimony that the jury was to take account of in weighing the degree of credit that it should be given. The disclosure of the act to her mother on the morning of 1 October greatly corroborated the testimony of Sarah Sutton 'provided the jury believed that fact to be as it was represented by Sarah Sutton and her mother'. The postponing of the fact from her husband until 13 October had contrary tendency unless 'the jury were satisfied it was attributed to the reason assigned by the mother and daughter'. He stated that weighing this evidence was crucial.

He continued, saying that Sarah Sutton knew she was ill between 1 and 13 October and it was very material to find out if possible whether or not she knew the real nature of her disorder or considered it merely as a renewal of her old complaint. He said that if it was the former 'it would become a material object of inquiry' whether the evidence of the mother was not calculated to prop the falling reputation of the daughter and whether the concealment of eleven days was not ended by Sarah Sutton's consciousness of her having a venereal complaint, which could no longer be concealed and which could leave infidelity no longer doubtful. On the other side, if Sarah Sutton really believed it was the return of an old complaint, her mother's advice along with the stress she was experiencing might have delayed the disclosure to the husband until 13 October. Judge Carleton stressed that the credit of the mother had to be considered very carefully.

'Its establishment would give considerable additional strength to the evidence of Sarah Sutton; on the contrary, were the credit of the mother destroyed, the evidence of Mrs Sutton would have its most essential support withdrawn from it.'

The defence evidence concerning Sarah Sutton's demeanour subsequent to 1 October weakened her case but her husband's account of the stress she experienced tended to support it. Judge Carleton stressed to the jury that the case was a question of fact:

> If the jury had a reasonable doubt on their minds whether the prisoner was guilty of the foul crime with which he stood charged, then it was their duty to acquit him but on the other hand, if the jury, after maturely weighing and considering the evidence to support the prosecution and that produced by the prisoner to rebut that testimony, had not such a doubt on their minds as a reasonable man could have, but were convinced on their oaths that the prisoner was guilty, however painful it must be to their feelings to bring such a verdict against a man of family and education, such as the prisoner was, yet, it was their duty to do so.

The jury retired and Lord Carleton adjourned the court, which had been sitting for eighteen hours, for a short time. It soon became apparent that the jury would be unable to come to a quick decision. The court reopened at ten o'clock the next morning, Lord Kilwarden presided and heard other cases.[25] At about one o'clock that afternoon, the jury sent a letter to the judge which he declined to read. The jury was called in and Lord Kilwarden told them it was 'most irregular' to send a letter to any person while they were enclosed to consider a verdict. When asked if they had decided on a verdict, they answered that they had not and they were not likely to. Kilwarden told them they had to return and decide a verdict. After four hours, a verdict was agreed. The verdict was guilty but with a recommendation to mercy. Judge Carleton, who had returned to the court by this time, asked if it was from any doubt in their minds that they recommended mercy. The jury replied it wasn't but was based on the 'previous uniform good character of the prisoner'. The verdict was recorded.

Before the sentence was read out, Thomas Lidwell spoke. He thanked Judge Carleton for his patience and his humanity in the way in which he dealt with and discriminated the weight of evidence that had been produced in the trial. He also thanked the sheriff for the 'respectable jury' he provided. Significantly, and ominously, he said, 'When that awful moment shall come in which I shall be about to return to my God, I will then make a public declaration of the facts. Till then I will forbear.' However, there is no record that he ever said anything more.

Lord Carleton acknowledged the jury's recommendation for mercy to which he replied that it was an additional instance of the humanity with which he was treated. Lidwell requested that he be allowed as much time as possible to settle his affairs and property, which were considerable. The sentence was then pronounced. 'You, Thomas Lidwell, are to be taken from the bar of the court, where you now stand, to the place from whence you came, the gaol, there your irons are to be knocked off; and from thence you are to be conveyed to the common place of execution, the gallows, where you are to be hanged by the neck, until you are dead; and the Lord have mercy on your soul.' The date set for the execution was Wednesday, 10 May 1800. It was noted by a reporter that the lord lieutenant sometime after the trial was 'graciously pleased to respite the prisoner until further orders'. The outcome of the case was reported in some newspapers of the day:

> ... at Naas assizes Mr Lidwell, whose trial excited extraordinary attention, was found guilty of the charge on which he was indicted but the verdict was accompanied by an earnest recommendation to the Royal Mercy.[26]

On 9 May it was reported that 'on making enquiries, we find it necessary to contradict a paragraph which appeared in the newspapers respecting Mr Lidwell, now under sentence of death at Naas, and who was stated to have received a pardon; no pardon nor respite has been issued and this execution stands for the 14th inst'.[27] The *Freeman's Journal* reported:

We understand that Mr Ledwell [sic], now under sentence of death at Naas, was ordered by the judge [for] prosecution on Thursday next – and 'tis rumoured, that petitions highly recommended have been forwarded to the Throne, to save the life of this unhappy culprit – the public, however, may be satisfied, that the strict accustomed justice of government, will, on report of the trial, finally operate – or should any circumstances appear in the prisoner's favour, that the Government's Clemency will, in like manner, attempter justice with mercy.[28]

Discussions took place but the execution did not proceed on 10 May as originally planned, or on 14 May. A further report stated: 'A respite for Lidwell, under sentence of death in Naas Gaol was sent thither on Tuesday last. It is said he is to be transported for life.'[29]

However, it is doubtful if Lidwell was transported at all. His brother, John Lidwell, referred briefly to the trial in his 1804 pamphlet but does not mention the outcome. There is a belief that, if Lidwell was transported, the inheritance of his property would have strongly interested his brother especially as he had strong grievances about his own rights in this area because their father favoured Thomas over him in respect of the property. In the circumstances of the time, it is quite possible that he served only a light sentence and it is possible that Thomas didn't even suffer that ignominy.

This case must have caused a major split not only between the Lidwells and Suttons, but also must have had a detrimental effect within each family. Their lives could never be the same again. Not much is known about what happened to these branches of the families after the trial. Thomas Lidwell had no son as far as the records show. There is a record of a will for Thomas Lidwill of Carlow for 1809 which is probably that of the accused.[30] Mrs Julia Lidwell, Thomas' wife, died in 1827: '…at Castle Connell, Co. Limerick at an advanced age. Mrs Lidwell, relict of Thomas Lidwell of Clonmore Esq., was sister to the late De Courcy O'Grady, Kilballyowen, Esq. and grand-daughter of Lord Kinsale.'[31]

As to the Sutton family, there is only one record of Mrs Sarah

Sutton at Clonmines, County Wexford, 'widow of the late Jacob Sutton of Ballyarnan (Ballylannon) Esq, born 21 May 1811, died October 27 1855'. The date of birth does not correspond with the Sarah Sutton in the case, but it is possible that the inscription on the tomb might not have been clear.[32] There is a record of a Mrs Naomi Reade who died on 12 April 1833. Probate was granted to Frances Theodoria Reade, possibly a grand-daughter. Frances Reade died in 1878 and probate was granted to Anne Reade.[33] Judge Carleton recognised Mrs Naomi Reade as a very important and crucial witness in the case. It does seem that both families departed from their midland homes and resettled in new surroundings.

From the seventeenth century, a strong tendency emerged which placed a new and heightened importance upon the values of family life and to deplore any aristocratic or libertine conduct which would put domestic security at risk.[34] This was stressed in the court in the opening prosecution speech. Anna Clarke's finding that a certain amount of libertinism remained in some areas of masculine and elite culture are borne out in the detail of the trial, such as references to Mr Sutton's 'libertinism' and 'gallantry', his dalliances with harvest girls, his bedfellow in Sarah Sutton's absence, and the suggestion that the disorder could have come from him.[35] Joshua Sutton's admission that he never 'met a woman that was not as willing as myself' and Lidwell's terrible behaviour and Sarah Sutton's fear that he would abduct her illustrate the point. It is noteworthy that the fear of abduction was not mentioned in Sarah Sutton's sworn statements at the beginning of the trial. When questioned as to why she did not tell Mrs Lidwell or Mary Grady of what had occurred, she said she did not wish to upset the family by mentioning abduction.

Sarah's own conduct came under scrutiny and what is especially telling is her absence from the family home from the 15 May until September 1799. According to Dr Blair she refused to be brought home by her husband although she had been cured in the first three weeks. The defence, surprisingly, did not make much of this and the reasons why she stayed away are not explored. To arrive at Osberstown House on the day after the Lidwells moved in could have been construed as unusual but it could also illustrate the intimacy that existed between the families. The familiarity of Thomas Lidwell's actions and his very telling plea – 'I wish to God, my Sally, you would consent to live with me forever' – suggests that there had been a relationship, at least in his eyes if not Sarah's. If there was it went horribly wrong for the parties involved and the accusation of rape may have been a case of damage limitation.

Living in a time when the preservation of women's chastity was very important, it effectively meant the restriction of women's sexuality to situations controlled by men, especially husbands and fathers.[36] Sarah Sutton was the victim twice over. She suffered violence from one man and she had to place herself under the patriarchal authority of her husband, who was a determined man and issued proceedings in her name. Sarah Sutton was at least treated with dignity in the court, she was not asked to give a detailed account of the act of rape itself.

As to the verdict, the 'respectable members' of the jury obviously found the decision-making process in this case very difficult. Having listened to eighteen hours of testimony the jury reported after a few hours that they were not likely to reach a decision. However, after they were sent back, there was a guilty verdict after three hours, which was surprising given that once there was a reasonable doubt Lidwell could have been acquitted. But, if Lidwell had been acquitted, Sarah Sutton's reputation would have been in tatters.

Carolyn Conley in her study of nineteenth-century magistrate's courts in England found that, if the accused rapist had an ostensibly respectable background, particularly if he was middle or upper-middle class, the courts sought to preserve his status in verdict and sentencing.[37] Lidwell's case affirms this, as he was recommended to mercy due to his previous good character. He would have had the resources and contacts to make a very strong plea for clemency and there was every chance he would not serve his sentence. Conley points out that later in the nineteenth century, it was not the commission of the sexual assault but serving a jail sentence of hard labour in the company of common criminals which damaged a man's respectability.[38]

The trial of Thomas Lidwell offers a glimpse into the social mores and political relations of early nineteenth-century Ireland. The case offers an examination of the role and position of upper-class women in domestic and public spheres in a patriarchal society. The outcome of the trial raises questions about the judicial system and its treatment of the propertied classes whose status and respectability it would appear were to be protected above all else.

'Those in whom you trust will always be the first to betray you'

Ballyconnell, County Cavan, 1855

FRANK SWEENEY

A STORY IS OFTEN related in the Tubberlion-Duffin region of west Cavan, four miles south-west of Ballyconnell town, about a man from the fertile lands who married into the Duffin area in the olden days.[1] While turning the unyielding soil in the cropping fields, he was heard to curse loudly the night he happened to stray to a dance in the area. He then cursed the consequence that saw him walk a local girl, whom he later married, to her home, before saving his most vigorous outburst for the heavy wet fields from which he was expected to derive a living. His departing words were a lament that he had been sentenced to remain tied to such harsh soil for the rest of his days. However, there were others whose attachment and commitment to the land and soil of Tubberlion-Duffin were very different and the intensity of such people in protecting their long-held rights and perceived entitlements to their beloved harsh and heavy land was to challenge many accepted tenets and have disastrous consequences.

One such person was Charlotte Hinds. In 1853, as she travelled from her Dublin residence at 13 Ontario Terrace, Rathmines, to take over the Tubberlion estate, which comprised 171 acres, and the adjacent Tubberlion-Duffin estate of 160 acres, her emo-

230

tions must have been filled with long memories and many regrets for the wrongs and weaknesses of the past which had destroyed her father's stewardship over the lands in west Cavan.[2] But Charlotte was a woman of steely determination and her firm resolve was that her stewardship would ensure that such errors would never occur again. The two estates had been in the Hinds' family for many years but her father, Ralph, had the misfortune of being in occupation during the turbulent years from 1815 until the end of the Great Famine, a period fraught with rural unrest, agrarian violence, secret societies, sectarianism, economic instability and finally the distress of the Famine and its consequent dislocation.

The pressures falling on landlords of this era continued to mount incessantly. After 1815, agricultural prices fell drastically and tenants' pressured their landlords to reduce rents and improve tenancies. In such an uncertain climate, some landlords coped better than others and the difference between those who practised professional and effective estate management and those who sailed close to the reefs of collapse became quickly apparent so that by 1844 '1,322 estates with a rental of £904,000 (possibly a tenth of the whole) were being managed by the courts, usually in preparation for sales to pay off creditors'.[3]

Ralph Hinds was one such unfortunate landlord. He had fallen into bad times through unpaid rents, difficulties with his tenants, the Famine upheaval and 'personal weaknesses'. Such were his problems that the debts on the estate led to its being taken out of his hands and placed in administration. Following his death in 1847, Charlotte took over his affairs. By that time, she was in her late fifties and had never been married – she refused to let the Tubberlion lands go without a fight as 'the property had been possessed by the family and name for centuries'.[4] The estate was not put up for sale and within a few years she was able to produce sufficient funds to settle outstanding debts and succeed in having the estate returned to her own personal ownership.[5]

No doubt embittered by her father's fate at the hands of his tenantry, Charlotte immediately took stern control of the estate.

She demanded that rents be paid on the due date and that arrears be settled within given periods. She insisted that the farms on the estate be worked to their full capacity so that rents could be paid. The bad habits and sloppy practices indulged in by the tenants during her father's time were no longer to be tolerated. However, not all of the tenants were willing to adopt her stern measures. Many had become used to a certain drift born out of the culture of secret societies during the years before the Famine and the threat of force. Ralph Hinds, like many other small landlords of his type, found himself incapable of resisting the tenants' power or breaking the silent actions taken against him. But Charlotte had not come to repeat her father's failure. In 1853, the situation on her estates was so serious that she left her home in Dublin and, together with her 'intimate companion' Miss Catherine Lyng, went to live in a cottage on the estate in Tubberlion in the midst of her tenants.

She immediately took direct control of the estate. When her instructions were not followed, she issued stern warnings. If these were not heeded, she dispossessed some tenants and took direct control of their farms herself. She had regular ejectment orders processed through the courts and no tenant was allowed to build up the type of arrears that had destroyed her father. It was said that 'Miss Hinds dealt with great vigour amongst those over whom she had control' and again, remarks were passed about the 'high head with which she ruled'.[6] On an estate that had grown used to arrears and certain panache in manipulating the landlord system to its own benefit, this new enforcement was not well received. Murmurings of discontent were soon followed by threats. A fire, which damaged Miss Hinds' property, was a warning to her that her methods were not acceptable but, when that did not deter her, a further missive was sent to her that she would be murdered if she did not change her ways and her attitudes towards her tenants. However, Charlotte only prepared further ejectment orders and made it plain that she would not be intimidated.[7]

On Friday, 12 October 1855, Charlotte Hinds went in her jaunting car to the market in Ballyconnell, as was her practice each market day. Her servant, James McKeon, aged about seventeen, had been in her employ for about eight months and was driving the horse. On the return journey, they met Andrew Reilly, an elderly tenant of the Hinds' estate who was lame. Charlotte Hinds ordered that McKeon stop the horse and Reilly was given a seat, taking up position on the same side as McKeon with Miss Hinds on the other side. As they entered Curran Lane, which led to Charlotte Hinds' house, McKeon got down from the car because the road was in bad repair and started to lead the horse. They passed the house of a person named McAuley and were nearing the end of a wood, which was seven or eight acres in extent, when two men emerged from the trees and passed close to the horse's head on the side nearest the wood. Then a scream rang out and, when McKeon looked around, he saw Charlotte Hinds standing on the roadside with the assailants in the act of striking her on the head. She fell to the ground. Then a shot rang out. At this, the horse bolted and McKeon ran with the animal in an effort to hold her back. Andrew Reilly was thrown from the car and fled into the wood. Another shot then rang out and McKeon said that he thought he heard a third.

The assassination attempt took place very close to the houses of McAuley, Masterson and Thomas Dunne, all tenants on the Hinds' estate and there were more than twenty houses situated on both sides of the lane in close proximity to the scene of the crime.[8] Yet, there were few people about at the time because most of the tenants had gone to the market in Ballyconnell. After the attack, the assailants ran back into the wood. Two men were seen soon afterwards emerging from the far side of the wood and making their way towards the River Scalan. They crossed the river in a small boat and went off in the direction of Newtowngore in County Leitrim.[9]

McKeon raised the alarm back at the Hinds' home and Miss Lyng and some others came rushing to the scene. They found Miss Hinds lying on the ground with her thumb, forefinger and wrist broken and two pistol bullets lodged in her skull – but she was still alive and conscious and told them that Red Pat Bannon, who had been a resident on her estate and was once an employee on her land, was one of the attackers. A door was brought to the scene and Charlotte was borne to her home where she fought bravely for four days before dying at 12.30 p.m. on Tuesday, 24 October 1855.[10] During her periods of consciousness, she continued to insist that Red Pat Bannon was one of her attackers and that the other assailant 'was a smart man'. A small sword and the butt of a gun were found at the scene of the assault.

McKeon was the chief witness to the event and, when the police arrived a short time after the attack, they immediately put him under arrest on the presumption that he was involved in the crime. McKeon was somewhat confused about the events, however, for he was not sure whether two or three men were involved. Later, he said that he saw two men strike and knock Miss Hinds down and then stand over her while striking her. McKeon was taken away by the police and lodged in Cavan Gaol and did not appear again until a fortnight later when he attended the inquest and testified that two men had attacked Miss Hinds. When Andrew Reilly gave evidence, his story differed materially from that of McKeon in that he was certain that the unnamed man did not strike Miss Hinds at all and he swore that it was Red Pat Bannon who actually hit her. The witnesses also differed about the demeanour of the second man – McKeon stated that he was disguised and had a stick and Reilly stated that he was not disguised and had no stick. Both were fairly certain, however, that Red Pat Bannon had been wearing a straw hat.

The RIC soon discovered that Red Pat Bannon was nowhere to be found and very soon a countrywide alert was issued for his apprehension. A full description was published in the police magazine, *Hue & Cry*, on 18 October 1855 in which he was described as 'a native of Tubberlion, County Cavan, parish of Templeport, twenty-six years of age, five feet six inches tall, slight make, fair complexion, grey eyes, red hair, wearing frieze coat, whitish trousers, cicatrice on back of leg, smart appearance; walks erect, shoulders inclining backwards, deserted the Cavan Militia on 22 June 1855'.[11]

On 27 October, Head Constable Gibson left Cavan for Derry-lin Barracks, County Fermanagh, where Storey Parks, a deserter from the Fermanagh Militia, was being held in custody, having been arrested that day on Innisleague Island in Loch Erne. Parks gave information that a man on the run from the law arrived on the island on 13 October, the day following the attack on Charlotte Hinds. He had given his name as John Keenan and he said that he had attacked his employer, a native of Fermanagh, with a hatchet. From the description of Keenan given by Parks, Head Constable Gibson felt confident that the man described was Red Pat Bannon. Parks was brought back to Cavan Gaol and questioned by the local resident magistrate, Nicholas Kelly, who was also satisfied that Keenan was in reality Bannon. Further enquiries informed them that Keenan had left Innisleague on 25 October and was staying with a man named John Hutthakins between Lisnaskea and Roslea. The house was searched at 4.30 a.m. on 28 October but there was no sign of Bannon.[12]

Charlotte Hinds' murder caused uproar both locally and nationally. The British press went into a frenzy of rage that a landlord who was a decent woman should be shot dead in such a manner and they demanded all sorts of recriminations to improve the wayward civilisation of the Irish race. Any shade of sympathy shown in any newspaper for the perpetrators of the crime or the tenants on the Hinds' estate was seized upon and the guilty organs excoriated. Some papers wrote that Miss Hinds was murdered because she was a Protestant, others blamed the local parish priest 'of being the chief mover and cause of the foul crime'.[13] The *Belfast News-Letter* wrote:

> *There is not a crime committed in any of the rural districts of Ireland or in the Romanist country of which the priests are not in a few ways fully cognizant, as well as of its authors but where is the instance in which a priest has caused even the most atrocious criminals to be brought to justice?*[14]

The British newspapers treated the death as being typical of the Irish peasantry at that time and many suggested that more murders were to be carried out during the coming year. The *Belfast News-Letter* continued its coverage of the outrage with the words: 'One of those hideous massacres that show the utter debasement of the Irish peasant and the moral disorganization of the priest-led multitude took place on Friday evening in Curran Wood.'[15] There were even suggestions that the government should take the collection of rents into its own hands and that every soul on the property where a murder had been committed should be ejected.[16] The *Daily Express* accused the local *Anglo Celt* newspaper of giving unfair and biased coverage of the horrific event and 'abetting the outrage' and *The Times*, while more balanced in its coverage, accused the people of the area of being:

> … *apathetic towards Miss Hinds' death and the hunt for the perpetrators and regretted to add that the people of the countryside seemed to be perfectly aware of what was about to take place and what was taking place. Everybody skulked out of the way during the preparation of the crime.*[17]

The Times had no doubt but that the Ballyconnell region had still retained its Ribbonism and secret societies. It was said that Miss Hinds' tenants presented themselves at the market in Ballyconnell on the day of the assassination attempt ostensibly in order to give themselves alibis. As soon as news of the shooting reached the market town, it reported that 'the liveliest exultations were displayed – women even openly rejoiced that this unfortunate lady had been so barbarously handled by the Ribbonmen'.[18] The *Belfast News-Letter* had no doubts about the consequences which should follow. 'Give these bloodstained ruffians and their abettors a lesson which may remain engraved on their memories for many a long day.'[19] *The Times* wrote:

> *An agrarian murderer is just a murderer – a murderer of a very foul and abominable class. He commits his crime not under the influence of momentary passion but deliberately and of aforethought. He murders too from the basest of motives – that he may resist the payment of a just debt.*

The Galway Vindicator took serious exception to *The Times* 'for the virulence and vindictiveness which has always characterized it in any matter where Ireland was concerned'. It then accused *The Times* that it:

> … *stirs the ashes of the dead O'Connell and desecrates the grave of him whose memory is yet green and cherished amongst millions of living Irishmen. And why? In order to identify him with the Cavan murders and to trace the shooting of Miss Hinds up to the teaching, when alive, of the great Irishman. 'By him,' said the oracle, 'a certain halo was cast round the skulking Ribbonman as he crouched behind a stone dyke in the twilight to shoot his enemy in the back.'*[20]

The gentry of Cavan were equally outraged and called a meeting in the courthouse attended by Lord Farnham, J. P. Maxwell, MP, and the important society members of the county. The fear that 'Ribbonism' was behind the outrage struck terror into the meeting because, some time previously, a landowner named Smyth had been very brutally murdered in Ballyhaise and it was thought that the motive for this crime was agrarian. However, in order to quell anxiety within the county, the speakers at the meeting deemed the outrage to be an isolated incident rather than part of a system. It was firmly stated that no county had been more peaceful than Cavan for years and this act must have come on suddenly in such a manner 'that it must have been the act of some persons maddened by their passions'. But they were not saying 'that the Ribbon conspiracy had no seat in the county'. The meeting passed motions condemning the crime and its perpetrators and determined that they would root out the Ribbon system. It was then decided to have an additional police station installed in the immediate vicinity of Tubberlion. This would have to be funded by the estate tenants and the burden would fall heavily on many of them. Finally, they declared that 'in spite of the reign of terror rents will be collected'. A subscription list was opened to help with the resolution of the crime and £544 was subscribed on the spot and a reward of £500 was offered for the capture of the perpetrators.[21]

Henry Grattan, Charlotte Hinds' direct landlord, was outraged at the crime. He informed the *Belfast News-Letter* that he had forgiven tenants on the lands where the outrage had been perpetrated '... rents due by them amounting to one thousand pounds. I hereby give them notice that I shall call for the arrears due these two years to November next and I shall insist on getting either the rent or the land.' Grattan then offered £100 reward.[22]

However, Thomas Dunne, a prominent tenant on the Hinds' estate, was not intimidated by invective from the meeting or from the Cavan landlords' condemnatory letters and outpourings in the various newspapers during the weeks following Charlotte Hinds' death in which the tenants of the county in general, and of the Tubberlion estate in particular, were severely castigated as outlaws and unprincipled vagabonds without a trace of decency. Dunne was thirty-one years old, had been married for two years and was the father of one child, and was one of Charlotte Hinds' closest neighbours. He was regarded as being very comfortable as he received a large dowry from his wife when he got married.[23] In the year before Charlotte Hinds' death, he had sold a farm on her estate for £150 and, shortly after her death, he disposed of another farm on the Tubberlion estate which he had purchased from Miss Hinds for over £100.[24] However, it was his success in 1854 that set him apart in the community. He stood in the Bawnboy Board of Guardians election against David Veitch, a prominent gentry member from the area, and won an unexpected and astounding victory.[25] Miss Hinds had been outraged at his success and she entered the election campaign the following year, compelling her tenants to vote for Veitch rather than Dunne who eventually lost the contest. The election issue, and more especially her interference, caused much resentment among her tenants.

Dunne challenged the invective of the upper classes and wrote to the *Anglo Celt* on 3 November 1855 about conditions on the Hinds' estate. He stated that none of the tenants who remained on her lands were allowed to fall into arrears and none owed more than one year's rent on the previous November day. Nearly all of them owed only half a year's rent, which fell due on November day. Significantly, Dunne finished his letter by stating:

I can appeal to Mr Moses Netterfield who has been our agent and he must admit that, during the many years he held the office of Petty Sessions Clerk and keeper of the Bridewell at Ballyconnell, he never knew a summons to be issued against me nor a cell door to be locked upon me and I am sure the peaceable character of the other tenants stands equally high.

Miss Hinds' companion, Catherine Lyng, replied to this letter the following week stating that Dunne had his facts wrong. On the figures supplied to her by Moses Netterfield she stated that four tenants were two years in arrears, four tenants were one-and-a-half years in arrears and eleven tenants were one year in arrears. Miss Lyng apologised to the editor for taking up his time with the matter stating that she would not have responded at all 'if the character of the writer [Dunne] were as well-known in the place where your newspaper circulates as it is in the locality in which he himself resides'.[26] Dunne countered the following week stating that Miss Lyng's information was incorrect and he demanded that the names of those in arrears be published. However, no further correspondence was entered into.[27]

Despite the intensity of the RIC investigations, a veil of secrecy shrouded the proceedings in the months after Charlotte Hinds' death and little information was divulged. However, it was obvious that Nicholas Kelly, the local resident magistrate, was deeply immersed in the case and was co-ordinating the inquiry's various strands. Then new evidence reached Cavan that gave hope that Red Pat Bannon had been captured on the road between Armagh and Newry.

A man wearing a straw hat had been seen near Newry and suspicion fell on him immediately. When it was discovered that he could not explain why he was travelling through the area, feelings hardened against him. After his arrest, he was brought back to Cavan but he immediately burned all the clothes he had been wearing, giving rise to the belief that he must have committed some terrible crime. He gave various names but it emerged later that he might be a man named Hassett, who was a deserter from the Limerick Militia. Later, he said that he was a native of Wicklow. He seemed to fit the description of the man wearing the straw hat who had killed Miss Hinds so he was charged with being an accomplice in the murder. He was lodged in Cavan Gaol and was committed from week to week. However, as time passed all parties gradually reached agreement that he was not the murderer at Tubberlion and he certainly was not Red Pat Bannon.[28]

The hunt for Red Pat continued relentlessly in various locations from Donegal to Cork and eventually to Scotland and England with Constable Gorby, assigned to follow every lead no matter where it might take him. The *Belfast News-Letter* reported that, on the night of the assault on Charlotte Hinds, Red Pat left the area and walked the whole way to Dublin.[29] But this was speculation and, as every lead to Red Pat petered out, the police became more and more desperate.

Eventually, a new strategy was decided upon. The RIC methodically arrested local men and imprisoned them in Cavan Gaol where the young servant, James McKeon had been detained since the day of the attack. Michael Bannon, a brother of Red Pat, Black Terence (Terry) Bannon (no relation to Red Pat), Felix Prior, John Logan and James Reilly, all tenants on the Hinds' estate, were imprisoned at various times in the weeks following the attack and were not released again. By the 17 January 1856, there were eight or nine men from the Tubberlion area incarcerated in Cavan Gaol, but no charges were made against any of them.

Thomas Dunne was also arrested as was James Murphy, a native of County Leitrim, aged about thirty and a father of four children.[30] Murphy was said to be a 'peaceful and industrious' man although he did have a reputation as he was once charged with beating a man very severely on the way home from Ballinamore Fair although he was later acquitted of the charge. He used to work on either side of the Cavan–Leitrim border from time to time, ploughing with a Mr O'Hare occasionally. Murphy lived in Crockavaddy for a time and worked as a herder to Mr Dolan of Carrigagh though he had been working all winter on the public road in the Tubberlion area.[31]

The arrests of Dunne and Murphy were regarded as significant in Tubberlion and the feeling set in that the authorities must have been getting information from someone already arrested because all were aware that the resident magistrate, Nicholas Kelly, was working tirelessly both inside and outside the prison in order to gain convictions. The prisoners were kept in solitary confinement, were denied visits from the Catholic priest and were prevented from going to mass on Sundays, a matter which was reported to the government. Mr Knipe, solicitor for Dunne, applied for copies of the sworn statements against his client several times but was told on each occasion that none had been made as all the parties had been committed for further examination. This delaying tactic and veil of secrecy continued throughout the winter months and nobody knew what evidence the police had obtained because no statements were available for scrutiny nor was there any information coming from within the prison because the excuse given at all times was that investigations were ongoing.

Word arrived in Cavan in mid-March 1856 that, instead of the accused being tried in the normal way at the spring or summer assizes, a special commission would sit in April to try the cases of Thomas Dunne and James Murphy. A special commission was 'the Queen's prerogative' which was only used in cases 'where a crime had been committed of a grave character and such as to endanger the safety and tranquillity, and well-being of society'.[32] This was unwelcome news because of the massive cost which would fall on the county as a result. The cost would eventually be extracted from the ordinary tenants in increased rents and the feeling among many of these same tenants was that extraordinary steps were being taken by the government in an effort to bypass the normal justice mechanism in order to secure convictions. It had been almost fifty years since a special commission had sat in County Cavan.[33] The official line was that special commissions 'were essential to the peace and tranquillity of the country which, from the prevalence of crime, it is important that its course be immediately arrested'.[34] In this instance, there was little reason to arrange a special commission for the murder committed six months previously, but the determination of the authorities to proceed was soon apparent when the grand jurors were summoned to attend under a penalty double that which had applied on any previous occasion.[35]

When the special commission opened proceedings at Cavan on 9 April 1856, under Chief Justice Monahan and Justice Moore, the courthouse was crowded to suffocation.[36] It became known that two defendants – Thomas Dunne and James Murphy – were to face murder charges, although all the others were still in gaol on various charges that were yet to be specified. James Murphy was tried first on the charge of having murdered Charlotte Hinds. 'He was dressed with care and though he took considerable interest in the proceedings he did not appear alarmed.'[37] The crowded courtroom waited anxiously to hear the evidence against the accused and wondered if the police had managed to break some of the prisoners and extract full confessions from them.

The first witness was the young servant, James McKeon. He gave detailed evidence of the events on the day of the murder and then identified James Murphy as the assailant who attacked Miss Hinds. His evidence was much more concise than the confused accounts he had given previously. The two men mentioned in his earlier evidence had now disappeared and only Murphy figured in his account. According to McKeon, Murphy beat Miss Hinds, Murphy stood over her, Murphy carried the pistols and Murphy fired the shots that eventually killed her. All McKeon's evidence incriminated Murphy and, despite severe cross-examination, he could not be diverted from his course.[38] However, he insisted throughout that he could not identify Red Pat Bannon as one of the attackers.[39]

Andrew Reilly, the lame man, told the court that Miss Hinds 'was the best natured woman in the world'.[40] He then went on to say that during the attack he saw one of two men with a short lump of a stick in his hand striking Miss Hinds about the head. He was nine or ten steps from one man who he knew as Pat Bannon and was always known as 'Red Pat'. Bannon had a cap on his head with the peak pulled down and the other man wore a straw hat and frieze coat. He knew Red Pat but had never seen the other man who had the pistol before because his head was covered with his coat. He failed to identify Murphy in court.[41]

Black Terry [Tarry] Bannon then took the stand. The *Anglo Celt* described him as:

> … *a low thick-set man; his complexion is swarthily yellow; his eyes sunken, his eyebrows shaggy, immediately impending over them; his countenance long, meagre and pock-pitted, while a mop of hair covers his bullet shaped head.*[42]

Within a few minutes of Black Terry's evidence, the throng knew that the game was up for it was soon apparent that he had turned approver, or 'king's evidence' as it was called, during his time in prison. He told the court that he was living in Tubberlion during the previous October on Miss Hinds' land. On the night of 9 October 1855, he had purchased a bottle of whiskey in Cosgrove's public house and brought it to Thomas Dunne's home. There he saw Dunne, a strange man, and Pat Smith and Phil McCartin. The following day, he again saw the stranger at Dunne's house. Dunne then sent him to John Logan for some detonating pistols and, when he brought these back to Dunne's home, Dunne told him to go to Ballyconnell for some powder and caps. He brought these back to Dunne and the strange man, who he now knew to be James Murphy, told him to charge the pistols but later warned him that he was putting too much powder into one of them.

On that same day, he went to Felix Prior and got another pistol which he also brought to Dunne. The next morning, Friday 10 October, he was digging potatoes when James McKiernan arrived and the two of them went to Curry's house where they collected £10 to which Black Terry added £2 in his possession. Black Terry had subscribed £1 himself which he had got from his brother who owed him £20 as part of the brother's marriage settlement.[43] He then got a small boat, called a cot locally, and rowed about in the river until two men emerged from the wood in great haste. These were Red Pat Bannon and the stranger, James Murphy.

When the attorney-general asked Black Terry if he could see the stranger in court, Bannon asked him, 'Where will I look?' He was told to look about him. 'He looked all about the court and after looking everywhere but in the right place, at last he identified Murphy.'[44] He took the two men into the cot and ferried them across the river, they having first told him that they 'had done the job' at the corner of Curran Wood. He then gave £8 to Red Pat Bannon and £4 to James Murphy. When they got to the other side of the river the two men swapped their headdresses and made off in the direction of Newtowngore in County Leitrim. Before they left him, they said that they had lost a small sword and the butt of a gun at the scene of the assault. When the sword was produced in court, Black Terry identified it as the one which he saw in Dunne's home on the night he saw Murphy there. Terry Bannon was cross-examined and admitted that he had been told by the police that a substantial reward was available for giving evidence. The *Anglo Celt* recorded that 'the aspect of the witness was most sinister and repulsive; his mode of giving evidence hesitating and astute in a very great degree'.[45]

Patrick Heavey, servant man to Thomas Dunne, said that he saw his master arrive home from the Longfield Fair with a stranger who he kept in the house. He never saw the man before or since. When pressed if he saw the man in court before him, Heavey looked around but failed to identify Murphy. He did admit, however, that he saw Dunne speaking to Red Pat Bannon a few days before the attack.[46]

Many more minor witnesses were then called to confirm various details of the evidence given by previous witnesses. All of them attested that Red Pat Bannon and the stranger were in the locations already described leaving no doubt but that Black Terry Bannon's evidence was substantially a true record of what had happened. The RIC had been fastidious in piecing together every detail of the crime and having witnesses to corroborate every aspect of the evidence.[47]

Mr Dowse, for the defence, then outlined the details of the crime. He told the jury that the principal evidence of the crown was to come from a person who had become an approver. He warned the jury that they should use the greatest caution before giving even the slightest credence to the approver, Terence Bannon. He, upon his own showing, was cognisant of the foul crime – he participated in it – he paid the murderers and proved himself the most depraved character that ever disgraced this or any other locality.

John Logan, who had been in gaol during the previous two months for giving the pistols, took the stand and denied vehemently that Terry Bannon had ever come to his house nor had he been given any pistols because he had none to give. His two daughters, Mary and Margaret, corroborated all of his evidence.

Mark Bannon was then called. He told how there was another Mark Bannon living in Tubberlion who had been ejected by Miss Hinds. His own father, James Bannon, had been put out of his home by Miss Hinds as well, even though he was only a cottier with a house and garden. Mark Bannon then told how he had been approached by Black Terry Bannon with a proposal that they should act jointly in an effort to collect the reward and point the finger of suspicion at James Reilly and Thomas Dunne. Another witness, Daniel Reilly, told how Black Terry approached him with the same proposal to collect the reward.

The jury retired and after an absence of about two hours, returned with a guilty verdict on James Murphy. It was almost seven o'clock and the prisoner was ordered to be removed.

The court sat again at 9.30 a.m the following morning, Friday, 11 May, when a panel for the jury was sworn in and Thomas Dunne was charged with procuring and inciting Pat Bannon and James Murphy or either of them to kill and murder Charlotte Hinds on 12 October 1855. Although Dunne was only thirty-one years old, he looked considerably older when he came into the court and was described as being 'careworn and emaciated and [had] laboured under an illness for some time past.' During the attorney-general's opening speech, Dunne fainted once and had to be attended by the doctor on two other occasions. He pleaded not guilty to the charges.[48]

When the jury was called to be formed, Dunne was told that he could challenge twenty of the panel peremptorily and any more against whom he could show cause. He, accordingly, did challenge twenty and, having done so, wanted to object to a juror called William Nixon. The crown objected to Dunne's attorney asking William Nixon any questions and because Dunne had no witnesses to prove the cause of the challenge, the court ruled that he would have to accept Nixon on the jury.[49]

The attorney-general opened the case with a speech of one hour and ten minutes but as he concluded one of the jury, Thomas Teevan, complained of being unwell. He was examined by a doctor who later pronounced that Teevan was unable to take further part in the proceedings. Consequently the judge discharged the jury and Teevan was allowed to withdraw. The other eleven jurors were then re-sworn in and another juror named John Edgars was called from the panel and was sworn in. The attorney-general then asked Edgars if he had heard his opening address from the body of the court and he stated that he had. Dunne was not told that he could challenge Edgars. If proper procedure had been followed a full new jury should have been called from the original panel and Dunne should have been given the right to challenge them as if they were the original jury.[50]

James McKeon again gave evidence as before. 'He appeared to be pert and sullen, crying when asked about being taken himself and being in gaol.'[51] At the hearing the previous October McKeon had stated that on the day of the attack he saw two 'boys' beat Miss Hinds with sticks and then stand over her. At the trial he stated that only Murphy beat her. In court McKeon said that during the hearings in October he had been confused or that the information must have been taken down incorrectly. Andrew Reilly then came to the stand and said that Pat Bannon had a stick but the other man had a pistol. He knew Red Pat since he was on his mother's knee.

Black Terry Bannon was then called and was led by the attorney-general through the conspiratorial aspect of the case with which Dunne was charged. He said that the whole conspiracy began in the month of August 1855 when he spoke to Dunne about the conduct of Miss Hinds towards some of her tenants and the ejectments that had taken place and the evictions and court cases which were to follow. Dunne himself had got notice from Miss Hinds to attend court regarding his land and rent. Having discussed the matter for some time Dunne told him that if some money could be collected he would get a man to shoot Miss Hinds. Black Terry said that he would put in £2 himself but Dunne replied that this would be no use because much more than that would have to be collected. Dunne then set out a plan. He sent Black Terry to big Jane Donohy, who lived on the Hinds' estate in Tubberlion and was married to another Terry Bannon, with the instruction to get £4 or £5 from her. She was to be told that the money was to put an end to Miss Hinds' cruelty. When asked, however, Big Jane would only give £2.

At this point in his evidence, Thomas Dunne became weak again and had to be attended by the doctor. After some time, he was able to resume. However, the interruption did nothing to impede Black Terry's outflow of evidence. He related how he saw Dunne with another neighbour, James Curry, cutting a white-thorn hedge near Dunne's house one day. Bannon joined them and mentioned that he had £4 now, his own £2 and Big Jane's £2. Dunne told James Curry that he was to take the £4 from Black Terry and keep it safely. Curry refused to take it saying he did not want to have anything to do with the intended shooting. Dunne would not accept his refusal and, after some further talk, Curry was persuaded to take the money. Dunne then told Curry that he would be expected to put up £3 or £4 himself and that he must hold the money until a man was found who was willing to shoot Miss Hinds. Dunne then sent Black Terry to Felix Prior of Ned a week or ten days later with the firm instruction to get £3, £4 or £5 from him but he got no money from him that time. Black Terry told Dunne that Prior gave nothing and was not willing to have anything to do with the conspiracy but, a few days later, Dunne sent him back to Prior again and, on this occasion, he got £1 from him.[52]

On Wednesday, 10 October, Black Terry went to Dunne's house in the evening where he saw Dunne, his wife, Patrick Heavey, the servant man, and old Frank Smyth. A while later, old Frank's son, Pat (Dunne's first cousin), came in. Phil McCartin and Pat Lunny were there also. John McKiernan then came in. There was no drink in Dunne's house so Black Terry went to Cosgrove's public house and got five naggings of 'whishkey' which he brought back to the house. James Murphy was in the house too. They all had a drink in Dunne's when he came back and then, some time later, the men started going home. But the stranger was still there.

The following morning, Black Terry met Dunne who instructed him to go to Tomas Bannon and later to John Logan's house in Derryhassan for pistols. Dunne followed him out and told him that the stranger was the man he got to shoot Miss Hinds. He went to Logan's house early in the morning but he only got the pistols from Logan later in the day. On Thursday, Dunne, McKiernan, Smyth and McCartin went to various houses in the locality looking for more pistols but got none. When they returned to Dunne's house, they felt that they were still short of pistols so they discussed the issue. They got word that Felix Prior had a pistol so McCartin, Smyth and McKiernan went to his house late at night and got his pistol.[53]

On the Friday morning, Black Terry was digging potatoes until one o'clock. Then McKiernan called for him and they went to James Curry's house and got three sovereigns, a £3 note and five single notes. Bannon had £2 himself which he added to the £10 he collected from James Curry making £12 in all. One of these pound notes he got from Felix Prior. Black Terry then went off to the canal and waited there until Pat Bannon and Murphy arrived and he gave them the money. One of the men was carrying the two pistols he got from Logan but he could not identify the man. They went off through Scalan towards Newtowngore and he went home to his brother's house.

He met Dunne a few day afterwards and Dunne told him he was sorry 'the likes ever happened as their lands would be robbed paying cesses'. Black Terry had then 'taken the sodality after

Holy Eve' and some days later, he was taken into custody. He had no house or land of his own and worked most of the time at the canal and the remainder for his brother.

The resident magistrate, Nicholas Kelly, told him that, if he told all he knew, he would not be sent to jail but, if he didn't, he would face hanging or transportation to Australia. Black Terry said that he never had a conversation with Mark Bannon or with James Reilly about the reward money. He admitted, under cross-examination, that, before he gave his information and agreed to make his confession, he had talked to Moses Netterfield, Charlotte Hinds' agent, and David Veitch who visited him in gaol, though Veitch 'had no great regard for Dunne because they were rival candidates for a Poor Law Guardianship and Dunne beat him'. He was first brought to Ballymagauran Barracks, then to Ballyconnell and then to Cavan when he was first arrested. He finally admitted that he had many chats with Nicholas Kelly before he made his statement, about two months after his arrest.

The next witness was James Curry who told the court that he did not want to get involved in the plot but Black Terry Bannon had said to him that 'any one who would not give help it would be worse for them'. On the morning of Miss Hinds' death, John McKiernan came to him as he was stacking turf. After speaking to McKiernan, he went to James Reilly and got a £3 note from him. He gave all the collected money to McKiernan and Black Terry Bannon on the day of the assault. He saw Thomas Dunne some days later and Dunne remarked to him that it was an unfortunate job. Dunne appeared uneasy. Curry then stated that he was a favourite tenant of Miss Hinds and that she had been very kind to him. He then confirmed that he had been arrested on 11 January and, under further questioning, confirmed various aspects of the conspiracy already detailed by Black Terry.[54]

John Flynn when questioned recollected the fair day at Longfield. He saw Dunne and a stranger at the Scalan river on the evening of the fair. Dunne asked him for his gun and powder but he told him that he had sold it. He advised Dunne that if he had anything bad afoot he should take care as the country was very unsound.

The solicitor, Edward McGauran, was the next to take the stand. He said that he was employed by Dunne to defend charges and demands for rent due to Miss Hinds which were levied by her agent, Mr Moses Netterfield. He gave Dunne a copy of a civil bill to be served on the clerk for the crown. Dunne came to him in October to have the statements entered but he did not do so due to the upheaval resulting from Charlotte Hinds' death.

The jury were out for an hour and a quarter and returned with a unanimous verdict of guilty on Thomas Dunne. Then the judge addressed the prisoner:

> *It appeared early in the course of the trial that during the month of August last, as a tenant residing upon the property of Miss Hinds, you, with several others of the tenants upon the property, entered into a conspiracy, the object of which was to deprive her of her life. The means which you devised or, at least was a party to devising, was the collection of a small sum of money, about £12 or £14, in order to lure assassins for the purposes of perpetrating that dreadful outrage which you then contemplated. You aided in the collection of this sum – you probably subscribed yourself some small sum of money towards it … It is one of the unalterable judgments of the Almighty Dispenser that when persons are implicated in such offences with others, those in whom you trust will always be the first to betray you. Accordingly, in the present case, scarcely was the crime committed than two or more of the persons implicated in it came forward to give evidence against you and several others of their companions engaged in the same outrage.*

During each of the four days of the hearing, the court was deeply thronged but the biggest crowds were present for the passing of the sentences. The judge sentenced Thomas Dunne and James Murphy to be hanged in Cavan Gaol on 16 May 1856 – seventeen years after the last execution in Cavan.[55] The prisoners received the sentences standing in the dock with great calm and firmness. 'Both prisoners exhibited the utmost composure and seemed less affected than any others in court. Murphy did not offer to make any observation but presented the same tranquil appearance that he exhibited throughout the trial.' Dunne asked:

250

'Will your lordship allow my body to be given to my people?' The justice explained that the law required that Murphy, having been found guilty of murder, would have to be buried within the precincts of the gaol but that Dunne's body, having been found guilty of the lesser crime of conspiracy, could be released to his next of kin.[56]

Dunne then addressed the court, 'I have no enmity or ill will to any man and I hope we will die, as we are going to die, innocent. I never sided or assisted since I was born in the case of which I am convicted now on the perjured evidence of those who imbrued their own hands with the blood of that woman and who have turned upon me now. I never gave a shilling since I was born to have the deed done. I absolve all my enemies.' The two prisoners were then removed.

'Upon the application of the Attorney-General their lordships ruled that Felix Prior and John Logan, persons mentioned in the course of the trials, as having been implicated to some extent, should be discharged, upon giving bail themselves of twenty pounds each and two sureties each in ten pounds'. With regard to three men from the Tubberlion area, who were charged with being in a riot during a fair in Ballyconnell in which a man lost his life, it was ordered that they might be liberated on giving bail. The riot was said to result from factions within the Tubberlion area concerned in Miss Hinds' murder. Another man charged with the homicide of the person alluded to in Ballyconnell should remain in custody as the crown would not consent to have him liberated on bail.

After the sentences were passed, a rumour swept Cavan town that Black Terry Bannon was to be charged with the murder of Captain M'Cloud some fourteen years earlier. The *Anglo Celt* reported that the story was 'swallowed most greedily'.[57]

Thomas Dunne immediately entered a petition to the lord lieutenant outlining his grievances with the conduct of his trial. His first objection was to the juror Nixon whom he would have set aside, because he was the man that Dunne believed was 'deeply prejudiced against him' and he stated that he had been informed that Nixon was the personal friend and companion of Mr Moses Netterfield who was the agent of the late Miss Hinds and was one of the most active persons in getting the prosecution against him.

Dunne then mentioned the withdrawal of the juror, Thomas Teevan, and his replacement by Edgar. Dunne argued that he was not told that he was entitled to challenge the new juror. He argued that a full new jury should have been called from the panel and that he should have been given the right to challenge each of them.[58]

A petition was organised locally and was signed by the Catholic bishop of Kilmore, the priests of the parishes of Ballyconnell, Maguiresbridge and Bawnboy, and many people including members of both Protestant and Catholic communities. It was sent to the lord lieutenant, the Earl of Carlisle, and stated that the only evidence upon which Murphy and Dunne were convicted was that of the boy McKeon whose identification of Murphy was so essential a link in the chain of proof. They pointed out that, while McKeon swore in the witness box in the most express terms that he only saw one man, Murphy, strike his mistress, he previously stated and swore that he saw the two men striking her, the two men knocking her down, the two men standing over her and this upon three occasions within an interval of some months. They added that McKeon's evidence differed greatly from the old man, Andrew Reilly, who had sat upon the car with him. Reilly stated that the second of the two men, who was Murphy, was disguised and had no stick, it being the other man, Red Pat Bannon who struck Miss Hinds and knocked her down. McKeon's version of the affair was that Murphy had a stick, was quite undisguised and felled Charlotte Hinds to the ground. The petitioners were also unhappy with McKeon's confusion after the murder when he did not seem to know how many men had been present.[59]

During the days prior to the execution date, a number of workmen were engaged each day outside Cavan Gaol erecting, arranging and eventually painting the scaffolding upon which the two men were to be hanged. However, it was deemed unlikely that either would actually be executed on 16 May as Dunne's appeal was being considered and might even go to the House of Lords.[60] A meeting took place of the lord chancellor, the chief justice, Judge Moore and the solicitor general on 13 May 1856 and, as they 'could find no reason to be dissatisfied with the verdict in either case', they issued the standard reply of 'let the law take its course'. The attorney-general refused leave for further appeals so the sentences of hanging on Murphy and Dunne stood.[61]

A few days before the hanging, those who had turned approver were moved away from Cavan by the authorities. The *Anglo Celt* reported that:

> *Tarry [sic] Bannon, this notorious individual and James Curry, the other approver in the case of Miss Hinds, left for Dublin this morning, hooted and hissed by a large crowd who would have handled him [Bannon] more roughly only a large body of police came to his rescue. Mr George Gallogly, governor of Cavan Gaol and a turnkey who accompanied him, were armed with pistols and a dagger which they presented at the assailants but had no occasion to use them. When Tarry was just getting out of town he received a parting farewell in the shape of a general burst of indignant feeling – one man actually falling on his knees and giving him a curse for all eternity. About a quarter of a mile from the town, he went into a house waiting for a coach but, when the mistress found out whom she had, she ejected him summarily by sundry blows from a creepy stool and the application of a pitchfork to his nether parts. Heavey and the boy McKeon went away a few days ago. We understand that they will be kept in durance until it is seen whether Red Pat and others of the persons charged with committing the murder or conspiring to it can be made amenable.[62]*

The day of the execution, Friday, 16 May 1856, was an exceptionally fine day. On the previous Sunday, the Catholic clergy advised their flocks that they should remain at home and spend a few moments in prayer for the repose of the souls of the unhappy men. At 10 a.m., there was hardly a stir in Cavan town but between that hour and noon, the roads leading from Butlersbridge, Kilmore, Ballyjamesduff and Ballyhaise became densely congested with crowds hurrying to the scene of the terrible drama that was about to be enacted.

At twelve noon, the 8th Huzzars, who had been parading the streets all morning, headed for the gaol. They were followed by a crowd of about 800 in all, mostly young boys and girls but some elderly persons were present too. But the *Anglo Celt* was not impressed by the demeanour of these young people:

> It was a sad sight to see parasols and veils, bonnets and mantillas of a really fashionable description in requisition for such an occasion. Something exceedingly morbid there must have been in the dispositions of the wearers and one might not hesitate a firm conviction that those who were present in the circumstances were there very little to their own credit.[63]

> The Cavan Militia together with the Monaghans [Monaghan Militia] and a company of the 6th Huzzars as well as 180 policemen were stationed at various positions commanding the access roads to the town. During the day, however, there was not the least necessity for such a display of force. There was no breach of the peace or any rush that would involve danger.[64]

At an earlier hour of the morning, Father Thomas Mulvaney, the Catholic parish priest and chaplain to the gaol, celebrated mass in the prison at which both the convicted men assisted and they received communion as they had done, separately, on the previous days. Father John McEnroe then celebrated mass which was also heard by the two men. After mass the convicted men, who had not seen each other since the trial, were brought together by mutual request. They kissed affectionately and expressed their full forgiveness for any wrongs, real or imaginary, which either had sustained or was supposed to have sustained at the hands of the other. They expressed their entire willingness to die, offering the pain and the ignominy of their death in atonement for their sins.

Murphy had resigned himself to his fate the day his sentence was passed, claiming that he had lived long enough. The *Anglo*

Celt reported that 'he suffered much from his bad health and was gone so deep into consumption that if the execution were to take place three weeks later, the hangman would have been spared the gruesome task'. During his time in prison, Murphy made no statements either to confirm or deny his guilt nor indeed about any other subject and it was believed that the expectation that he might make a last minute confession or statement was the reason why so many people turned up for his execution. However, he held his own counsel to the very end.[65]

At precisely one o'clock, the press-room door opened. The hangman reached out and drew in the rope which he adjusted around the neck of Murphy who was dressed completely in white, with gloves of the same colour. Attended by Father Thomas Mulvaney, Murphy came forward with a composed step and knelt for some time in prayer. At Murphy's appearance, a loud cry was made by the watching multitude which could easily be heard a mile from the scene. Dunne, who was in his cell with Father McEnroe heard the cry and exclaimed, 'There goes poor James. May the Lord have mercy on his soul.' When he got up from his prayers, the 'cap' was fitted over his eyes and face and he was placed on the scaffold by the executioner who, returning, drew the bolt. Murphy hardly made a struggle – a few shrugs of the shoulders – and all was over. The body was left hanging for approximately forty minutes.[66]

However, not all the people witnessing the hanging were in sympathy. One man exclaimed as Murphy dropped, 'You'll never kill another Hinds.' A second was heard to shout at the same moment, 'Pop goes the weasel.' It was reported that a body of people '... who stood along the Farnham Road, laughing and jeering, taunted a most respectable Roman Catholic gentleman who was driving by at this time to look up if he dared thinking, doubtless that the sight in which they themselves exulted would deeply pain him. There was obviously an element of Protestant triumphalism as opposed to Catholic mortification involved in the spectacle.'[67] The *Belfast News-Letter*, however, showed some sympathy towards Murphy. 'The deportment of Murphy was marked with every appearance of severe contrition which gained him the pity and compassion of all who came in contact with him. Murphy said more than once that he forgave Dunne and hoped that God would forgive him also.'[68]

The great majority of the crowd left after Murphy's hanging and when Dunne made his appearance, the place was almost entirely in the possession of the military and police.[69] Shortly before two o'clock, the executioner went to Dunne's cell and commenced to dress and pinion him. Dunne kissed each article as it was presented. Arriving at the press-room, accompanied by Father McEnroe, he kissed the rope as it was being placed around his neck. He was covered in a brown dress and wore white gloves. He was then immediately placed on the 'drop' and within seconds his body was suspended. He appeared to suffer less than Murphy, due to the fact that he got a greater length of rope and had therefore further to fall. The *Belfast News-Letter* had little sympathy for Dunne saying that: 'Dunne continued to manifest the same sullen, hardened demeanour which has characterised him throughout.'[70]

Dunne's body was also suspended for forty minutes and was then given to his sister who was present. It was brought off in the direction of the graveyard in his Tubberlion homeland on a cart because no undertaker in the Cavan area would provide a hearse.[71] The cortege was accompanied for part of the journey by the Huzzars who returned almost immediately when there was no sign of trouble. On Dunne's own instructions, the funeral procession moved via Ardlougher in order to avoid any incidents in Ballyconnell where the monthly fair was taking place that day. On the following day, Saturday, his funeral took place in a peaceful and orderly manner. When George Gallogly, the governor of Cavan Gaol wrote to the authorities confirming that both men had been executed he also pointed out that neither man had made any confession or admission of either of guilt or innocence.[72]

Many of the respectable shopkeepers in Cavan town kept their doors closed until after the executions and, in many of the private houses which looked on to the gaol, the window blinds were drawn. However, normality soon re-established itself. 'There was nothing to mark the evening in town beyond the presence of a greater number of strangers in the streets. The public houses were full and the laughter and jest most pronounced and it was obvious that the executions were not well over until they were practically forgotten.'

However, exciting news came to town during the evening that Red Pat Bannon had been arrested in Drogheda. A policeman from the Cavan district left immediately by coach in order to identify him and convey him back to Cavan.[73] But by the time he reached Drogheda, the resident magistrate in that town had discharged him and his whereabouts were then unknown. Once more, the Cavan public had been deprived of the opportunity of seeing the by now infamous Red Pat.

On the Sunday following the hangings, a declaration was posted up at the chapel signed by Hugh Brady of Creehan to the effect that he had not acted as hangman for either Dunne or Murphy. It was countersigned by Robert Erskine, JP, who added that he had reason to believe the statement to be correct. Whoever the hangman had been, the high sheriff of Cavan gave him a shilling to buy a drink after he had performed his duties and a piece of the rope used in the executions as a memento. However, it later emerged that, on the evening prior to the executions, the original hangman refused to perform the deed when his demands for more money were turned down. He apparently had refused to do the two executions for the price of one. When all negotiations failed, another volunteer hangman was called upon and 'he rendered efficiently as well as willingly'.[74]

Excitement once again mounted in Cavan a few weeks later when news reached the county that Red Pat Bannon had definitely been captured in Dundalk. The *Anglo Celt* reported that: '...a man with red hair asked for a ticket at the steampacket office in Dundalk. When asked for his name, he replied, "Pat Bannon". He was immediately taken into custody.'

When examined, he was found to have a cut or a sore on his leg which he said was caused by a dog who had once attacked him. He was taken to court but was discharged. The *Anglo Celt* reported: 'It has since transpired that he is not Red Pat Bannon. On being liberated, the man departed for England on Thursday last.'[75] From that point onwards, the trail of Red Pat ran into the sand.

Within six months, the efficient and enthusiastic Nicholas Kelly, resident magistrate of Cavan town, had received the reward for his work. He was granted '… a good service pension of £100 a year for the zeal and ability exhibited by him in reference to the Miss Hinds outrage. We understand that the pension came to him quite unsolicited and unexpected by him.'[76]

In the following October, the *Anglo Celt* told of its amazement to learn that 'Tarry [*sic*] Bannon is living at this moment in Tubberlion without the least molestation and Heavey, Thomas Dunne's servant man, is in gaol here for the present, both having returned from a summer sojourn on the seaboard and amid the wild yet glorious scenery of Wicklow'.[77]

The years passed, but the reward for Red Pat Bannon was never collected. With the closing of each decade after the murder of Charlotte Hinds, the antagonism and bitterness within the community became slowly submerged in the turmoil of life and newer struggles. Emigration carried many of the younger generation away for good. People grew old. Some died. Communities changed and the facts about Charlotte Hinds' murder became blurred and distant, though a residual gall remained.

As the century ambled towards its final years, the political and social climate had changed drastically in Ireland. Gladstone's Home Rule bills and the various land acts had stirred the tenant farmers and the Conservatives' policy of creating decent loyal citizens by 'killing home rule with kindness' weakened the landlords and aristocracy. Intense emigration, the opening of the countryside by road and railway, the outrages during the Land League years followed by the intense growth of nationalism and the continued dilution of the landholding structure had changed Irish society beyond recognition from the days of Charlotte Hinds. But then, a ghost from the old days returned. On 25 April 1898, forty-three years after Charlotte Hinds' death, Owen Coyle, a publican in Shercock, County Cavan, saw a man going into Mrs Baker's public house. Some hours later, the same man came over to his bar. The man was drinking heavily but did not say anything. On the following Wednesday evening, Coyle was sitting at the fire in his own public house when the man came in fairly drunk. After some time he made a remark about Miss Hinds. He inferred that he was accused of the murder. He was under the influence of drink when he came in again on Friday evening. Coyle recognised him and the first thing he said was, 'You are Red Pat Bannon'. The man replied, 'I am Red Pat Bannon'. Coyle could not be sure whether Bannon then said, as he held up his hand, 'I am the man' or 'I am the shot.' Two regular customers, Tom Traynor and Edward Mooney, were present when this had been said.

Word quickly spread in the neighbourhood that Red Pat was about and was drinking heavily. It was not long until the RIC became aware of his presence and Sergeant Coholan arrested him in Shercock on Sunday night, 1 May 1898, and charged him with having murdered Charlotte Hinds in 1855. Coholan said that Bannon was the worse for drink when he was arrested. He appeared like a man who was continuously drinking.[78] After his arrest, Bannon told Coholan that he was arrested and charged with the crime in Dundalk in 1856 but was let go from the court and made his way to England that night.

When charged Bannon said, 'All right, I beat the police for the last forty years and I'll beat them again. I beat them from Donegal up. I knew the men were shadowing me all day.' That was all he said. Coholan examined the wound on the leg and it corresponded with the *Hue & Cry* description.

A few days later, Red Pat Bannon appeared in Bailieborough court charged with the murder of Charlotte Hinds on 12 October 1855. The *Anglo Celt* described Bannon as being stout with reddish complexion, wearing a 'Yankee beard' and exhibited signs of nervousness in the court. When the charge was read to Bannon, he replied that he never heard of the locality of Tubberlion in his life.[79]

The publican, Owen Coyle, was the first witness called. He told the court that Bannon had come around about twelve years before that with his son and daughter. He believed he and his family lived in Liverpool. When cross-examined Coyle replied that Bannon had said, in a swaggering way, 'I'm the man'. He also boasted to him that he had been arrested and charged with the crime in Dundalk but was discharged by the magistrates and had gone to England.

Patrick Duffy, another publican, said Bannon had come into his premises on Wednesday, Thursday and Friday evenings. On one evening Bannon said that the Shercock people believed he had shot Miss Hinds. Duffy said 'perhaps you did' at which Bannon hung his head and laughed. On Sunday evening, 1 May, Bannon again repeated the story about Hinds saying she was a tyrant that deserved all she got and that she was burning in hell at the present time. He said she coerced her tenants to vote for some candidate in an election and that two men suffered for it. He was asked by Duffy if he had been in Shercock a year earlier and he said he was. He was remanded until the following Wednesday.

A big attendance appeared on the following Wednesday, including a daughter of the prisoner who came over from Liverpool. A description of Patrick Bannon was read out from *Hue & Cry* of 18 October 1855.

Joseph Gorby, a constable in the RIC in 1855 in Ballymagauran, was then called and he said, 'I believe he is Red Pat Bannon'. Gorby had been engaged in the investigation of the case. When asked if he was positive that the man named Bannon who he was sent to arrest in 1855 was the man now in court, he replied, 'I would not be sure but he is like the man. He got away.' Gorby told how he had followed Bannon to Glasgow and then spent nine months looking for him. He knew him before the murder as he was hired next door to the barracks. He had picked Bannon out in the Bridewell yard that very morning. Gorby's final evidence was to confirm that he did not know that a man named Red Pat Bannon had been arrested in Dundalk in May 1856.

Bannon's leg was then examined in court and the slight scar

was pointed out. Sergeant Coholan said that as well as the *Hue & Cry* information there was a general rumour through the village that he was boasting about who murdered Hinds forty years ago. Bannon was remanded until the following Tuesday. When the case resumed, there was much legal argument in the absence of the jury. The prosecution needed more time. District Inspector Locke asked for a remand of eight days to produce an important witness. McBreen, solicitor for Bannon, objected, saying:

> I am in a position today to prove that he [Bannon] never saw Curranwood and that he is a native of the parish of Knockbride, four miles from here. If you heard the evidence I can give, you would have no doubt about refusing information.

Mr Starkie, resident magistrate, then set down severe restrictions on the presentation of evidence when he told the prosecution that the depositions used in the former case back in 1856 could not be used in this case because the prisoner was not present when they were taken. He further added that a dying declaration, such as that allegedly made by Miss Hinds in 1855, must be proved again in the present court. Eventually, the case was remanded for a week on application of the prosecution, which stated that they were seeking their most important witness. McBreen objected saying he would produce witnesses to say they were with Bannon at the time of the murder. However, the remand was granted. McBreen then made application for bail for Bannon but it was rejected.[80]

There were throngs of people present both inside and outside the courthouse in Bailieborough when Bannon again appeared. Mr Locke, for the prosecution, then stood up and said, 'We have submitted the case to the law advisors to the Crown and they consider [that] we are not justified in proceeding any further against the prisoner and I am instructed to ask you to discharge him.'

Magistrate Gibson then said, 'There is not sufficient evidence before us to return the case for trial and, under the circumstances, we discharge the prisoner.'

Bannon calmly said, 'Thank you.'

Gibson then said to him, 'I hope it will be a lesson to you in future to keep from drink.'[81]

After forty-three years on the run, Red Pat Bannon left Bailieborough a free man and returned with his family to Liverpool.

Notes

Abbrevs: CSO = Central Statistics Office; NAI = National Archives of Ireland

And be hanged by the neck until you are dead

1 For a dramatic Dublin example of this see Bob Reece, *The Origins of Irish Convict Transportation to New South Wales* (Palgrave, Basingstoke, 2001), pp. 62–3.

2 Victor Gatrell, *The Hanging Tree: execution and the English people, 1770–1868* (Oxford University Press, Oxford, 1994) and James Kelly, *Gallows Speeches from Eighteenth-Century Ireland* (Four Courts Press, Dublin, 2001).

3 Gatrell, *The Hanging Tree*, p. 8, n. 14.

4 Frank Sweeney, *The Murder of Connell Boyle, 1898* (Four Courts Press, Dublin, 2002).

5 Mark Finnane, *Insanity and the Insane in Post-Famine Ireland* (Croom Helm Ltd, London, 1981), pp. 130–6.

6 For example Michelle McGoff-McCann, *Melancholy Madness: a coroner's casebook* (Mercier, Cork, 2003), pp. 250–1, 255–67.

7 W. E. Vaughan, *Landlords and Tenants in Mid-Victorian Ireland* (Oxford University Press, Oxford, 1994), p. 143.

8 Gatrell, *The Hanging Tree*, pp. 470–4.

9 Vaughan, *Landlords and Tenants*, pp. 142–9.

10 *Ibid.*, pp. 189–202.

I don't care where I am brought to, so long as you don't take me to hell

1 *The Irish Times* reported the housekeeper's name as Mary Ronane: *The Irish Times*, 13 July 1881, p. 3.

2 *Freeman's Journal*, 13 July 1881, p. 6.

3 Nugent & Co., *Full Report of the Horrible Murder in Naul* (Dublin, 1881).

4 *Freeman's Journal*, 18 July 1881, p. 3.

5 *The Irish Times*, 18 July 1881. Report of Threatening Mowers with death.

6 William Jacob is referred to as both a sub-constable and sub-inspector in the reports relating to this case.

7 *The Irish Times*, 6 August 1881.

8 *Freeman's Journal*, 26 October 1881.

I flatter myself we have strangled the evil in the bud

1 See *note* 3 below for an explanation of the Molly Maguires.
2 According to the Devon Commission (1847) conacre in Leinster and Ulster was usually for potato crops alone while in Connacht and Munster the crops included oats, hay, flax as well as potatoes.
3 Molly Maguires was a Catholic, agrarian, secret society (1835–55) that directed its campaigns against bailiffs, process-servers, landlords and their agents. The movement spread to the anthracite mines of Pennsylvania as an offshoot of the Ancient Order of Hibernians, where it gained great strength and notoriety in the years after the American Civil War.
4 Ribbonmen emerged in 1826 and were named after their identifying green ribbons. The mission of the Ribbonmen was to prevent the exploitation of tenant farmers and achieve a reduction in the payment of tithes, dues to the clergy, the price of conacre and other perceived problems. Roscommon was one of the counties where it thrived.
5 *Roscommon and Leitrim Gazette*, 16 May 1846.
6 Revd Edward Nangle (1799–1883), Church of Ireland evangelist, arrived in Achill with famine relief in 1831 and stayed on to found a Protestant mission there.
7 Various letters between the 'British Association for the Relief of Destitution in Ireland', Henry Brennan, PP, Kilglass and Captain Wynne, Poor Law inspector, *Roscommon and Leitrim Gazette*, 2 August 1848.
8 Mr Blake, resident magistrate, Elphin, to Dublin Castle, 29 November 1847. Outrage Papers, Roscommon, 1847.
9 Gay Lloyd of Croghan to T. S. Redington, Dublin Castle, 29 November 1847. Outrage Papers, Roscommon, 1847.
10 Memorial of magistrates of the County Roscommon to his Excellency George Williams, Earl of Clarendon, Lieutenant Governor and General Governor of Ireland, 25/853, NAI. Outrage Papers, Roscommon, 1847.
11 Editorial, *Roscommon and Leitrim Gazette*, 4 December 1847.
12 *Ibid.*
13 Letter of Father Brennan, PP, Kilglass to His Excellency, the Earl of Clarendon, Lord Lieutenant of Ireland. NAI, 29 December 1847. It was government policy at the time that any disturbed area, which the administration deemed required extra policing, was liable for the extra expenditure involved.
14 Threatening letter received by Fr Henry Brennan, PP, Kilglass'.

NAI, 6 December 1847.

15 *Roscommon and Leitrim Gazette*, 13 November 1847.

16 Notice issued under signature of T. S. Redington on behalf of the lord lieutenant, dated November 1847. Outrage Papers, Roscommon, 1847.

17 Letter of Mary MacNamara to his excellency, the lord lieutenant, Dublin Castle, 28 March 1848. NAI, Outrage Papers, Roscommon, 1848.

18 Letter of Constable William O'Brien to Sub-Inspector Heath, Roscommon, 27 April 1848. NAI, Outrage Papers, Roscommon, 1848.

19 Report of Resident Magistrate Blake, Elphin, 22 May 1848. NAI, Outrage Papers, Roscommon, 1848.

20 *Roscommon Journal*, 26 February 1848.

21 *Ibid.*

22 The information on the trial of Owen Beirne obtained from the *Roscommon Journal*, 15 July 1848.

23 Report of crown solicitor Peter Keogh containing an extract of the legal opinion obtained from the attorney-general in relation to the Lloyd murder case, 6 October 1849. NAI, Outrage Papers, Roscommon, 1849.

24 For the Mahon affair see Patrick Vesey, 'The Murder of Major Mahon', MA thesis in Local History (NUI Maynooth, 2003).

25 Report of crown solicitor, Peter Keogh, 20 November 1849. NAI, Outrage Papers, Roscommon, 1849.

26 Petition of James Coughlan, Roscommon, 28 April 1848. NAI, Outrage Papers, Roscommon, 1848.

27 Patrick Rooney to His Excellency, Lord Clarendon, Governor and General Governor of Ireland, 30 September 1848. NAI, Outrage Papers, Roscommon, 1848.

28 Report of crown solicitor, Peter Keogh to the inspector of constabulary at Roscommon, 10 November 1848. NAI, Outrage Papers, Roscommon, 1848.

29 Thomas Padden to his excellency, Lord Clarendon, 21 September 1848. NAI, Outrage Papers, Roscommon, 1848.

30 Mr Blake magistrate, Elphin, to the under secretary, Dublin Castle, 7 April 1848. NAI, Outrage Papers, Roscommon, 1848.

31 Report of crown solicitor, Peter Keogh, 30 November 1849. NAI, Outrage Papers, Roscommon, 1849.

32 Letter of crown solicitor Peter Keogh to Constabulary Office, Dublin Castle, undated. NAI, Outrage Papers, Roscommon, 1849.

The eagerness of the lower orders to press the case against the prisoner

The *Sligo Champion*, *Sligo Chronicle* and *Sligo Independent* each gave extensive coverage of all events relating to this case and the succeeding trial; this chapter draws extensively on these three newspapers.

1 R. O'Rorke, *History of Sligo town and county* (James Duffy & Co., Dublin, 1889).

2 Bridewell means a secure place of detention for persons awaiting trial. The name is derived from a London jail situated near a well used for washing clothes.

3 Tadhg Kilgannon, *Sligo and its Surroundings* (Kilgannon & Sons, Sligo, 1926), p. 257.

4 *Sligo Champion* from January to August 1861 contains ongoing reports about all aspects of this case.

5 The tea-tree (*Leptospermum petersonii*) has papery bark. Species have aromatic oils that are used germicidally and for perfume.

6 'Tick' derives from the Old English word for 'sheath' which was used for the enclosure of straw, flock or other bedding material and subsequently, for the enclosure of a mattress.

7 The pseudo-science of phrenology was an attempt to determine the character and abilities of a person through an examination of the shape and size of portions of the skull. The theory was initiated by Franz Gall and was developed further by Jojann Gall in the late eighteenth century.

8 *Sligo Independent*, 19 January 1861.

9 Some idea of the distance that was considered normal for walking is contained in the Gaol Minute Book for 1872 which records the fact that the Board of Superintendence refused to reimburse the constabulary for hiring a car to take a prisoner from Ballina to Sligo, a distance of some forty miles, since the board claimed that the prisoner was considered fit enough to walk, presumably accompanied by a policeman.

10 *Sligo Champion*, 17 August 1861.

11 The press-room was an ante-room where the condemned person was prepared for execution.

12 *Sligo Champion*, 24 August 1861.

13 J. C. McDonagh, *History of Ballymote and the Parish of Emlaghfad* (Champion Publications, Dublin, 1936), p. 148.

Notes

They have been sent back to their desolate home, broken spirited and hopeless

1   Oral source, Daniel Dowling, Glenmore, County Kilkenny.

2   Griffith's Valuation, County of Kilkenny, townland of Shanbogh.

3   Registry of Deeds, 1872, 23/151, Memorial of Deed of Conveyance to Thomas Boyd.

4   *Ibid.*

5   NAI, Landed Estates Court sales, Vol. 105, No. 23.

6   Registry of Deeds, 1872, Memorial of Deed of Conveyance to Thomas Boyd. Memorial of an Indenture of Mortgage between Thomas Boyd and Rev. Edmond Walsh.

7   Montgomery-Massingberd, Hugh (ed.), *Burke's Irish Family Records* (Arco Publishing Company, New York, 1976), pp. 160–1.

8   Registry of Deeds, 1872, 23/152.

9   Census of Ireland 1901, Household Schedules, County Kilkenny, parish of Rosbercon, townland of Raheen.

10 Margaret Forristal's farm was the largest, comprising 123 acres, Anastasia Holden had 110 acres, Richard Phelan held 106 acres, Michael Phelan 88 acres, whereas John Shea's farm comprised only 25 acres.

11 NAI, Landed Estates Court sales, Vol. 105, No. 23.

12 *Wexford People*, 11 August 1880.

13 Oral source, Daniel Dowling.

14 *Wexford People*, 18 August 1880.

15 *Ibid.*, 11 August 1880.

16 *Wexford Independent*, 11 August 1880.

17 Mahon was later imprisoned for Land League activity and spent two months in Kilmainham Gaol with Charles Stewart Parnell and other Land League leaders in 1881. He was released on health grounds and emigrated to Australia in 1882 under an assumed name as a paid agent of the Land League. He was eventually elected to the Australian parliament as a member of the Labour Party and served as Postmaster General, Minister for Home Affairs and Minister for External Affairs. In 1920, he was expelled from the federal parliament after he attacked British policy in Ireland in the wake of the death on hunger strike of Terence McSwiney.

18 Roche, Cecil R, *Report on the Trial of Walter Phelan and John Phelan in the Queen's Bench Division of the High Court of Justice in Ireland*, 27, 28, 29 and 39 June 1881 (1881).

19 *Wexford People*, 11 and 14 August 1880.

20 *Ibid.*, 14 August 1880.

21 *Ibid.*, 18 August 1880.

22 Robert Leigh was the owner of a huge estate near Wellington Bridge in south County Wexford.

23 *Wexford People*, 18 September 1880.

24 *Ibid.*, 11 September 1880.

25 *Ibid.*, 25 August 1880.

26 *Ibid.*, 28 August 1880.

27 *Ibid.*, 11 September 1880.

28 *Ibid.*, 18 and 22 September 1880.

29 *Ibid.*, 16 October 1880.

30 *Daily Express*, 11 September 1880.

31 Gahon, John V., *The Secular Priests of the Diocese of Ferns* (Editions de Signe, Strasbourg, 2000).

32 In a letter to the journalist Hugh Mahon in Australia in May 1883, Father Furlong wrote that his parish priest had taken the earliest 'decent' opportunity to have him removed from New Ross, using the pretext of his ill health. NLA, Ms 937, papers of Hugh Mahon, letter from Father Patrick Furlong to Hugh Mahon, 6 May 1883.

33 *Wexford People*, 22 September 1880.

34 Sweeney, Frank, *The Murder of Conell Boyle* (Four Courts Press, Dublin, 2002).

35 *Wexford People*, 15 and 18 December 1880.

36 NAI, crown book at assizes, County Kilkenny. Spring 1863–Spring 1885.

37 NLA, Ms 937, papers of Hugh Mahon, letter from Walter Phelan to Hugh Mahon, 18 March 1881.

38 *Wexford People*, 26 March 1881.

39 *Ibid.*, 2 April 1881.

40 NLA Ms 937, papers of Hugh Mahon, letter from John Colfer to David Lynch, 26 May 1881.

41 *Wexford People*, 29 June 1881.

42 Roche, *Report on the Trial of Walter Phelan and John Phelan*.

43 Bourke, Angela, *The Burning of Bridget Cleary* (Pimlico, London, 1999).

44 *Ibid.*

45 *True Detective* magazine, March 1985, reproduced illustrations from penny dreadful, *Famous Crimes*.

46 *Wexford People*, 9 July 1881.

47 Urwin, Margaret, *A Co Wexford Family in the Land War* (Four Courts Press, Dublin, 2002).

48 *Wexford People*, 16 July 1881.

49 NAI, CSO RP 4776/1882. Grounds of suspicion against John Phelan,

arrest recommended, warrant of arrest issued, arrest and discharge.
50 *Wexford People*, 27 July 1881.
51 *Ibid.*, 27 July 1881.
52 *Ibid.*, 23 July and 10 August 1881.
53 *Ibid.*, 30 July 1881.
54 *Ibid.*, 27 August 1881.
55 *Ibid.*, 7 January 1882.
56 *Ibid.*, 8 March 1882.
57 *Ibid.*, 7 June 1882.
58 *Ibid.*, 26 January 1884.
59 St Canice's Hospital, Kilkenny, admission papers to Kilkenny District Lunatic Asylum, admission application, certificate of magistrate and PLG and medical certificate in respect of Walter Phelan, 18 February 1883.
60 Census of Ireland 1901, Household Schedules, County Kilkenny, townland of Shanbogh.
61 Montgomery-Massingberd, *Burke's Irish Family Records*, pp. 160–1.
62 *Wexford People*, 29 December 1900 and headstone at St Mary's Cemetery, New Ross.
63 *Ibid.*, 12 March 1904.
64 NAI, CSO RP 21727/1887. Evictions at Ballykerogue.
65 Last will and testament of Thomas Boyd, probate granted June 1904.

Put the saddle on the right horse

1 Liam Price, *Placenames of County Wicklow* (Institute of Advanced Studies, Dublin, 1945). Borkle means borderland.
2 *Leinster Leader*, 20 May 1893.
3 *Ibid.*
4 *Ibid.*
5 *Ibid.*
6 *Irish Daily Independent*, 18 May 1893.
7 *Ibid.*, 20 May 1893.
8 *Ibid.*
9 Woodquest = woodpigeon.
10 *Wicklow Newsletter*, 8 July 1893.
11 NAI, CSORP 10236. John Conran, prison report, 17 July 1893. Unless otherwise stated the narrative is generally based on this document.
12 *Leinster Leader*, 9 December 1893.
13 *Irish Daily Independent*, 9 December 1893.

14 NAI, CSORP 10236. John Conran, prison report, 1893.

15 *Irish Daily Independent*, 9 December 1893.

16 *Leinster Leader*, 27 May 1893.

17 NAI, CSORP 10236. John Conran, prison report, 1893.

18 *Freeman's Journal*, 7 December 1893.

19 *Ibid.*, 9 December 1893.

20 *The Irish Times*, 8 December 1893.

21 *Daily Express*, 28 December 1893.

22 There were eleven Protestants on the jury.

23 The Bradley murder happened in Mullingar and gained much notoriety during these years.

24 NAI, CSORP 10236. John Conran, prison report, 20 December 1893.

25 *Ibid.* In 1893, John Conran was the holder of lot 11 in the townland of Borklemere. The actual will made by Conran was presumably destroyed in the Custom House fire as were all wills made prior to 1905. In 1894, Pat Conran was the registered holder of the farm. (Valuation Office, Irish Life Centre, Dublin 1.)

26 *Ibid.*

27 *The Irish Times*, 27 December 1893.

28 Dropsy is the old term for oedema.

29 NAI, CSORP 10236. John Conran, prison report, 10 October 1896.

30 NAI, CSORP. John Conran, prison report, June 1897.

31 NAI, CSORP. Jon Conran, prison report, 23 July 1897.

But the stairs is not sound, sir!

1 F. G. Hall, *The Bank of Ireland 1783–1946* (Hodges Figgis, Dublin, 1949), p. 504.

2 D. George Boyce, *Nineteenth Century Ireland: the search for stability* (Gill & Macmillan, Dublin, 1990), p. 98.

3 Ruán O'Donnell, *Robert Emmet and the Rebellion of 1798* (Irish Academic Press, Dublin, 2003).

4 *Ibid.*, p. 116.

5 Charles Dickson, *The Life of Michael Dwyer* (Brown & Nolan Ltd, Dublin 1944), p. 396.

6 O'Donnell, *Robert Emmet and the Rebellion of 1798*, p. 137, 139.

7 Dickson, *The Life of Michael Dwyer*, p. 397.

8 O'Donnell, *Robert Emmet and the Rising of 1803*, p. 116.

9 Helen Landreth, *The Pursuit of Robert Emmet* (Whittlesey House, London, 1948), p. 238, 239.

Notes

10 Emmet's father, Dr Robert Emmet, was a successful doctor living on St Stephen's Green in Dublin. He was a specialist in fever cases and, in 1770, was appointed state physician for Ireland and was a governor of Swift's Hospital for the insane. He died in 1802 and his wife, Robert's mother, died just days before Emmet's execution. The Emmet family in Ireland suffered greatly by reason of Robert's rebellion. See Patrick M. Geoghegan, *Robert Emmet: A Life* (Gill & McMillan, Dublin, 2002), p. 56, 220.

11 Geoghegan, *Robert Emmet: A Life*, p. 189.

12 O'Donnell, *Robert Emmet and the Rising of 1803*, p. 187.

13 Dr George Little, *Malachy Horan Remembers* (Gill & Son, Dublin, 1945), p. 109.

14 Weston St John Joyce, *The Neighbourhood of Dublin* (Dublin, 1921: republished Skellig, Dublin, 1988), p. 208.

15 Jim Herlihy, *The Royal Irish Constabulary* (Four Courts Press, Dublin, 1997), p. 28.

16 *Ibid.*, p. 30.

17 W. D. Handcock, *The History and Antiquities of Tallaght* (Tower Books, Dublin, 1976), p. 75.

18 *Ibid.*

19 *Ibid.*

20 Little, *Malachy Horan Remembers*, p. 39.

21 St John Joyce, *The Neighbourhood of Dublin*, p. 208.

22 Stephen Trombley, *The Execution Protocol* (Anchor, USA, 1993), p. 13.

23 O'Donnell, *Robert Emmet and the Rising of 1803*, p. 165.

24 Thomas Galvin is reported to have previously worked for the Duke of Leinster in Kildare and to have been sentenced to transportation for life sometime before 1798. Like others of his time he agreed to become executioner in preference to a lifetime in Botany Bay. He lived until 1830. O'Donnell, *Robert Emmet and the Rising of 1803*, p. 166.

25 Handcock, *The History and Antiquities of Tallaght*, p. 75.

26 O'Donnell, *Robert Emmet and the Rising of 1803*, p. 277.

27 Little, *Malachy Horan Remembers*, p. 110.

28 Handcock, *The History and Antiquities of Tallaght*, p. 76.

29 *Ibid.*

Every word stated by the prisoner may be taken *cum grano salis*

1 S. Lewis, *A Topographical Dictionary of Ireland* (Quintin Publications [reprint], 3 vols, London, 1837), ii, p. 442.

2   J. M. Hunter, 'Style and form in gravestone and monumental sculpture in County Tyrone in the seventeenth and eighteenth centuries', in Charles Dillon & Henry Jefferies (eds), *Tyrone: history and society* (Geography Publications, Dublin, 2000), p. 298–9.

3   Lord Killanin & Michael V. Duignan, *The Shell Guide to Ireland* (Ebury Press, London, 1967), p. 395.

4   Lewis, *A Topographical Dictionary of Ireland*, ii, p. 442.

5   A. Day & P. McWilliams (eds), *Ordnance Survey Memoirs of Ireland* (Queen's University, Belfast, 1993), v, p. 12.

6   William Macafee, 'The population in County Tyrone 1600–1991', in *Tyrone: history and society*, p. 453.

7   *Ibid.*, p. 445.

8   Day & McWilliams, *Ordnance Survey Memoirs of Ireland*, p. 6.

9   PRONI, TYR1/2C/1B. Trial transcript, p. 224.

10   PRONI. Trial transcript, p. 227.

11   *Freeman's Journal*, 1 July 1871.

12   *Ibid.*, 10 July 1871.

13   *Ibid.*, 20 July 1872.

14   *Ibid.*, 1 July 1871.

15   PRONI. Trial transcript, p. 233.

16   *Ibid.*, p. 278.

17   *Freeman's Journal*, 23 July 1873.

18   PRONI, TYR1/2C/1B. Trial transcript, p. 233.

19   *Freeman's Journal*, 3 July 1871.

20   *Ibid.*, 25 July 1873.

21   PRONI. Trial transcript, p. 248.

22   *Freeman's Journal*, 10 July 1871.

23   *Ibid.*, 17 August 1871.

24   *Ibid.*, 2 January 1872.

25   *Ibid.*, 20 July 1872.

26   *Ibid.*, 24 July 1873.

27   *Ibid.*, 23 July 1873.

28   *Ibid.*, 29 February 1872.

29   *Ibid.*, 18 July 1872.

30   *Northern Star*, 4 July 1872.

31   PRONI. Trial transcript, p. 254.

32   *Freeman's Journal*, 10 March 1873.

33   PRONI. Trial transcript, p. 237.

34   *Ibid.*, p. 239.

35   *Freeman's Journal*, 19 July 1872.

36   PRONI. Trial transcript, p. 239.

Notes

37 *Freeman's Journal*, 23 July 1872.
38 A sandwoman spread sand on the kitchen and pantry floors.
39 *Freeman's Journal*, 6 March 1873.
40 *Ibid.*, 10 March 1873.
41 *Ibid.*, 13 March 1873.
42 *Ibid.*, 14 March 1873.
43 *Ibid.*, 22 July 1873.
44 *Ibid.*, 24 July 1873.
45 *Ibid.*, 25 July 1873.
46 *Ibid.*, 29 July 1873.
47 *Ibid.*, 30 July 1873.
48 *Strabane Weekly News*, 23 August, 2001.
49 *Ibid.*, 14 September 2000.
50 www.historycoop.org/journals/25/01/04. Martin J. Wiener, 'Judges Vs Jurors: courtroom tensions in murder trials and the law of criminal responsibility in nineteenth century England', p. 24.

It's not fit for you to be keeping company with that unfortunate fellow

1   *The Western News and Weekly Examiner*, 11 October 1879.
2   *Ibid.*, 25 October 1879.
3   *Ibid.*, 4 December 1880.
4   Anne Coleman, *Riotous Roscommon: social unrest in the 1840s* (Irish Academic Press, Dublin, 1999), pp. 55–6.
5   *Land League meetings and agrarian crimes reported to the constabulary.* House of Commons 1881 (5), lxxvii, p. 793.
6   *The Western News and Weekly Examiner*, 29 May 1880.
7   *The Galway Vindicator and Connaught Advertiser*, 9 February 1884.
8   This account of meeting with Will Mahon in Burke's is based mainly on Cox's deposition before the magistrates in Galway on 15 February 1884, as reported in *The Galway Vindicator and Connaught Advertiser* on 20 February 1884 and *The Western News and Weekly Examiner* on 23 February 1884.
9   Judge Johnson's Report on the trial at Carrick-on-Shannon, in Michael Tansey's Convict Reference File, Misc. 1181, 1907, at NAI, p. 22.
10 *Ibid.*, p. 2.
11 *The Galway Vindicator and Connaught Advertiser*, 9 February 1884.
12 *Ibid.*; *The Western News and Weekly Examiner*, 29 May 1880 names Patrick Hickey as Will Mahon's brother-in-law.
13 Judge Johnson's Report, p. 26.
14 *The Western News and Weekly Examiner*, 25 October 1879.

15 Interview with Tom Kelly, Grange, June 2003.

16 *The Galway Vindicator and Connaught Advertiser*, 13 February 1884; *The Western News and Weekly Examiner*, p. 19.

17 Judge Johnson's Report, pp. 27–8.

18 Michael Tansey's Convict Reference File, Misc 1181, 1907, at NAI, 17303, A. Reed report, n.d. July 1884.

19 Chief Secretary's Office Registered Papers, at NAI 19546, 21165, 21604/1879; 267/1880.

20 *The Western News and Weekly Examiner*, 29 May 1880.

21 *Ibid.*, 19 June 1880.

22 *Ibid.*, 3 July 1880.

23 Details from proceedings at Ballinamore on 26 May 1880, *The Galway Vindicator and Connaught Advertiser*, 29 May 1880.

24 *Return relating to agrarian offences (Ireland), province of Connaught.* House of Commons 1881(13), pp. lxxvii, 607.

25 *The Galway Vindicator and Connaught Advertiser*, 11 December 1880.

26 In 858 of the 961 agrarian offences reported to the RIC in the province of Connacht during 1880, no offender was made amenable – *Return relating to agrarian offences (Ireland), province of Connaught.* House of Commons 1881 (13), pp. lxxvii, 607.

27 Valuation Office, Cancellation Books, 1/40577, Ballyforan townland.

28 *Return of outrages, County Roscommon, January 1879 to January 1880.* House of Commons 1880 (131), lx, 199.

29 Michael Tansey's Convict Reference File, A. Reed to G. Bowler, 23 July 1884.

30 *The Western News and Weekly Examiner*, 31 July 1880.

31 *Ibid.*, 1 April 1882.

32 Judge Johnson's Report, pp. 23–4.

33 Conversation with Frances Henderson (neé Tansey), Ballyforan, 13 February 2003.

34 *The Western News and Weekly Examiner*, 14 July 1883.

35 *Ibid.*, 15 July 1882.

36 *Ibid.*, 7 July 1883.

37 *Returns relating to agrarian crimes (Ireland): December 1880.* House of Commons 1881(6), lxxvii, 273.

38 *The Western News and Weekly Examiner*, 4 December 1880.

39 *Ibid.*, 14 July 1883.

40 Judge Johnson's Report, p. 23. Tom Casey was an 'approver' who received money for information in the case concerning the murder of five members of the Joyce family of Maamtrasna, County Galway,

on 18 August 1882. A cousin of the victims, Myles Joyce, believed to be innocent, was one of three men hanged for the crime on 15 December 1882. Shortly after Michael Tansey's trial, in 1884, Casey and Anthony Philbin, another approver, sensationally revealed that their testimony was false. This led to debate in the British parliament – but no reprieve was granted to five other men in jail for their part in the crime.

41 Michael Tansey's Convict Reference File. The phrase is used by Michael Tansey in his petition of 10 April 1895.

42 This John Rogerson was a cousin of Patrick Rogerson, convicted in the Weston House case. Patrick's brother, also named John, appeared as first defence witness at the Tansey trial.

43 *The Galway Vindicator and Connaught Advertiser*, 6 February 1884.

44 *Ibid.*, 8 March 1884.

45 *Ibid.*, 29 March 1884.

46 Michael Tansey's Convict Reference File, 17303 to the attorney-general, 25 July 1884.

47 *The Galway Vindicator and Connaught Advertiser*, 27 February 1884.

48 Lally's recollection of the conversation was uncertain because he changed 'it' to 'him' in later statements. See Judge Johnson's Report, p. 3 and *The Galway Vindicator and Connaught Advertiser*, 19 July 1884. 'Annagh' is an Irish word for a swamp or marshy area. The small townland between Muckloon and the Suck, adjacent to Ballyforan Bridge, is called Gortananny.

49 Judge Johnson's Report, pp. 39–42. Typescript copy of John Cox's deposition, 15 February 1884.

50 *The Galway Vindicator and Connaught Advertiser*, 6 February 1884.

51 *Ibid.*, 23 February 1884.

52 *The Western News and Weekly Examiner*, 14 July 1883.

53 NAI, ED2 112/32-33, Ballyforan N.S., roll number 1866.

54 *The Galway Vindicator and Connaught Advertiser*, 8 March 1884.

55 Michael Tansey's Convict Reference File, Petition by Michael Tansey, April 1899; Cox revealed this under cross-examination at Tansey's trial in Carrick-on-Shannon. See Judge Johnson's Report, p. 18.

56 *The Connaught People and Ballinasloe Independent*, 15 November 1884.

57 *The Galway Vindicator and Connaught Advertiser*, 29 March 1884.

58 *Ibid.*, 5 April 1884.

59 NAI, ED2/141/78, Ballyforan N.S., inspector's remarks 4 May 1883 and 10 September 1886.

60 *The Western News and Weekly Examiner*, 5 July 1884, account of the inquest; *The Galway Vindicator and Connaught Advertiser*, 12 July 1884. During Tansey's trial, it was revealed that Kennedy had become a crown witness.

61 General Prisons Board, Correspondence Register, at NAI 9010/1884, Governor of Galway Gaol to Dublin Castle, 3 July 1884.

62 Judge Johnson's Report, pp. 1–32.

63 *Ibid.*, pp. 8–9.

64 *Ibid.*, pp. 23–4.

65 Michael Tansey's Convict Reference File, 17303, 22 July 1884. The prosecution and police handling of this issue was scrutinised by Andrew Reed.

66 Michael Tansey's Convict Reference File, Statement by Constable Keegan, 22 July 1884. *Hue & Cry* was a police gazette circulated to all RIC barracks. The issues of 1 and 4 June 1880 carried details of the reward.

67 Judge Johnson's Report, p. 45.

68 General Prisons Board, Correspondence Register, at NAI, 9385, 9438, 9483, 9679/1884.

69 Michael Tansey's Convict Reference File, Petition to Earl Spenser, received 2 August 1884.

70 Michael Tansey's Convict Reference File, Reed to the attorney-general, 25 July 1884.

71 Michael Tansey's Convict Reference File, Second memorial by Marian Hawkes, 29 July 1884. First petition dated 28 July 1884.

72 Jarlath Waldron, *Maamtrasna: the murders and the mystery* (Edmund Burke, Dublin, 1993), chapters 11 and 12. See n. 29.

73 Michael Tansey's Convict Reference File, Note by 'M', Law Room Dublin Castle, 4 August 1884.

74 Michael Tansey's Convict Reference File, Declaration by Michael Tansey, 6 August 1884.

75 *The Galway Vindicator and Connaught Advertiser*, 9 August 1884.

76 Michael Tansey's Convict Reference File, Petition by Michael Tansey, 1895.

77 *The Connaught People and Ballinasloe Independent*, 7 March 1885.

78 *Royal commission on prisons in Ireland: Medical officer's report, Mountjoy prison, 6 May 1885*. House of Commons 1884–85 [C 4233], pp. xxxviii, I, 899.

79 Michael Tansey's Convict Reference File, Medical officer's report, 2 August 1899.

80 Michael Tansey's Convict Reference File, Petition by Michael

Notes

Tansey, 1895.

81   Michael Tansey's Convict Reference File, Petition to the lord lieutenant, 4 August 1899.

82   Michael Tansey's Convict Reference File, Memorial by Michael Tansey, 3 October 1907.

83   Conversation with Mrs Kathleen Tansey, 6 November 2004.

84   *Return relating to peace preservation acts (Ireland).* House of Commons 1878–79 (70), pp. lix, 369.

85   Michael Tansey's Convict Reference File, Memorial on behalf of Michael Tansey, 10 May 1899.

86   Judge Johnson's Report, p. 18.

Oh! Good God, is there no one to assist me?

1   *Hibernian Journal*, 30 October 1800.

2   *Freeman's Journal*, 29 April 1800.

3   *Lidwell's Trial An authentic report of the Trial of Thomas Lidwell, Esq. On an indictment for a rape committed upon the body of Mrs Sarah Sutton, wife of Jacob Sutton, Esq. of Portarlington, Queen's County. Tried at Naas Lent Assizes 1800* (Printed by Robert Marchbank for W. Wison, Dublin, 1800), held at NUI Maynooth. Unless stated otherwise the proceedings and quotations from the trial have been taken from this pamphlet.

4   Kelly, James, 'A Most Inhuman and Barbarous Piece of Villainy: an Exploration of the Crime of Rape in Eighteenth-Century Ireland' in *Eighteenth-Century Ireland*, vol. 10 (1995), p. 90.

5   *Ibid.*, pp. 94, 98.

6   Thomas Lidwell was born in 1750. His grandfather, John Lidwell, had married Eleanor Cooke (*d.*1754) and they had three children: Thomas (father of the Thomas of this story) who died in 1782, George and Eleanor.

7   In 1736 Thomas Sr married Jemima Cowley who was born in Clonmore, County Tipperary, and controlled most of the lands which were brought into the Lidwell family.

8   Lidwill, John, *The History and Memoirs of John Lidwill, Eldest Son of Thomas Lidwill Esq., late of Clonmore, in the County of Tipperary* (National Library, 1804).

9   Index to Marriage Licence Bonds, Cashel and Emly 1664–1857 (NAI).

10 Stephen, Leslie *et al.*, *Dictionary of National Biography* (London, Smith, Elder & Co., 1885–1901).

    Standish O'Grady, first Viscount Guillamore. On 28 May 1803, after the murder of Lord Kilwarden, he became attorney-general, and was one of the prosecuting counsels at the trial of Robert Emmet. He was one of the first to suspect the duplicity of Leonard McNally. On his retirement from the bench in 1831 he was created Viscount Guillamore of Cahir Guillamore and Baron O'Grady of Rockbarton, County Limerick, in the peerage of Ireland.

11 Costello, Con, *Kildare, Saints, Soldiers and Horses* (Naas, Leinster Leader, 1991), pp. 175–77.

12 Jacob Sutton's mother was Elizabeth and he had a brother Joshua.

13 *Leucorrhoea* or *Leukorrhea* is an abnormal white discharge from the cervix which may be caused by infections in the ovaries etc. Infections can be viral, parasitic or fungal and recurring infections are common (*New Encyclopedia Britannica*, 1976).

14 Marriage Licence Bonds for the Diocese of Ossory Ferns and Leighlin 1691–1845 (NAI).

15 O'Higgins, Paul, *A Bibliography of Irish Trials and Other Legal Proceedings* (Professional Books Limited, Abingdon, 1986).

16 *Ibid*.

17 Stephen, Leslie, *et al.*, *Dictionary of National Biography* (London, Smith, Elder & Co., 1885–1901).
   Plunket, William, Conyngham's first Baron Plunket, Lord Chancellor of Ireland was born in 1764 at Enniskillen. He was the fourth and youngest son of a Presbyterian minister. His debating skills and instant wit were noteworthy. He appeared for the prosecution in the trial of Robert Emmet in 1803 was charged with being unjustly harsh is this regard in order to win favour with the government. He was friendly with Robert Emmet's brother. He had an illustrious career. He died on 4 January 1854 and is buried in Mount Jerome Cemetery, Dublin. He married Catherine McCausland and left six sons and five daughters.

18 *Ibid*.
   William Ridgeway (d.1817), law reporter. He acted as one of the crown counsel in several state trials, notably in that of Robert Emmet in 1803. He died at Dublin, of typhus fever, while on circuit at Trim, on 1 December 1817. He had a high reputation as a lawyer and was a diligent and accurate reporter of legal cases.

19 Foster, R. F., *Modern Ireland, 1600–1972* (Penguin Books, London, 1988), p. 171.
   John Philpot Curran, born 1750, father of Sarah Curran, who was Robert Emmet's girlfriend. He was an eminent lawyer who defended Wolfe Tone and Napper Tandy and other United Irishmen,

but he would not defend Emmet because of his daughter's attachment to him. He treated her severely because of her engagement to Emmet.

20 *Ibid.*, p.169.
    Jonah Barrington, born near Abbeyleix in 1760, MP 1790–1800, opposed the Act of Union, appointed admiralty judge in 1798 but lost office because of misappropriation of funds in 1830.

21 *Ibid.*
    Leonard McNally, born 1752, lawyer, playwright and spy. Involved in setting up Society of United Irishmen and helped defend some of them in court. After his death it was discovered that he had been a spy for the government.

22 The jury consisted of Samuel Mills (foreman), Robert Montgomery, William Brunton, George Paine, George Pillsworth, John Haysted, Matthew Coates, Benjamin Braddill, John Chapman, Charles Fitzgerald, Samuel Leonard and George Leonard.

23 Lewis, Samuel, *A Topographical Dictionary of Ireland* (Genealogical Publishing Company, Baltimore, 1984 reprint).

24 Kelly, James 'The Abduction of Women of Fortune in Eighteenth-Century Ireland' in *Eighteenth-Century Ireland*, Vol. 9 (1994), p. 36.

25 D'Cruze, Shani 'Approaching the History of Rape and Sexual Violence: notes towards research' in *Women's History Review*, Vol. 1, No. 3 (1993), p. 389.

26 Stephen, Leslie, *et al.*, *Dictionary of National Biography*.
    Wolfe, Arthurs, first Viscount of Ireland, was born on 19 January 1738–39. He was the son of John Wolfe of Forenaughts, County Kildare. He was appointed chief justice of the king's bench and was created a peer by the title of Baron Kilwarden of Newlands. He was an advocate of the Act of Union. On 23 July 1803 while driving to Dublin Castle with his nephew and niece, his carriage was stopped in Thomas Street by rebels. Wolfe and his nephew were murdered. It was said that Wolfe was mistaken for Carleton, the chief justice of the common pleas, a judge of much sterner character.

27 *Dublin Evening Post*, 26 April 1800; *Hibernian Journal*, 30 April 1800.

28 *Hibernian Journal*, 9 May 1800.

29 *Freeman's Journal*, 29 April 1800.

30 *Belfast News-Letter*, 23 May 1800 (report taken from the *Freeman's Journal*).

31 Index to Prerogative Wills 1536–1810, NAI.

32 Dr Myles T. Shortall, descendant of Lidwell family (also provided information about Lidwell family history).

33 Cantwell, Brian J., *Memorials of the Dead South-West Wexford*, Vol. viii (REF 358), NAI. The tombstone is also mentioned in Hore, Philip, *History of the County of Wexford, Tintern, Rosegarland and Clonmines* (E. Stock, London, 1901), p. 219

34 Index to Diocesan Wills Ossory 1536–1858 (NAI).

35 Thomas, Keith 'The Double Standard' in *Journal of the History of Ideas*, Vol. 20 (1959), p. 204.

36 D'Cruze, Shani, 'Approaching the History of Rape and Sexual Violence', p. 380.

37 *Ibid.*, p. 379

38 *Ibid.*, p. 389.

39 Conley, Carolyn A., 'Rape and Justice' in *Victorian Studies* (Summer 1986), p. 529.

Those in whom you trust will always be the first to betray you

1   There are various spellings for these names. Toberlyon, Tubberlyon, Toberlion and Tubberlion. Duffin is pronounced Diffin locally.

2   *Griffiths Valuation*, County Cavan, Toberlyon and Toberlyon Duffin townlands.

3   K. Theodore Hoppen, *Ireland since 1800* (Longman, London, 1989), p. 36.

4   *Belfast News-Letter*, 23 October 1855, letter from J. T. Hinds, Killeshandra, a relative.

5   *Anglo Celt*, 18 October 1855.

6   *Ibid.*, 1 November 1855.

7   *Ibid.*, 18 October 1855.

8   *Belfast News-Letter*, 23 October 1855.

9   NAI, CRF, 1856, D 26.

10 NAI, CSORP, 1855, 9339.

11 *Hue & Cry*, 18 October 1855.

12 NAI, CSORP, 1855, 9415.

13 *Anglo Celt*, 29 November 1855.

14 *Belfast News-Letter*, 1 November 1855. This article was quoted from *The Standard*.

15 *Ibid.*, 17 October 1855.

16 *Anglo Celt*, 18 October 1855.

17 *Ibid.*, 25 October 1855.

18 *The Times*, 25 October 1855; *Anglo Celt*, 25 October 1855.

19 *Belfast News-Letter*, 23 October 1855.

20 *The Galway Vindicator*, 3 November 1855 in NLI Larcom Papers, ms. 7576.

21 *Anglo Celt*, 1 November 1855.
22 *Belfast News-Letter*, 19 October 1855. Letter from Henry Grattan.
23 *Ibid.*, 15 April 1856.
24 *Ibid.*, 15 April 1856.
25 *Anglo Celt*, 17 April 1856.
26 *Ibid.*, 15 November 1855.
27 *Ibid.*, 15 November 1855.
28 *Ibid.*, 3 January 1856.
29 *Belfast News-Letter*, 15 April 1856.
30 *Ibid.*, 15 April 1856.
31 *Anglo Celt*, 17 May 1856.
32 *Belfast News-Letter*, 12 April 1856, p. 1.
33 *Anglo Celt*, 17 April 1856.
34 *Ibid.*, 10 April 1856.
35 *Ibid.*, 3 April 1856.
36 *The Times*, 11 April 1856, p. 12.
37 *Ibid.*
38 *Belfast News-Letter*, 12 April 1856.
39 *Anglo Celt*, 10 April 1856.
40 *Belfast News-Letter*, 12 April 1856.
41 *Anglo Celt*, 10 April 1856.
42 *Ibid.*, 17 April 1856.
43 *Belfast News-Letter*, 15 April 1856.
44 *Anglo Celt*, 17 April 1856.
45 *Ibid.*, 10 April 1856
46 *Ibid.*
47 *Ibid.*, 17 April 1856
48 *Ibid.*
49 NAI, CRF, 1856, D26. Larcom to the lord lieutenant.
50 *Ibid.*
51 *Anglo Celt*, 17 April 1856.
52 *Ibid.*
53 *Ibid.*
54 *Ibid.*
55 *Belfast News-Letter*, 15 April 1856.
56 *Ibid.*
57 *Anglo Celt*, 22 April 1856.
58 NAI, CSORP, 1856, D 26.
59 *Ibid.*
60 *Anglo Celt*, 1 May 1856.
61 NAI, CSORP, 1856, D 26.

62 *Anglo Celt*, 15 May 1856.
63 *Ibid.*, 22 May 1856.
64 *Ibid.*
65 *Ibid.*
66 *Ibid.*
67 *Ibid.*
68 *Belfast News-Letter*, 19 May 1856.
69 *Ibid.*, 15 April 1856.
70 *Ibid.*, 19 April 1856.
71 *Ibid.*
72 NAI, CSORP, 1856, D 26.
73 *Anglo Celt*, 22 May 1856.
74 A. F. McEntee, *Memories of a lifetime in journalism in Cavan* (*Anglo Celt*, County Cavan, 1991), p. 26.
75 *Anglo Celt*, 12 June 1856.
76 *Ibid.*, 30 October 1856.
77 *Ibid.*
78 *Ibid.*, 7 May 1898.
79 *Ibid.*, 14 May 1898.
80 *Ibid.*, 21 May 1898.
81 *Ibid.*, 28 May 1898.

Contributors

Sean Bagnall, an accountant and lawyer, lives in Celbridge, Co. Kildare. He is a graduate of UCD and King's Inns.

Joe Clarke from Mountbellew, Co. Galway is an MA graduate in Local History of NUI Maynooth. He is the principal of Bally-foran N.S., Co. Roscommon. Previous publications include *Christopher Dillon Bellew and his Galway estates 1762–1826* (2003); and *Coosan School 1836–1988* (1988).

Susan Durack from Maynooth, Co. Kildare is a graduate of the Open University and an MA graduate of Local History of NUI Maynooth. She works in the library in NUI Maynooth.

Raymond Gillespie is a senior lecturer in Modern History and coordinator of the MA in Local History degree course at NUI Maynooth.

Catherine Mullan of Lusk, Co. Dublin is a graduate of NUI Maynooth. Published works include: *Vernacular Buildings of East Fingal* (co-author, 1993); *History of O'Brien Institute* (1996). She is presently completing an M.Litt. on Land Transfer in Fingal 1900–39.

Seán O'Sullivan, born in Clare, is a graduate of UCD and a retired principal of Valleymount N.S., Co. Wicklow.

Austin Stewart, a native of Co. Tyrone, is a teacher and author and lives in Celbridge, Co. Kildare. He is a graduate in Local History from NUI Maynooth. Previous publications include *Coalisland, County Tyrone in the Industrial Revolution 1800–1901* (2002).

Frank Sweeney is a retired teacher, born in Co. Donegal and living in Rockbrook, Co. Dublin. He is an MA graduate in

Local History from NUI Maynooth and is the author of *The Murder of Conell Boyle* (2002).

Margaret Urwin, a native of Ballymitty, Co. Wexford, lives in Dublin. She is a graduate of the Open University and a MA graduate in Local History from NUI Maynooth. Her published work include *A County Wexford Family in the Land War* (2002).

Padraig Vesey, Castlerea, Co. Roscommon is a full-time farmer. He is a graduate of UCG and an MA graduate in Local History from NUI Maynooth.

Edward Wylie-Warren, born in India, is a chartered surveyor who lives in Dromore West, Co. Sligo. He is an MA graduate in Local History of NUI Maynooth.